Introduction

It never fails to amaze me just how many motorhome enthusiasts, hand on heart, tell me: "Buying a motorhome changed my life."

I've heard tales of saved marriages and new romances, strengthened family ties and more time with the grandchildren, new friendships and emotional re-unions – all attributed to making one simple decision: 'Sod the Carribbean cruise, let's buy a motorhome.'

Many people buy a motorhome with the intention of using it for just a few weeks a year, but once aquired, new possibilities open up and suddenly it becomes a way of life. As well as providing an almost limitless range of holiday options, 'the van' often offers solutions to problems you didn't even know you had: accommodation for that wedding in Somerset? No problem. A spare bedroom for unexpected guests? Easy. An extra apartment for that family holiday in Spain? Certainly.

In a surprisingly short space of time, after a few dry runs, you'll almost certainly have the confidence to start planning your first big adventure. It might be a solo enterprise or something you do with new motorhoming friends, but adventure isn't too strong a term. Because regardless of whether your plans involve a weekend rediscovering a stretch of coastline where you enjoyed childhood holidays or a embarking on a six-month sojourn in Southern Europe, it's the freedom, flexibility and, above all, the spirit of adventure that makes motorhoming such a life-changing experience.

We hope this book persuades you to climb aboard and enjoy the ride!

Buying a motorhome will change your life.

How to use this book

This book is not intended to be a definitive guide to the complex and infinitely varied world of motorhomes; it aims merely to dispense a few useful tips and pointers with the odd suggestion for further reading.

Its primary purpose is to inspire would-be nomads to take the plunge by joining the growing legions of motohomers in the UK and offer friendly impartial guidance on the sometimes complex choices facing them.

However, its secondary function is to encourage both newcomers and seasoned motorhomers to get the most out of their vans by exploring new frontiers – both at home and abroad.

So to ease navigation, we've split the book into two parts: The CHOOSING section details every aspect of the buying process – from determining which type of motorhome best suits your individual needs, to drawing up a shortlist of vehicles and establishing where you are most likely to find your perfect van. It's designed mainly for newcomers, but we hope it's also useful for people thinking about trading up down or sideways.

Then we come to the USING section, which should serve as a useful companion to planning your first – or 131st – motorhome adventure.

There's plenty of practical information about where to go and what to do when you arrive, plus advice on setting up the van for habitation and how to trouble-shoot common problems.

We've also included checklists of the essential items you'll need to consider taking along with you and a country-by-country guide to some of Europe's most popular destinations.

▶ ***For answers to more specific questions and the very latest advice, visit: www.outandaboutlive.co.uk and click on the 'Forums' link***

Contents

Should we or shouldn't we?

Motorhoming isn't for everyone and it's important to establish whether the lifestyle is going to suit you BEFORE investing thousands of pounds in a new or used van.

If you've never camped or caravanned before, it's strongly recommended that you hire a motorhome for a taster session before taking the plunge.

Even then, it's important to remain realistic about the practicalities of owning a motorhome. A few days' spent barbecuing in the sunshine on a short break in a hired motorhome in July is a very different proposition from spending a week huddled around the heater whilst it pours down outside in the middle of February.

Research suggests the majority of first time buyers spend between six and 12 months weighing up all the pros and cons and deciding which model and layout best meets their needs before signing on the dotted line.

In short, buying and owning a motorhome is a long-term commitment and not something to be entered into lightly, but do your homework thoroughly, select a van that suits your needs and the rewards are potentially huge.

MOTORHOMES ARE GREAT FOR:

- Extended holidays
- Touring the UK and Europe
- Weekend escapes and short breaks
- Visiting friends or family without imposing on them
- Use as a base for activity holidays
- Taking pets along with you
- People with mild to moderate mobility issues
- Using as an office on wheels

MOTORHOMES ARE LESS GOOD FOR:

- Large families (more than four)
- Parking on a permanent pitch
- The annual two-week holiday – but nothing else

FREQUENTLY ASKED QUESTIONS

Can we afford it?

On the face of it, motorhomes may seem like an expensive purchase, but when placed into context, they can make an extremely shrewd investment.

Try looking at it this way. How much do you spend a year on holidays – including short breaks and weekends away?

Multiply that figure by three and you'll arrive at a number. Write it down.

Now work out the purchase cost of your ideal motorhome. Motorhomes don't depreciate as quickly as cars, so bear in mind that the van should still be worth a significant proportion of what you paid for it in three years' time. Subtract a realistic future value from the purchase price and you'll arrive at a second number. Write it down.

Now compare this figure with the one you wrote down earlier. If the former is greater than the latter, you can afford to fund a motorhome over three years from your current holiday expenditure.

Surprisingly few motorhome purchases are funded with credit finance however. Most buyers fund the purchase from lump sum pension payments, inheritances or equity release from their homes.

Ongoing costs aren't too onerous. Your van will need servicing once a year and an annual MOT inspection. Insurance premiums tend to be on a par with a family car and unless you're using it as a second car, diesel bills shouldn't be too steep. Typical pitch fees range from £5 to £20 a night and you can spend as little – or as much as you like on food.

Motorhome holidays could be cheaper than your current holiday costs – even if you include the purchase price

Could we swap the second (or primary) car for a motorhome?

If you're contemplating a camper or van conversion, it's feasible to run this sort of motorhome as a second car. Fuel consumption shouldn't be much higher than an estate car and as long as it has rear travel seats with seatbelts, you should still be able to carry up to three passengers and more luggage than the typical estate car.

The downsides are parking difficulties in supermarkets, town centres and multi-storey car parks and potential issues with garaging it or getting it into the driveway. Some enthusiasts happily use a van as their sole mode of transport and as long as you have the space and are comfortable manoeuvring a larger vehicle on a regular basis, this can be a cost-effective option.

Many dealers are happy to accept cars in part exchange against a motorhome, but make sure you establish a fair value for the car before you start haggling over the price.

Do we have the space to store it on our drive or nearby?

With the exception of the most compact campers and microvans, few motorhomes will fit in the standard garage, so they tend to spend most of their lives outdoors on driveways. If you live on a modern housing estate, it's important to check whether the developer placed any restrictions on parking caravans or motorhomes in driveways. On-street parking is a far from ideal option – if only because during long periods of being laid-up, the batteries will slowly lose their charge and it's useful to be able to hook up the van to the mains for a top-up before you head off for a trip.

If you have no alternative but to place the van in storage when it's not in use, unless you can find a friendly farmer with a big, dry barn, this could significantly increase the cost of ownership.

If you do have to pay for storage, check the security measures in place and make sure you can get access to the van with the minimum of notice.

Are we both happy to drive such a large vehicle?

Today's modern motorhomes drive very much like cars and differ only in terms of their size, height and all-round visibility from the driver's seat.

Many less confident drivers still view the prospect of getting behind the wheel of such

A camper van could replace your existing car, it's easy to store and provides you with holidays

a large vehicle with trepidation and spending a significant proportion of your holidays in a state of mild anxiety is not an ideal recipe for a relaxing break.

Sharing the driving significantly eases the burden if you are intending to cover large distances in Europe and the other consideration is what happens if the sole driver falls ill or sprains an ankle? We've heard of several cases where couples have been charged hefty repatriation fees to ship a motorhome back to the UK after the driver was incapacitated and their partner, while legally entitled to drive the motorhome, flatly refused to do so.

The solution for nervous drivers is to enrol on a motorhome manoeuvring course. Both Clubs offer these popular courses and we'd strongly recommend that all newcomers to motorhoming book a place before heading off on their maiden voyage.

Log onto www.caravanclub.co.uk or www.campingandcaravanningclub.co.uk for more details.

How much use will we really get out of it?

If you're contemplating the purchase of a motorhome as a vehicle for the annual two-week holiday and don't envisage using it for anything else, it's likely to turn out to be an expensive acquisition.

The mathematics of motorhome ownership dictate that the more you use it, the cheaper it gets and most owners actually find themselves using their vans much more frequently than they anticipated.

As well as broadening people's holiday horizons, motorhomes are fantastic accessories for a whole range of shorter-haul applications. City breaks, walking holidays in the hills, visiting family and friends and even attending major sporting events or concerts and festivals suddenly become more accessible and affordable when you don't have to worry about the hassle and expense of finding accommodation.

And once you start making friends with your fellow motorhomers, you'll find the invitations to come along to try exciting new experiences start coming in thick and fast.

Take a look at the forums on www.outandaboutlive.co.uk to get a taste of what MMM readers get up to in their motorhomes!

Will other members of the family be able to make use of it?

It may sound overly altruistic, but many people justify their outlay on a motorhome by making it available to other members of the family.

Using the equation in the first question in this section, if your motorhome is enjoyed for an additional month by children, grandchildren or other relatives, then it begins to look like even better value.

Think of it as a timeshare offer: if you paid for two weeks in September and the company threw in a month in July for free for anyone to use, you'd be pretty happy with the deal.

Bear in mind though, that buying a van which is suitable for the wider family will almost certainly

Your next step could be a visit to your local dealer...

dictate the purchase of a four-berth motorhome with a family-friendly layout, which is likely to cost more and be less practical as a second car or daily runabout.

It's also important to clearly communicate your expectations regarding any contributions towards the upkeep of the van and the standards of care exercised when using it.

CRUNCH TIME

So you've considered all of these questions, together with any additional factors which relate to your individual circumstances and discussed your ideas with the wider family.

You've established you can afford a motorhome and you have somewhere to store it safely and at least one of you is happy to drive it.

You know you're going to make extensive use of it and have already started drawing up a list of must-see destinations.

...or a motorhome show perhaps

The next step is entirely down to you: forget the whole idea and book a world cruise or start searching for your ideal motorhome. Only you can decide, but if you opt for the latter, the rest of this section of this book is dedicated to helping you find the best vehicle for your needs.

With a motorhome the world is your oyster!

Motorhome base vehicles

JUST about any commercial vehicle and a number of MPVs have the potential of being converted into a motorhome, but in practice, the popular motorhomes of today revolve around just a few proven models.

These are referred to in the industry as 'base vehicles' or 'platforms' because they are what the entire motorhome is built upon.

The big manufacturers like Swift and Explorer Group tend to focus on one platform, but some of the mid-sized converters will work with two or more base vehicle manufacturers. Some of the smaller converters are prepared to work with a wider range of platforms, but they too develop their favourite based upon which vehicles best meet their customers' needs and are the most straightforward to convert.

On the following pages are details of the most common base vehicles. Others do crop up however and if you are proposing to buy second-hand, you may well encounter some rarer vehicles and it's worth checking the precise specifications of these so you know exactly what you are buying.

FIAT DUCATO/PEUGEOT BOXER/CITROEN RELAY

Fiat was the first of the major van manufacturers to recognise the importance of the motorhome market and has worked closely with the major converters to produce a motorhome-friendly base vehicle.

Fiat Ducato

Fiat Ducato cab

The all-conquering Ducato was wholly revamped in 2006, complete with a specially designed motorhome chassis, a unique engine option and a Pan-European breakdown recovery and support network – Fiat CamperAssist.

These special efforts have been embraced both by UK and European motorhome manufacturers and the Ducato and its almost identical sister vehicles from Peugeot and Citroen are more popular than ever.

The X2/50, to give the SEVEL-built vans from Fiat, Peugeot and Citroen their correct title, has a pleasant cab with intuitive controls and an almost car-like seating position – thanks to redesigned seats and mountings.

Available in a wide choice of weights and lengths, the Ducato also has a good range of diesel engines and they are all very easy to drive thanks to the flexible engines and light clutch and gearshift.**a**

SPECIFICATIONS: FIAT DUCATO

ENGINE OPTIONS:

Common-rail turbodiesel 2.0-litre (100bhp), 2.2-litre (120bhp) 2.3-litre (130bhp), 3.0-litre (157bhp)

OVERALL LENGTHS:	WEIGHTS:
4.96m	3000kg
5.41m	3300kg
5.99m	3500kg
6.36m	4005kg

VOLKSWAGEN TRANSPORTER

The iconic status enjoyed by the original VW Camper has kept Volkswagen at the forefront of the van conversion market with converters of all sizes maintaining a strong preference for using the Transporter as a base vehicle.

Established UK converters such as Auto Sleepers and Devon continue to use the Transporter T5 to underpin their products and such is the continuing appeal of the badge that Volkswagen itself has muscled in on the action with its own camper – the California.

Superb build quality, exceptionally frugal TDI engines, car-like handling and the option of four-wheel-drive mean the Transporter looks likely to remain a favourite in the van conversion market for years to come.

The Transporter range only extends to 3200kg however and the bigger Crafter has yet to find favour with converters who specialise in coachbuilt motorhomes.

Volkswagen Transporter

Volkswagen Transporter cab is very car-like

Volkswagen's California

SPECIFICATIONS: VW TRANSPORTER

ENGINE OPTIONS:
Direct injection turbodiesel 1.9-litre (102bhp) 2.5-litre (130bhp and 174bhp)

OVERALL LENGTHS:	WEIGHTS:
4.89m	2800kg
5.29m	3000kg
	3200kg

The Ford Transit cab

FORD TRANSIT

Ford's enduring Transit remains a popular base vehicle with everyone from tiny specialist converters to the big continental manufacturers.

The Transit's huge range of chassis lengths and weights make it especially suited to everything from compact campers and van conversions, right up to 4,000kg-plus coachbuilts with rear wheel drive.

In its latest incarnation, the Transit's angular cab doesn't appeal to everyone, but the combination of a supple chassis, excellent TDCi engines and the option of front or rear wheel drive add up to a compelling package for converters to work with.

The Transit isn't perhaps as easy to drive as the Fiat family of vehicles and with standard seats, the seating position isn't as car-like, but the cab feels classier and overall, the vehicle feels somewhat more solid than comparable Fiats.

However, the Transit costs significantly more than the Fiat, so expect to pay slightly more for a Transit-based motorhome – particularly at the budget end of the market, where the price premium is not as easily absorbed by the converter.

Ford Transit

SPECIFICATIONS: FORD TRANSIT

ENGINE OPTIONS:
Direct injection turbodiesel 2.2-litre (85bhp, 115bhp and 140bhp) 2.4-litre (100bhp, 115bhp and 140bhp)

OVERALL LENGTHS:	WEIGHTS:
4.86m	2600kg
5.23m	2800kg
5.68m	3000kg
6.40m	3300kg
	3500kg
	4600kg

MERCEDES SPRINTER

Fiat's concerted efforts to court the motorhome converters has seen Mercedes lose ground in the motorhome market in recent years.

Would-be customers of more upmarket motorhomes still like the cache of the three-pointed star on the grille, but converters have found it increasingly difficult to justify the price premium at the middle and budget ends of the market.

Like the Transit, the Sprinter offers a huge array of chassis and engine options – all of them rear wheel drive – which appeals to converters of larger A-class motorhomes and it also remains popular with some of the smaller van conversion specialists.

Mercedes Sprinter

SPECIFICATIONS: MERC SPRINTER

ENGINE OPTIONS:
Common rail turbodiesel 2.1-litre (88bhp, 109bhp, 129bhp and 150bhp) 3.0-litre six-cylinder turbodiesel (184bhp)

OVERALL LENGTHS:	WEIGHTS:
5.24m	3000kg
5.91m	3500kg
6.94m	4600kg
7.34m	5000kg

Sprinter-based motorhomes tend to feel more truck-like on the road and can feel a little ponderous compared with their Ducato or Transit-based competitors, but some motorhomers don't regard this as a drawback in a larger vehicle and the big 3.0-litre six-cylinder turbodiesel is a class act.

The arrival of an all-new Sprinter is not far away and expectations of the new vehicle will be justifiably high.

RENAULT MASTER

When the new Master first appeared in 2005, several converters jumped at the opportunity of offering customers a brand new van which exhibited more car-like driving characteristics.

Thus the Master has become a popular option for builders of van conversions, compact coachbuilts and low-profile motorhomes.

The Master has a decent spread of chassis lengths and weights and although the engines

Renault Master

aren't quite as lively as those of its main competitors, they are more than adequate and there's an automatic option with the flagship 150bhp version.

The seating position is more upright than the Fiat's and the large, almost horizontal steering wheel is more akin to a truck's, but the Master's dashboard doesn't intrude as far into the cab as its competitors', so there's marginally more room

Renault Master

SPECIFICATIONS: RENAULT MASTER

ENGINE OPTIONS:
Common rail turbodiesel engine 2.5-litre (100, 120bhp and 150bhp)

OVERALL LENGTHS:	WEIGHTS:
4.89m	2800kg
5.39m	3300kg
5.81m	3500kg
5.89m	

in front lounge van conversions, where space is at such a premium.

With the Master, Renault has established a significant foothold in the motorhome conversion market – and it looks like it is here to stay.

AND SOME OTHERS YOU MAY ENCOUNTER...

Inside the Fiat Scudo

Fiat Scudo

Fiat Scudo
The all-conquering Ducato's little sister – potential for camper-style van conversions and small coachbuilts.

Iveco Daily
Large, truck-like stablemate to the Ducato.

Iveco Daily

Volkswagen Caddy
Car-like van which some smaller converters favour for micro-campers.

Renault Trafic
Smaller version of the Master and base vehicle for Adria's acclaimed 3-Way.

Mazda Bongo
Privately imported from Japan then converted in the UK, these compact campers are attractively priced.

AND FINALLY...

A word about engines. Don't be tempted to go for a smaller capacity engine to save cash and improve fuel economy. Although the smaller engine option may have seemed lively enough on the test drive, how will it cope when the van is fully laden with a full compliment of passengers, full water tanks, fresh gas cylinders and all the luggage for an extended break?

Under such a burden, a smaller capacity engine could actually use more diesel than a more muscular unit, so don't be tempted to skimp on the horsepower.

The weight of a typical four-berth coachbuilt motorhome increases by between 15 and 25 per cent once fully laden, so to be on the safe side, you need to be convinced that the engine has at least 10 per cent more power in reserve to propel your van comfortably. As a rule of thumb, allow at least 35bhp per tonne of motorhome and you shouldn't be far out.

Types of motorhome

MOTORHOMES come in all sorts of shapes and sizes – ranging from tiny delivery-van based single-berth vehicles to massive American behemoths.

You can buy ready-converted vehicles off-the-shelf from specialist motorhome dealers or go direct to a motorhome conversion specialist if that bespoke feel appeals to you.

Some of the smaller converters will even offer design and build packages which allow the customer to specify precisely what features and details they want included. Others will allow the customer to source a new or used base vehicle themselves and bring it to the converter for the complicated job of transforming it into a motorhome.

Clearly, your choice of motorhome is going to be heavily influenced by your budget. Membership of the motorhome fraternity can start as low as a few hundred pounds, but you are unlikely to get anything usable for less than a couple of thousand pounds.

In the following pages, we examine the main categories of motorhomes, plus a few interesting sub-species.

We also explain the pros and cons of each genre and give a rough idea of what you can expect to pay for both new and used examples of each type of motorhome.

MICROVAN

These tiny one or two-berth vehicles are a relatively new category of motorhome, but it's an area of the market which is growing for a variety of reasons. Broadly, they fall into two subsets: delivery-van based conversions – usually adapted for motorhome use in Britain – and microcar-based Japanese imports.

The latter are privately imported second-hand by specialist dealers and converted for camping use in the UK. These are usually well-maintained, low-mileage vans with high specification at eye-catching prices. It's worth bearing in mind that there may be issues with repairs and insurance and trading them in or selling them on in the future may be problematic.

Japanese imports have established something of a cult following in the UK however – epitomised by the success of the absurdly named Mazda Bongo (see under Campers).

Typically, microvans incorporate very basic overnight accommodation comprising a bed or two, a gas hob, sink and running water, table and possibly a form of heating. Toilets are usually of the basic chemical variety and headroom is provided by means of an elevating roof with fabric sides. Extra living space can be provided in bespoke awnings which attach to the rear or side of the van.

These tiny campers are finding favour with two distinct groups: experienced motorhomers who have lost their partners but want to continue camping and younger folk who want a cheap alternative to B&B accommodation whilst pursuing outdoor activities.

The Romahome R10 Solo

bürstner
£34995
FA07 YNG

Used examples can be bought comparatively cheaply and their compact proportions make them viable as sole transport for couples.

HERE'S THE DEAL

PROS:
Cheap to buy, great fuel economy, drive like cars, will comfortably fit into most garages and driveways

CONS:
Cramped and basic accommodation, unsuitable for lengthy tours, cold in winter

EXPECT TO PAY:
From £5,000 for a used Japanese import to £25,000 for a brand new

COMPACT COACHBUILT

These quintessentially British motorhomes are usually the products of small specialist converters who manufacture in small volumes and take a bespoke or even custom-built approach to making motorhomes.

Based on a small panel van chassis such as the Fiat Scudo, they are miniature versions of full-size coachbuilts and generally offer a little more space than the van conversions to which they are an alternative.

The converter takes the basic vehicle and adds on a custom-built GRP habitation compartment into which the customary refinements are added. Ingenious converters with years of experience usually manage to cram a surprising amount of kit into these compact alternatives to a full-blown coachbuilt – including comprehensive kitchens and washrooms and the full spectrum of gas, electrical and water services.

The Nu Venture Nu Rio

They are significantly lighter than full-size coachbuilts and usually have lower payloads and it's unusual to find a realistic multiberth version capable of accommodating more than a couple.

The continental equivalent of this approach is the 'van'. To the untrained eye, these can be difficult to distinguish from a low profile or full-blown coachbuilt motorhome, but they basically follow the same principal of mounting an insulated habitation section onto a van chassis – generally a short wheelbase version of the Ford Transit or Fiat Ducato.

They are narrower than a full-size coachbuilt, but will sleep up to three people and often have two fully functional travel seats in the habitation section, so they can be used as a second vehicle for a driver and three passengers.

HERE'S THE DEAL

PROS:
Easier to drive and manoeuvre than full-size coachbuilts, high quality accommodation, well-insulated bodies for year-round use

CONS:
Can still feel cramped, only marginally cheaper than full-size coachbuilts, occasionally awkward looks

EXPECT TO PAY:
£10,000 – £15,000 for used examples; £25,000 and upwards new

CAMPER

The iconic Volkswagen Camper van epitomised this genre in the 60s and 70s and it looks poised to make a bit of a comeback as the next generation of 'cool campers' trade in their socially and environmentally unacceptable 4x4s for vehicles which will genuinely enhance their lifestyles.

With this in mind, Volkswagen took the conversion of a camper for the 21st century in-house and now sells the beautifully built and intelligently packaged California through its dealer

Mazda Bongo

Volkswagen California

Autocruise Pulse

network. Based on the VW Transporter van, the California looks fantastic, drives like a large car and – in TDI diesel form – returns car-like fuel economy.

A number of the big boys and dozens of smaller converters offer infinite variations on this theme, whose beauty is its ability to serve as both a family car and weekend getaway vehicle.

The basic camper traditionally comprises a double bed and basic cooking and dining facilities and a compact loo. Elevating roof derivatives will, additionally, sleep a couple of youngsters in the roof bed and, like the micro campers, living space can sometimes be extended with the addition of a bespoke awning.

On the downside, adults can't stand up in them and in terms of the space and facilities on offer, they look expensive in comparison with full-size van conversions and coachbuilts.

A cheaper alternative is the increasingly popular Mazda Bongo and its ever-growing crowd of imported alternatives. These similarly-sized vans are shipped in second-hand from Japan and converted into campers over here. They aren't quite as cool or clever as the California, but they fulfil a similar function and with prices starting at less than £10,000, they are significantly more affordable.

HERE'S THE DEAL

PROS:
Very cool, will double as a family car, easy to drive and manoeuvre, good fuel economy, fantastic resale values

CONS:
Cramped accommodation, limited ability as a long-term tourer, expensive to buy

EXPECT TO PAY:
From £10,000 for decent used campers. Treat anything below this price with caution. New prices start at around £30,000 for the more basic VW Transporter

Auto-Sleepers Trident

2003 Murvi Morello

VAN CONVERSION

This category accounts for a huge proportion of the motorhomes on British roads and continues to be an extremely popular new purchase.

Basically, the converter takes a pretty much standard panel van, upgrades the windows, insulates the body and installs all the habitation equipment.

These compact and flexible vehicles are usually fitted with a sliding nearside door, which restricts the number of layout options, but makes access easy as the step isn't too high off the ground.

The two cab seats traditionally rotate to combine with seats in the habitation to create a lounge/diner and the beds are typically longitudinal twins or doubles in this area, or a transverse double towards the back of the vehicle.

Most van conversions offer a reasonable kitchen and a functional washroom with sink, loo and shower and, unlike Campers, even six-footers can generally stand up in them.

They drive almost as well as cars and fuel economy continues to improve with the latest diesel engines. The new generation of vans from Fiat, Peugeot, Citroen and Ford has seen the widespread introduction of refinements such as cruise control, cab air conditioning and even automatic gearboxes and if fitted with the latest high performance turbo-diesels, these motorhomes have absolutely no issues keeping up with motorway traffic – as anyone who has been tailgated by a delivery driver in one of the 'white vans' upon which they are based will testify.

On the downside, levels of insulation aren't on a par with the best coachbuilts, so they can be cold in winter, and despite having decent payloads, many van conversions have precious little meaningful storage space. They can also look expensive in terms of the accommodation offered.

Trigano Tribute

Bilbo's Celex

Space is still at a premium when more than two are on board, but they are excellent for weekending and short breaks and many enthusiasts happily take them on extended tours of the continent.

Both the small converters and large manufacturers are very serious players in this market and there are some genuinely excellent vehicles out there. Some derivatives have three or four berths, but realistically, van conversions are best suited to couples, which explains why they are so popular in the UK.

HERE'S THE DEAL

PROS:
Fairly compact, easy to drive, reasonable fuel consumption, high-top versions have good headroom

CONS:
Can be cold in winter, few layout options, can look expensive compared with full-size coachbuilts

EXPECT TO PAY:
From £15,000 for an elderly, but well-maintained used example. Nearly new vans start at just under £30,000 and high-spec new models can comfortably top £50,000

Knaus Sun Ti

LOW PROFILE

This relatively new genre was only introduced to the UK around 2004, but has really caught the motorhome-buying public's imagination. It's basically a coachbuilt motorhome based on the customary light van base vehicle, but the habitation section is only a few inches taller than the top of the cab. Sufficient headroom is achieved by using a specially adapted 'step down' chassis, which reduces the ground clearance of the habitation, thus freeing up more headroom.

Swift Bolero 600EK

This adapted chassis has a roll-bar incorporated into its tweaked suspension system, which offers better ride comfort and improved handling.

After initial resistance to the low-profile concept, they have become increasingly popular over the last three or four years and most British manufacturers now feature a low-profile in their model ranges.

While multi-berth derivatives are available, the low-profile is more suited to couples. They offer more space, a wider range of layouts and better insulation than the typical van conversion, but in some cases, actually cost less than these smaller vehicles.

As well as better manners on the road, low-profiles are more aerodynamic and less likely to fall foul of height restrictions on back-roads or ferries. Many owners report superior fuel consumption to overcab designs and they certainly feel less intimidating to drive.

Excel 590EK

HERE'S THE DEAL

PROS:
Good looks and competitive prices, good ride and handling characteristics.

CONS:
Few multi-berth layouts, less storage than full-size coachbuilts

EXPECT TO PAY:
Because of their relative newness and sudden popularity, used examples are hard to find, so expect to pay at least £20,000 for a good used example. New models start at around £35,000.

CLASSIC COACHBUILT

This is the definitive home on wheels or caravan with an engine – whose fundamentals date back to the earliest days of motorhoming when enterprising embryonic converters first bolted a box onto the back of a commercial vehicle.

Their popularity has waned in the face of cooler or more compact alternatives making the most of new designs and technology, but this is still the cheapest means of building a motorhome with sufficient space to live in for weeks at a time.

Every major manufacturer offers one or more examples of the coachbuilt style, many of which provide sufficient accommodation for a family or four to share in comfort.

The key to fitting in four is the overcab or Luton' which sits on top of the cab to provide a large double bed. Like the rest of the habitation section, it's robust and well insulated.

Rotating front seats and settees then form a roomy front lounge – although the latest thinking is converging on a dinette arrangement to allow for the provision of two forward-facing travel seats with full three-point seatbelts.

The classic layout is for the kitchen to stretch across the rear of the van with a small washroom in the corner, but there are huge variations on this basic theme.

The overcab coachbuilt also comes in many lengths – from sub-six-metre compacts to huge twin axle versions which will sleep up to six.

With such a cumbersome front end and a high centre of gravity, overcab motorhomes are not noted for their aerodynamic, driving and handling characteristics, but they manage to cram in more

Swift Escape 624

The overcab coachbuilt has more space per person

space per person than just about any other type of motorhome.

They're also a relatively cheap option, with prices starting at between less than £15,000 for a very serviceable four-berth. £15,000 to £20,000 buys a fairly recent example and – until Sterling's recent slide – the cheapest new examples cost only a little over £25,000.

HERE'S THE DEAL

PROS:
Loads of space, plenty of layout options, loads of storage, flexibility, affordability

CONS:
Pedestrian looks, poor performance, can feel unwieldy to drive.

EXPECT TO PAY:
From under £15,000 used. £27,000 - £30,000 new.

A-CLASS

Owning an A-class is viewed by many as the pinnacle of motorhoming aspiration as the unique design strips away many of the clues to their origins as humble commercial vehicles.

The converter takes the basic van chassis, engine and gearbox and constructs a completely new body on top. This body is traditionally much wider than the standard van and integrates the cab seamlessly with the habitation area.

The complexity involved in their construction means A-classes are understandably more expensive than a conventional coachbuilt, but it allows the converter to maximise the space inside and make the best use of that additional space.

German manufacturer Hymer has elevated this approach to an artform and while its products are eye-wateringly expensive, the sheer number of aging Hymers still in active service bears testament to their durability.

One of the biggest advantages of the A-class is that the wider cab can accommodate a full-size drop-down double bed – offering all the advantages of an overcab bed, without the need for the addition of a clumsy Luton. This means the typical A-class can feature two, large double beds, making them genuinely luxurious four-berths.

There's also enough space in most for an abundance of lounge cum dining space, a well-equipped kitchen and a comfortable washroom with separate shower.

Eriba Jet 613

Hymer B564

Other characteristics are a huge panoramic windscreen and an elevated seating position offering a commanding view of the road. Many incorporate recessed lockers in the side skirts and secret storage lockers under the floor plus extensive roof racks and rear ladders for further storage.

A-classes do have their drawbacks however: most are at least 7ft wide and 11 or 12 feet tall. The challenges of installing their own doors mean that many models dispense with one or both of the cab doors – and have the only opening door on the 'wrong' side. They also tend to be significantly more expensive to maintain and repair.

UK converters have traditionally struggled to wrest dominance of the A-class market from the big European manufacturers and Sterling's slide against the Euro has rendered new A-class motorhomes even more expensive in the last year or so.

HERE'S THE DEAL

PROS:
Space, luxury, cache.

CONS:
Price, size on the road, maintenance and repair costs

EXPECT TO PAY:
Even 10-year-old examples will fetch in excess of £20,000, but left-hand-drive examples with odd layouts can be bought more cheaply. While some compact A-classes can be bought for around the £40,000 mark, £50,000 is a more realistic starting point for a full-size new A-class.

However, there is a buoyant market for quality used A-classes – many of which have been lovingly looked after with the same commitment usually reserved for a cherished classic car by their enthusiastic owners.

AMERICAN RECREATIONAL VEHICLE (RV)

Despite their intimidating dimensions and incorrigibly thirsty engines, these spectacular vehicles find favour with a significant minority of enthusiasts who insist they get more bang for their bucks in these huge behemoths.

Work out the cost per square foot and the US RV fans are absolutely right – with their slide-out extensions and colossal floorspace, these enormous vehicles do deliver and they don't cost as much as many people first assume.

The real costs however, are those associated with keeping what amounts to a medium-sized truck on the road. The large examples will return as little as 8mpg and servicing costs can be eye-watering too. Then there's the cost of storing it when not in use – as its hardly likely to fit on the average driveway. You'll also need to upgrade your driving licence to legally pilot anything over 7.5 tonnes.

They are also challenging to manoeuvre and few standard sites in the UK are geared up to accommodate RVs, meaning owners need to plan well ahead to pinpoint viable sites.

However, for spending six months touring Europe or escaping winter in Southern Spain, these massive motorhomes can combine similar accommodation to a small apartment with the freedom to roam – and that still appeals to an awful lot of people.

This is a Class B Winnebago Aspect

2004 Class A Winnebago Journey

A Class C Winnebago Outlook

AND FINALLY...

A word about payloads. This is a potential minefield for newcomers and we dedicate a whole chapter to it later in the book, Please read this, understand the implications and factor it into your choice of vehicle.

It's especially important if you are considering large, multi-berth motorhomes, want to carry a scooter or tow a small car behind your van. Similarly, even if there's just the two of you, but you want to take everything including the kitchen sink with you on a grand tour of Europe, please familiarise yourself with the complexities of what sort of payload your motorhome can legally carry.

HERE'S THE DEAL

PROS:
Space, value for money, accommodation, some even have baths!

CONS:
Running costs, lack of pitches, styling and build quality issues

EXPECT TO PAY:
£15,000 - £20,000 for a well-used but relatively rare 'van camper'. £30,000 - £50,000 for a used 30ft-plus RV with slide-outs.

Garages can be big enough for a scooter but check the payload

Towing a trailer, boat or even a car is possible but there are implications regarding your payload

Which layout?

CHOOSING the right layout is arguably the single most important aspect of the motorhome selection process.

Get it right and you're well on the way to years of happy travelling, get it wrong and you may end up having to trade in your first van for something more appropriate within six months – with all the attendant hassle and costs.

The problem is, there are so many different types of layout and so many variations on the same themes that it can be a bewildering decision.

The size of the motorhome tends to dictate the number of layout options available, so if you're in the market for a fairly simple van conversion, the layout choices are unlikely to overwhelm you, but it's still important to choose the right layout for your individual needs.

However, if you're considering something bigger, the range of layout options increases dramatically and it's important to be clear about your key criteria.

If you are completely new to motorhoming, the best way to establish some baseline requirements is to borrow or hire a motorhome to live in for a few days. In doing this, you will gain practical experience of what works for you and what doesn't.

You'll discover whether you're comfortable with a French bed or you really need an island arrangement, whether you're happy using site facilities or you want the privacy of your own washroom and what sort of cooking facilities you're comfortable using.

If you're really lucky, you may have inadvertently stumbled across the perfect layout for your needs; it's more likely however that you'll encounter certain aspects of your borrowed van that you simply can't live with. Make a list of these together with any aspects of the layout you liked and use them to draw up a shortlist of potential candidates.

If hiring or borrowing a van isn't an option, then study as many different layouts and look at as many different motorhomes as possible and try to put yourself in holiday mode to consider the practicalities. Who's going to sleep where? Is the washroom big enough? Does the kitchen meet our needs? Is there enough storage space for all our clutter? Is the lounge comfortable enough to stretch out and relax when the weather's rubbish?

Then split your requirements into essentials: e.g. four berths, four travel seats and desirables: e.g. fixed bed, big washroom, nice kitchen.

It then becomes a process of elimination which needs to be adhered to quite ruthlessly if you are to arrive at the right combination of van and layout.

NEW OR USED?

The complexity of the selection process can be further compounded if you want to buy used. Buying new allows you to specify exactly which layout you would like – as long as the manufacturer offers it.

Finding the perfect combination of base vehicle, make and layout on the used market is an altogether less predictable undertaking and the temptation may be to compromise on your ideals if an attractive alternative comes on to the market at the right price.

If you are satisfied you've done your homework properly, our advice is to resist the temptation to settle for a less than ideal layout and wait for the right one to come along – as it inevitably will in the fullness of time.

The other dilemma you may face is that of right layout, wrong vehicle – where you stumble across your ideal layout on a base vehicle or particular make which you've already discounted.

Again, we'd recommend holding out for the perfect combination, but if it's proving difficult to locate your ideal layout in the exact make and model of motorhome you've settled on, you may want to consider a compromise.

On the following pages, we highlight the main categories of layout and explain what they're good at and what they're less good at.

The first two chapters look at the inevitably restricted range of layout options available in the Camper and Van Conversions markets.

Subsequent chapters focus on the huge variations on offer among everything from low-profile to A-class motorhomes. The list is by no means comprehensive, but it should offer some useful pointers to inform your decision-making.

At the end of the day, all layouts are a compromise between competing priorities. Choose one that attempts to do everything reasonably well and it won't do any one thing brilliantly. So if you want the big fixed bed, the trade-off will be a smaller washroom or compact kitchen. Settle for a bed which you make up every night and you'll generally have more living space. Only you can decide what's best for your individual needs.

Camper layouts are of necessity, pretty straightforward

BASIC TYPES

Campers

While the base vehicles upon which they are based have evolved significantly since the early days of the VW Camper or Dormobile, the layout remains largely unchanged and there are relatively few variations on the basic theme.

Most campers are designed to sleep two on either the fold-flat rear seats or twin single beds. Rising roof versions may offer additional berths for a couple of small children, but the kids will otherwise have to sleep in a pup tent outside the van.

Typically, there's a run of basic appliances along the offside wall opposite the sliding side door, and a bench seat for two behind the front seats – which usually rotate to create a compact lounge/diner with a pedestal table.

There's usually a small wardrobe towards the rear and maybe a locker to store a portable loo for nocturnal emergencies. The main variation on this theme is the rear kitchen approach, where the kitchen and other services are divided across the back of the van, allowing for two individual travel seats behind the front seats. This layout potentially offers two single beds or a double made up by spanning the central gap between the two sets of seats.

Smaller, specialist converters offer subtle variations on these basic themes, but these usually involve fairly minor detail changes.

OVERVIEW

PROS:
Easy to drive, relatively cheap to run, stylish and flexible

CONS:
Lack of headroom, insufficient space for families on extended holidays, can be chilly in winter

IDEAL FOR:
Couples looking for a compact camper which doubles as an everyday vehicle. Young families with small children wanting a base from which to enjoy outdoor pursuits

BENCHMARK MODELS:
VW California, Westfalia Nugget, Auto-Sleepers Trooper, Autocruise Pulse

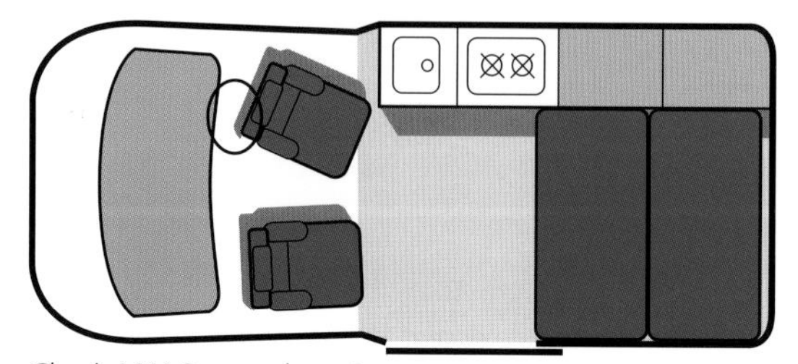

Classic VW Camper layout

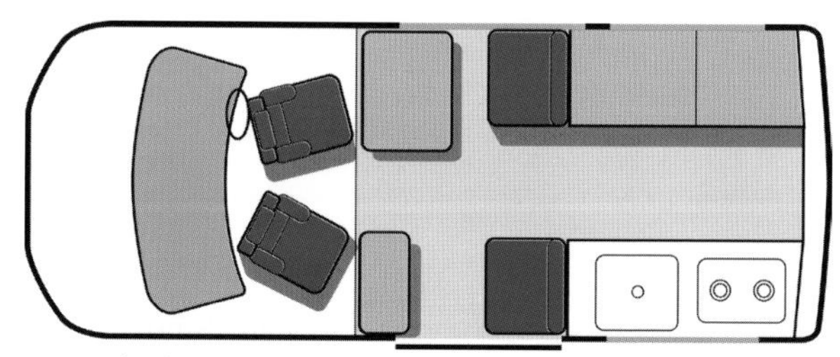

Rear kitchen camper

Van conversions

Fiat's wider, more motorhome-friendly Ducato has heralded something of a renaissance in the van conversion arena, and with both the small converters and big manufacturers piling into this growing sector of the market, there's a huge range of choice on offer.

The choice of layouts too, has increased significantly over the last two or three years, but essentially the range of options revolves around three basic configurations: rear lounge, rear kitchen and fixed bed.

Like the Camper, a van conversion can make a viable everyday vehicle, but the standards of habitation equipment and the space on offer can rival smaller coachbuilt motorhomes. Expect a decent kitchen, proper washroom with cassette toilet and in some cases, a fixed double bed.

Rear lounge

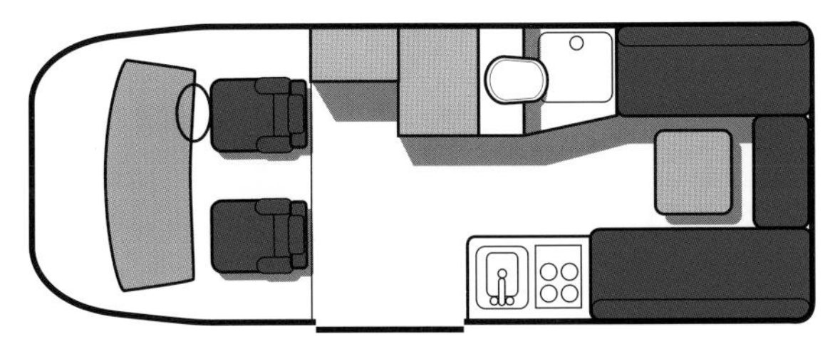

Rear lounge van conversion

The rear lounge option is a traditionally British approach to motorhome design and while it's comfortable and roomy, it's not a particularly space-efficient configuration – which sits uneasily in a vehicle where space is always going to be at a premium. Rear lounges convert to great double beds but they struggle to incorporate proper travel seats, so while the vast majority of van conversions are two or at most three-berths, only the driver and front seat passenger are able to travel safely in them, which restricts their viability as an everyday vehicle.

OVERVIEW

PROS:
Spacious and comfortable, clearly defined living, cooking areas separate from cab, big double bed.

CONS:
Inefficient use of space, no travel seats, impractical as an everyday vehicle.

IDEAL FOR:
Couple wanting a lighter and more compact alternative to a coachbuilt.

BENCHMARK MODELS:
Auto-Sleepers Warwick, Autocruise Rhythm, IH Tio

Rear kitchen

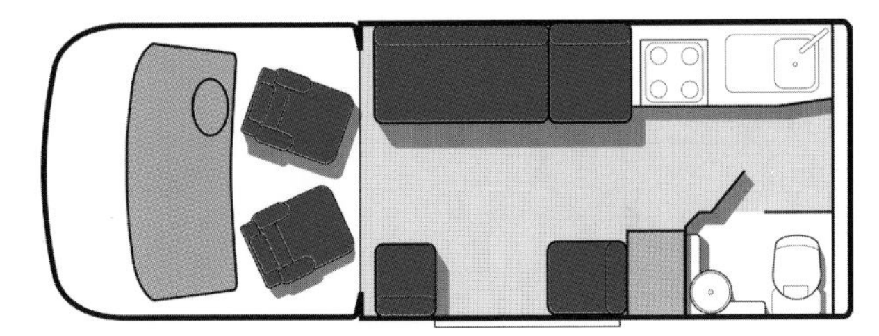

Rear kitchen and washroom, side settee

This configuration features a central lounge with the swivel front seats offering additional space for guests or reasonably comfortable lounging, while the kitchen and washroom are located at the rear of the van divided by the central isle.

There's usually a third, forward-facing travel seat inside the sliding door and a long bench settee opposite. It's a more flexible arrangement than the rear lounge approach, but possibly less well suited to stretching out in front of the TV or curling up

The Trigano Tribute crams a decent lounge, proper kitchen and washroom into what is essentially a delivery van.

The Murvi Morello is typical of the rear kitchen van conversion

OVERVIEW

PROS:
Three-seater flexibility and good use of space in shorter base vehicles

CONS:
Beds can be complicated to make up.

IDEAL FOR:
More active campers who want more storage and increased flexibility for everyday use.

BENCHMARK MODELS:
Auto-Sleepers Symbol, Murvi Morello, Autocruise Tempo

with a good book and the beds – either twin singles or a double – tend to be a little more hassle to make up.

Fixed bed

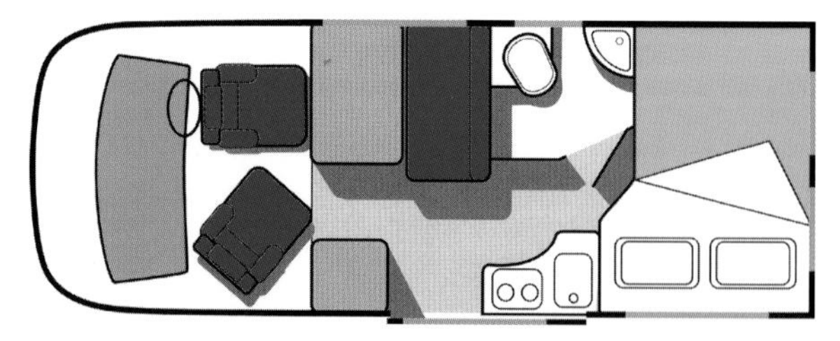

Rear kitchen and washroom, side settee

This continental approach has recently found favour with UK customers because of its wonderful flexibility, space efficiency and colossal storage capacity.

OVERVIEW

PROS:
Flexibility, four travel seats, fixed bed comfort, great storage, genuine potential for everyday use.

CONS:
Lounge is almost non-existent, kitchen and washroom are squeezed.

IDEAL FOR:
Couples who want the flexibility of a genuine all-rounder.

BENCHMARK MODELS:
Adria Twin, Hymer Car

By slotting in a fixed double bed transversely across the rear, models like the Adria Twin offer ample additional storage space underneath.

The kitchen and washroom sit amidships – and tend to be quite compact – while the lounge is reduced to a rather small dinette, but this allows for the provision of two forward-facing rear travel seats.

The fixed bed approach inevitably compromises the lounge, kitchen and washroom, but offers much more flexibility. Little wonder it's proved so popular in the last couple of years.

Rear lounges

As characteristically British as fish and chips, the rear lounge layout owes much of its DNA to the traditional touring caravan. Little wonder that this tried and tested layout has always been popular with motorhome converts with a caravanning background.

It's main strengths other than familiarity and availability are the comfort and space to stretch out and watch the world go by through a trio of panoramic windows.

It also offers the flexibility of a pair of single beds or a big double bed, although once made up, there's little remaining living space.

The rear lounge is, however, rather space-inefficient and it's difficult to integrate a couple of forward-facing travel seats into this layout – which is likely to curb its popularity in the future.

Auto-Trail Apache 634

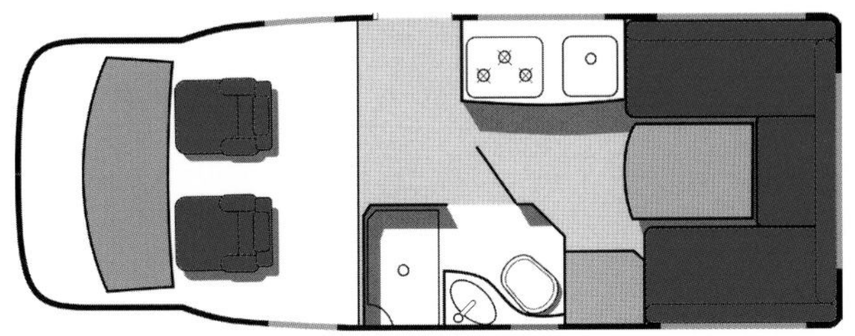

Rear U-shaped lounge

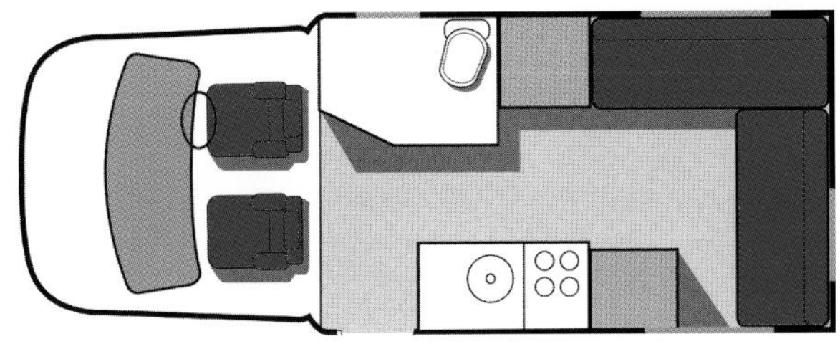

Rear L-shaped lounge

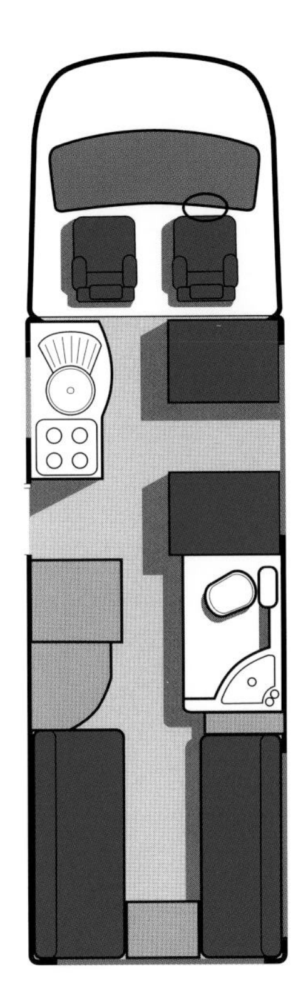

Rear lounge with front dinette

Some manufacturers have got round this failing by creating an additional lounge/diner with travel seats further forward, but this option inevitably squeezes the space dedicated to the washroom and kitchen and is usually only available on significantly longer base vehicles (7m-plus).

Key variations include U-shaped lounges with wrap-around seating instead of a caravanesque central chest of drawers and L-shaped affairs which free up additional space for the washroom, but this can compromise the seating and sleeping arrangements.

The sheer number of rear lounge vans out there will ensure this layout's continued popularity for several years to come, but the huge choice of cleverly packaged continental layouts offering a more balanced approach to living, cooking and storage space are likely to become increasingly popular.

OVERVIEW

PROS:
Great living space, excellent for entertaining, flexible beds.

CONS:
Lack of rear travel seats, limited storage space, small washrooms and kitchens.

IDEAL FOR:
Couples wanting a big lounge for entertaining at rallies and year-round indoor comfort.

BENCHMARK MODELS:
Auto-Sleepers Berkshire, Auto-Trail Apache

Front lounges

There's a significant amount of variation on the theme of the front lounge and – with increasing consideration being given to the provision of proper travel seats – some really clever innovation too.

In the most compact vans, the front lounge tends to be more of a lounge/diner with swivel front seats coming into play and the remaining seats arranged around a wall-mounted table. This means there are at least two forward-facing rear travel seats behind the table, which usually convert into a small double bed plus a long settee on the offside wall, which will form another bed. In family-orientated overcab models, the other two berths are located up the ladder into the Luton, while the washroom and kitchen sit along the rear wall.

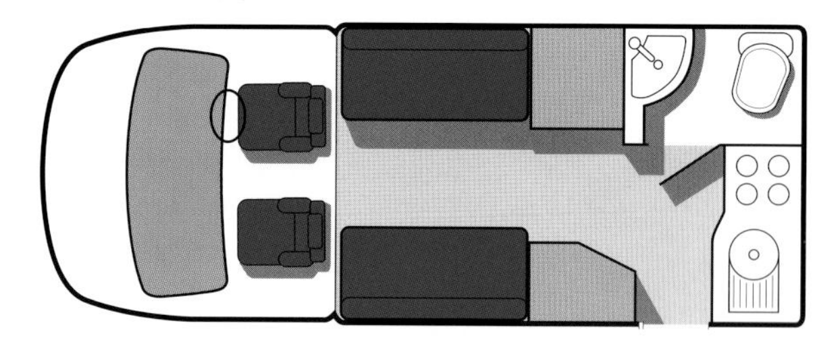

Front transverse lounge

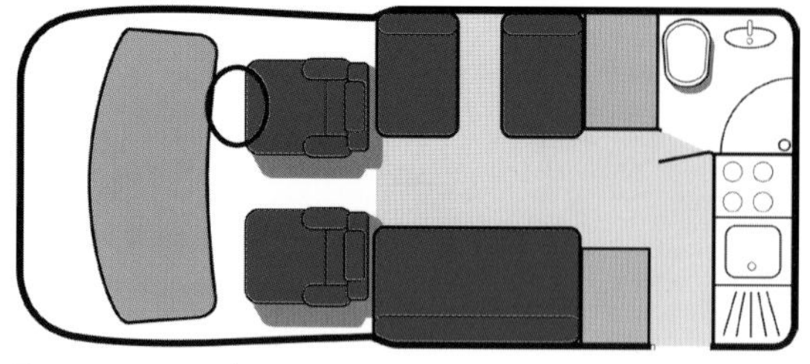

Front transverse lounge

One alternative which is enjoying popularity at the compact end of the is the market opposing settee approach which offers a really roomy lounge, but restricts the provision of travel seats. Some manufacturers – notably Auto-Sleepers with the Sigma and Nuevo – have got round this with some clever adaptations which are really worth a closer look.

Moving up the price range, the choices increases when you move into 7-metre-plus and A-class territory, where there's more space to play around with. Here you'll find more spacious lounges – some with integrated travel seats - and bigger kitchens, but these are significantly more expensive to buy and run.

A front lounge is a popular option

OVERVIEW

PROS:
Huge choice, clever solutions to seating, five-berth flexibility, up to four travel seats.

CONS:
Lounges with travel seats dominated by dinette, habitation door in kitchen.

IDEAL FOR:
Families wanting multi-berth accommodation with travel seats. Couples wanting a spacious lounge and a good kitchen.

BENCHMARK MODELS:
Ace Airstream 630EK, Swift Bolero 600 EK, Excel 590 EK, Auto-Sleepers Nuevo ES, Auto-Sleepers Sigma EK, Autocruise Starfire, Rapido 9048dF, Laika Rexosline 680

The key question is whether there are just the two of you with no real need for travel seats or you need a fully functioning four-berth, in which case, the provision of proper travel seats will be the foremost factor in shaping your decision. An important secondary factor is whether or not you want a fixed bed.

Fixed beds

The fixed bed revolution started in France – hence the soubriquet of French bed for the most common variety – and gradually caught on in the UK after much scepticism.

Many condemned the space-munching aspect of devoting such a large slice of a motorhome's already confined space to sleeping as, quite literally, a waste of space.

However, the virtues of having a comfortable, flat bed with a good mattress (although they vary considerably in quality) which doesn't require slotting together before you get your head down, continues to win converts seduced by the attractions of a proper night's sleep.

Fixed beds broadly fall into three categories: French bed, island bed and twin singles – each with their own set of pros and cons.

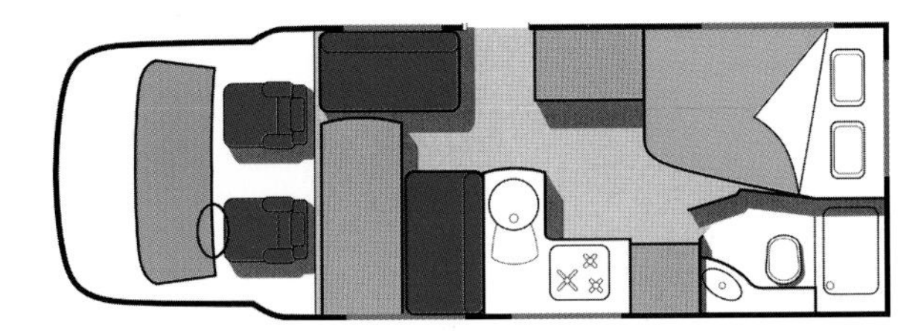

Euro fixed bed

French bed

The classic fixed bed layout incorporates a double bed offset along one side of the van or the other and usually slotted into the rear corner. Some larger vans place a full-width washroom behind the fixed bed, but more commonly, the washroom sits immediately adjacent to the bed, which typically has the outermost corner sliced away to ease access past the bed and into the washroom.

What happens forward of the bed varies, but typically you'll find an L-shaped kitchen and a half-dinette which faces the swivelling front seats to comprise a lounge/diner. The most common variation of this flips the L-shaped kitchen around and incorporates two opposing settees while another option is to relocate the kitchen immediately behind the front seats and introduce an L-shaped lounge opposite.

As well as the obvious superiority of a decent mattress which you don't have to make up every night, the fixed bed will usually have a sizable storage space underneath – although this can be compromised by habitation clutter such as water heaters or electrical consumer units.

OVERVIEW

PROS:
More comfortable than a converted settee, needs no making up, potential for storage underneath.

CONS:
Eats into living space, cramped washroom, access issues at night.

IDEAL FOR:
Couples who prize a good night's sleep above all.

BENCHMARK MODELS:
Autocruise Startrail, CI Carioca 694, Bürstner Delfin

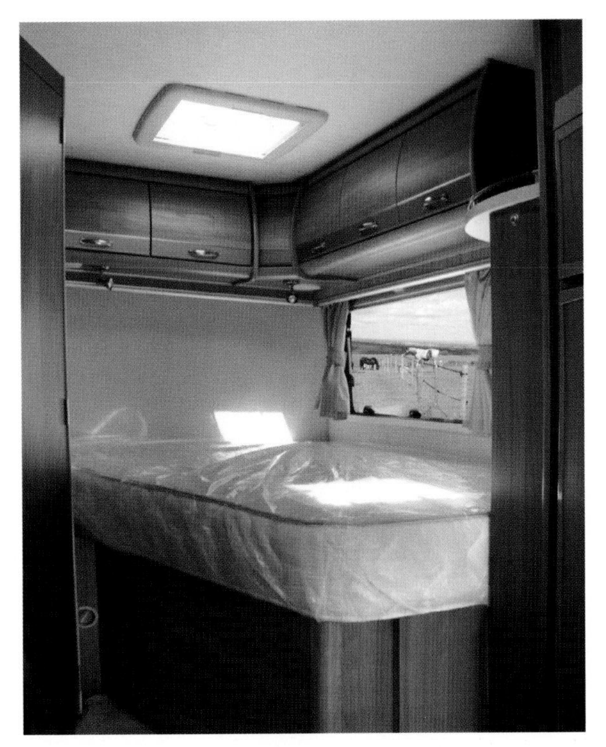

The rear fixed bed in an Autocruise Startrail

On the downside, the key consideration is whether you or your partner are athletic enough to clamber over one another to visit the loo in the middle of the night. And, while we're on the subject, washrooms in fixed bed models tend to be quite cramped and tiny with very little space for showering – unless you go for an end washroom variant.

In sub-6-metre compact models, whether you need two or four berths will have a major bearing on your choice of layout and if living space is a key priority, you may well conclude that the French bed is a luxury you can't afford.

Twin singles

One way of overcoming the French bed's biggest drawbacks: inefficient use of space and the problems of climbing over one another to get in and out, is to replace it with twin singles.

This decidedly practical approach may seem like a bit of an unromantic sleeping arrangement, but it's difficult to fault the logic.

Twin single layouts tend to fall into one of two categories: purpose-designed rear single beds and

Best of both worlds? Adria Compact's rear bed functions as twin singles or a huge double.

OVERVIEW

PROS:
Independent sleeping space for both parties, no assembly required.

CONS:
Rear bed versions eat up a lot of space, unromantic.

IDEAL FOR:
Couples who don't share the same sleeping habits, insomniacs who don't want to disturb their partners.

BENCHMARK MODELS:
Autocruise Augusta, Bürstner Travel Van, Lunar Roadstar 900, Swift Kon Tiki 675.

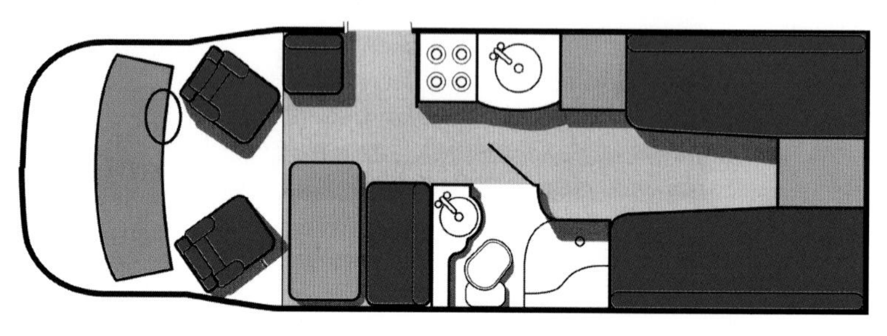

Fixed single beds

Single beds with full-width rear washroom

front lounge settees which double up as beds. The former are a continental innovation and often sit quite high atop a substantial rear garage, while the latter are an evolution of the traditionally British rear lounge configuration – but redeployed in a front lounge.

The height of fixed singles above rear garages means they are usually accessed via a set of steps – and many have the best of both worlds option of a slot-in central section turning them into a huge fixed longitudinal double. However, such a generous bed inevitably means the kitchen, washroom and especially the lounge are squeezed – and these vehicles aren't well suited for lounging around in.

The better option for those who like a big lounge is the British approach of opposing settees. This layout does restrict the provision of travel seats – although some manufacturers get round this by incorporating a forward facing half dinette with two seatbelts within the lounge.

How the rest of the space in the van is arranged largely depends on the size of the vehicle in question, with many placing a generous washroom at the back of the van while others – like Autocruise in the Augusta – separating the habitation into three distinct areas.

Island beds

The obvious solution to the French bed's intrinsic design defect of requiring slumberers to climb over one another to get in and out is to create space either side of the bed, which is exactly what an island bed does.

Unfortunately, an island bed tends to take up a lot of space, so this particular innovation was the sole preserve of big American Recreational Vehicles – until recently.

Over the last three years, island beds have become increasingly common – both in continental

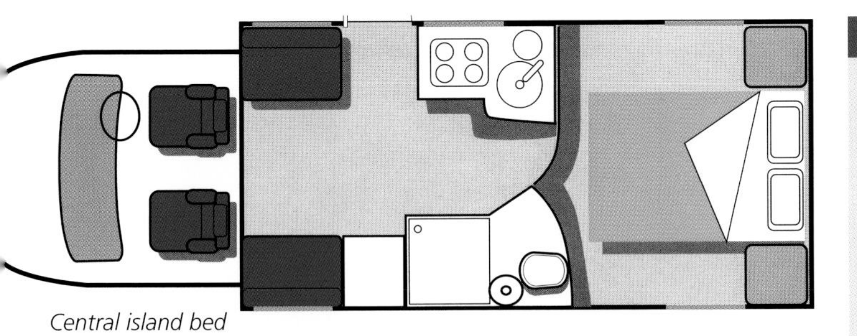

Central island bed

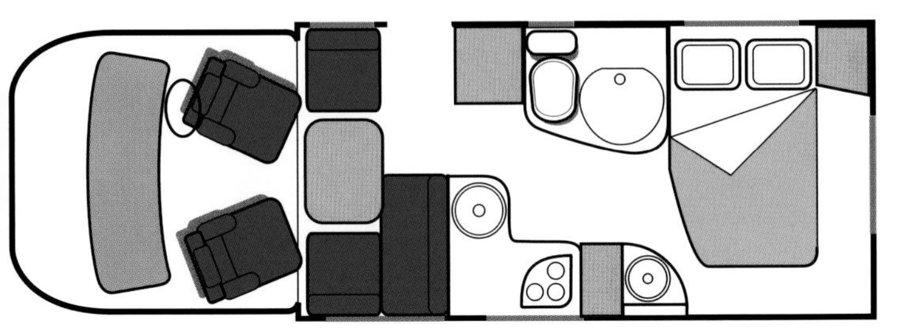

Transverse island bed

OVERVIEW

PROS:
Comfort, ease of access.

CONS:
Consumes even more space than a French bed.

IDEAL FOR:
Couples who are happy to drive a larger vehicle or sacrifice living space for a similar bed to the one at home.

BENCHMARK MODELS:
Auto-Trail Cheyenne 840D, Swift Kon-Tiki 669, Chausson Allegro, Autocruise OakmontTrooper, Autocruise Pulse

motorhomes and upmarket British vans – although for space reasons, they remain a rarity in the sub-7-metre market, with one or two notable exceptions.

The obvious place for a fixed island bed is right in the middle of the back wall of the habitation – usually with his 'n' hers wardrobes and bedside cabinets either side. However, an increasing number of manufacturers are experimenting with transverse island beds, usually with a small washroom in the rear corner, which can incorporate the benefits of an island bed within a shorter vehicle.

Opinions over how to sub-divide the remaining habitation remain divided, with some opting for an en-suite approach and others going for a completely separate washroom.

The island bed in an Eriba Car Emotion

Family-friendly layouts

Motorhomes are overwhelmingly popular with retired or semi-retired couples in the UK, but there is a slowly growing constituency of younger families who have bought into the freedom the lifestyle offers.

It's a different story on the continent, where affordable family-oriented layouts are an important part of the market and the British manufacturers are showing signs of waking up to this embryonic market over here.

It's the Europeans, however, who still offer the greatest choice of layouts in the four and six-berth stakes although many of these are aimed at the rental market and so tend to be 'no frills' overcab models.

Bunk layouts tend to revolve around three basic themes: fixed across the rear, fixed along one side or Pullman dinettes with a pull-out bunk. The most important considerations are how old the children are and whether the bunks are safe for them. Most manufacturers advise against very young children sleeping in top bunks and place an age limit on these, while some impose a weight limit on the upper bunk and in others, the bunks are simply

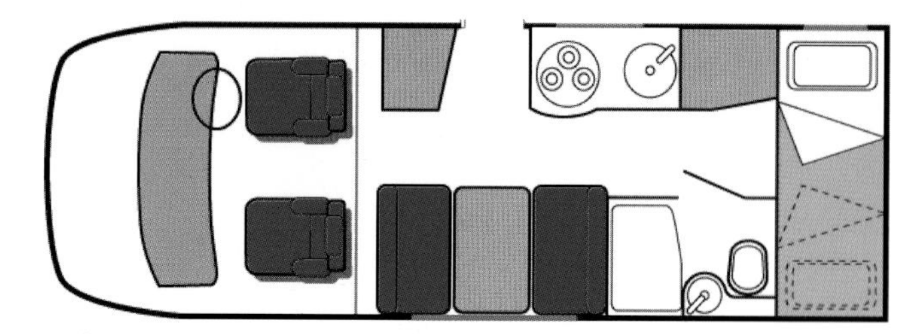
Transverse rear bunks

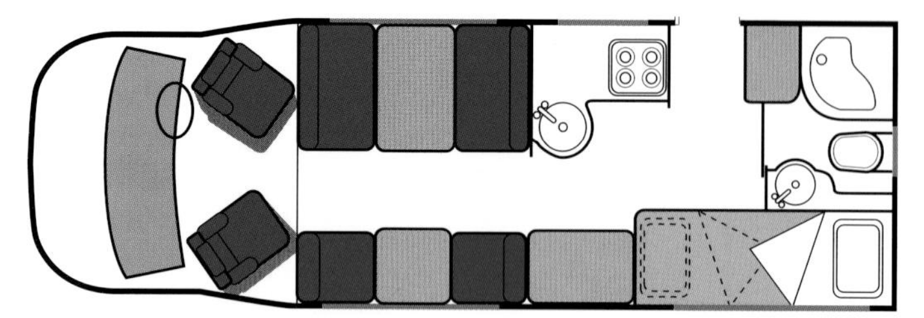
Rear bunks with twin dinettes

OVERVIEW

PROS:
Efficient use of space, flexibility to use as storage.

CONS:
Tend to be found in low-spec, budget vans – although there are exceptions.

IDEAL FOR:
Family motorhomers with more than two children.

BENCHMARK MODELS:
Rimor Katamarano 3, Chausson Flash 03, Bürstner Nexxo Family A694, Roller Team Auto Roller 700

Rear bunks

too small for children above a certain size. This can mean that the window during which a bunk layout is appropriate is quite small.

Check carefully the design specifications of the bunks in any models you consider and don't worry if you conclude that you would be better suited to a standard four-berth van without bunks – the choice of vehicle available – particularly on the used market – will be that much greater.

If you have more than two children however, bunks are probably the only way to go, and the best way to achieve accommodation for such a substantial clan is usually to split the lounge into two Pullman dinettes – a single and a double.

Garage layouts

The incorporation of a garage within the footprint of a motorhome is something that – until recently – many people associated with upmarket European motorhomes of 7-metres-plus or massive US RVs.

The truth is rather different and some sub-6-metre vans now boast quite capacious garages within very compact proportions

The appeal of a garage is obvious: it offers a substantial, secure storage space for a little runaround like a scooter, mountain bikes or even a motorbike, if that's your thing.

Check whether the garage has a loading ramp, lashing points and lighting

Some garages have access from both sides

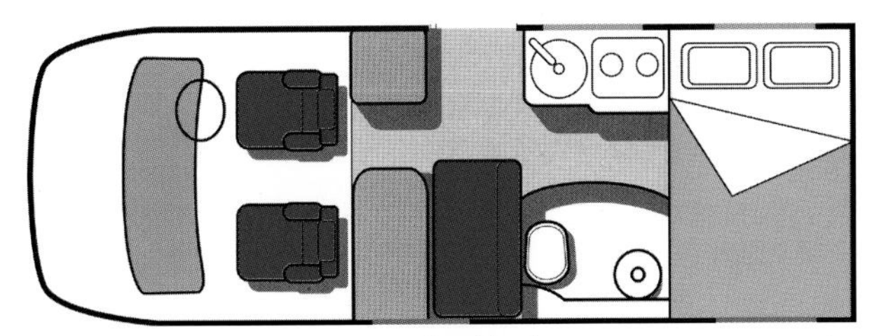

Compact 6-metre transverse fixed bed

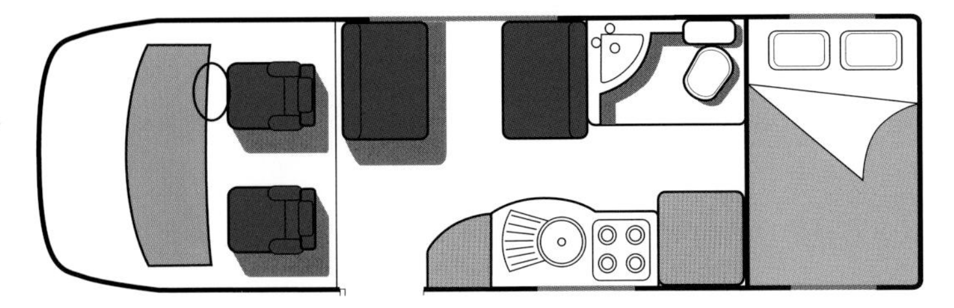

Garage with front dinette

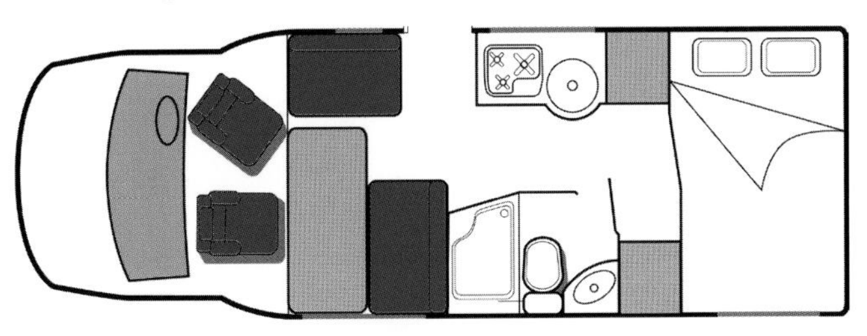

Garage with Euro lounge

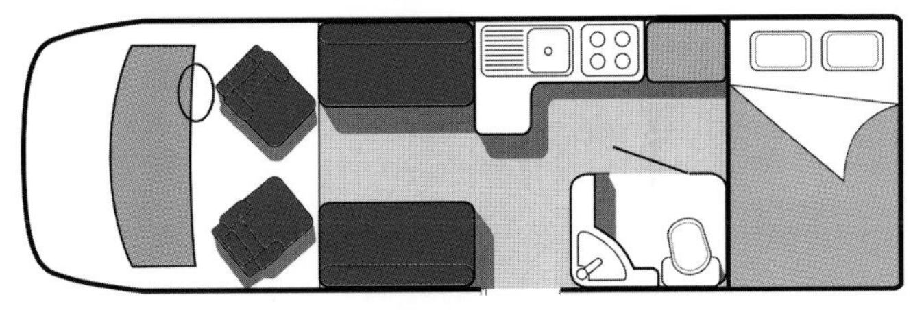

Garage with transverse lounge

Typically and almost without variation, European garage layouts involve rear fixed beds – usually slotted in sideways – but occasionally lengthways. In compact vans, this inevitably militates for a front lounge layout in which the kitchen and washroom are generally squeezed. In longer vehicles, there's less compression and some of the big tag-axle interpretations like Bürstner's A747, offer a huge garage, fixed bed, decent kitchen and washroom and a separate lounge – but this sort of luxury comes at a price and it's unlikely such a long vehicle will fit onto your driveway comfortably.

However, the increasingly popular 'van' class vehicle – again epitomised by Bürstner in its Travel Van – still offers a very usable garage in a compact sub-6-metre package.

But if you decide that a motorhome with a garage is the way forward, do take the following into consideration: if you're going to stow a scooter in there, check the van's user payload and ascertain whether a loading ramp is included. Also have a look at the flooring of the garage and check whether it has lashing points. Lighting is another important feature which may not be included as standard.

Finally, in these environmentally enlightened times, electric bicycles seem set to eclipse the scooter as a clean and green means to explore your environs but if you are contemplating the purchase of his 'n' hers bikes – check there's sufficient room to get them BOTH in the garage.

OVERVIEW

PROS:
Secure storage, ease of access, no need to tow a trailer.

CONS:
Eats into living space – especially in sub-6-metre vans.

IDEAL FOR:
People who want to pitch up and explore the locale by bike or scooter.

BENCHMARK MODELS:
Bürstner Travel Van 570G, Bessacarr E789, Adria Coral Compact, Autocruise Starblazer

And so to bed

Most motorhomes on sale in the UK – almost without exception - will sleep at least two people. However, the detail of the sleeping arrangements varies enormously.

If there are just the two of you, you'll be spoilt for choice, but what sort of beds do you need?

The best solution is a fixed island double bed allowing both parties easy, independent access without clambering over one another to get in or out.

Many fairly compact coachbuilts offer this option, but you're unlikely to find a van conversion with such luxury, and even in a coachbuilt, a fixed double eats up an awful lot of space.

A more common option, is an offset double or French bed, which usually slots into one corner of the van. The only drawback here is that the person nearest the sidewall has to climb over their partner to get out of bed.

It's a similar story with the transverse double bed, which is a common arrangement in many van conversions and to get around this issue, many manufacturers now offer twin bed arrangements. Inevitably, it means a slightly less intimate sleeping arrangement, but in practicality terms, a pair of singles is hard to beat.

A fixed island bed is luxurious but eats up space

A fixed French bed - Lunar Roadstar 786

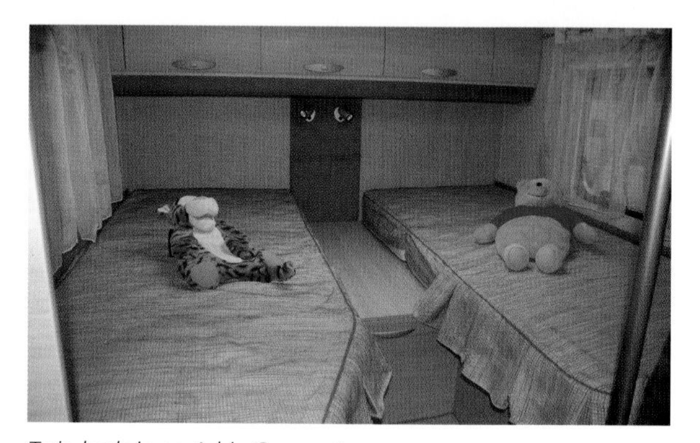

Twin beds in an Adria Compact

But the huge number of variations on the bunking theme don't stop here. One of the most space-efficient options, which is common in the classically British rear lounge layout, are the settees which converts into a large double at night.

This usually involves pulling out a slatted support or using the table as a base and using the seatbacks to fill in the gaps between the seats to form a big double bed.

It's a simple solution which maximises both living and sleeping space, but it does involve a fair bit of shuffling around immediately before bedtime – which puts a lot of people off.

In multi-berth motorhomes (vans with three or more beds), the dinette often converts into a double bed using a similar mechanism to the cushion-shuffling arrangement outlined above, but this is usually the secondary bed.

The primary bed in a four or five berth van usually involves some sort of overcab arrangement. In the aspirational A-class, this often takes the

Pull-down bed - Carthago Chic C-Line

form of the ultra space-efficient pull-down bed. This sits just below the roofline during the day, but then drops down on hydraulic arms to rest just above the level of the dashboard – making access relatively easy – although the resting heights of drop-down beds do vary substantially.

In more common, and substantially cheaper coachbuilts, the overcab bed is the primary sleeping space. The same access issues which apply to the fixed French bed – namely needing to clamber over one another to get in and out apply to the overcab, but there's an added complication: height. Many overcabs are well over four feet above the motorhome floor and accessed by a fairly narrow ladder.

They're fine if you're in the first flush of youth, but can be a bit awkward to access for people with any sort of mobility issues. Similarly, despite having a substantial safety net across the open side, many parents (or grandparents) remain uncomfortable with the idea of young children sleeping in the overcab.

Overcab bed - Swift Escape 624

Overcabs also vary substantially in terms of the headroom on offer and those with only small windows and no roof vent can feel a little like coffins!

Bed height can also be an issue in low-profile vans with rear garages, where the fixed transverse double is often set quite high off the floor.

In some upmarket 7-metre plus coachbuilts, you may find both a fixed bed and an overcab – giving the best of both worlds – but bear in mind the additional storage and manoeuvring implications of owning such a large vehicle.

Finally, there's the bunk option, which is relatively rare in the couples-dominated UK motorhome market, but common in the more family-friendly European arena. Typically, two or even three bunks will be racked along the back or side wall of the van. They make sense for children, but check carefully on any weight restrictions before adults use them.

KEY CONSIDERATIONS:

- Do you have any mobility issues?
- How likely is one or both parties to get up in the middle of the night?
- Are you happy to shuffle cushions prior to turning in?

HOW MANY BERTHS?

This may seem like a pretty obvious question, but there are one or two additional considerations which may need to be taken into account before arriving at a decision.

If there's just the two of you, there is a huge range of vehicles open to you – ranging from tiny little compact coachbuilts up to luxurious A-classes with spacious lounges, large washrooms and fantastic kitchens.

But what if you'd like to take the grandchildren for the odd holiday, or you'd like to be able to lend the van to relatives with children or take friends along with you?

If this sounds likely, then it will save money in the long run to opt for the additional flexibility offered by a multi-berth, rather than discovering you need extra beds at a later stage and having to trade up.

The other big consideration with multi-berths is where your extra guests will travel in the van – but that's something we address in greater detail in subsequent chapters.

Lounge and overcab beds - this Lunar Roadstar 786 sleeps up to six

What you get for your money

Membership of the motorhome club can cost surprisingly little if you're prepared to compromise on the latest creature comforts and rough it in an elderly camper.

The table below offers a rough indication of what you can expect for your investment. The values are approximate, so allow some leeway either side for haggling, but the second-hand values are all based on a sample of real motorhomes for sale in MMM Magazine.

At the time of writing, list prices of new vehicles,particularly European models, were adversely affected by the weakness of Sterling, prompting many dealers to quote prices in Euros.

This situation could revert back in favour of Sterling again in the not-to-distant future, but as it stands, imported motorcaravans will remain expensive in the UK and this could potentially increase the second-hand value of imported motorhomes under three years old.

For a more up-to-date indication of how much your ideal van is going to cost, visit the classified advertising section of the MMM website at www.outandaboutlive.co.uk

PRICE	VEHICLE TYPE	COMMENTS
Under £2,000	High-mileage van conversions, DIY van conversions and elderly coachbuilts.	Well, it's a step up from a tent, but accommodation will be basic and appliances dated. View DIY conversions with a degree of suspicion.
£2,000 to £5,000	Elderly coachbuilts and high mileage campers.	There are bargains to be had at this money – but expect things to go wrong.
£5,000 to £7,500	Reasonable campers – especially Japanese imports – elderly coachbuilts in good nick and interesting compacts.	A surprising range of choice here. Do your homework and look for service histories and authenticated mileages. Check for signs of water damage on coachbuilts and evidence of welding on van conversions.
£7,500 to £10,000	Serviceable coachbuilts and even elderly A-classes. Clean campers and quality used Mazda Bongos.	At this money, private sales usually represent better value for money. Do your homework and spend time quizzing the vendors. If they seem genuine, you could get a bargain. Never buy unseen.
£10,000 to £15,000	Top-spec Japanese imports, elderly LHD A-classes, well-used smaller US RVs, 5-10-year-old coachbuilts and van conversions	A huge choice of used vehicles opens up for this money. The trade-off is between buying something newer, but basic, or older, but more luxurious – but remember, the more toys a van has fitted, the more there is to go wrong!
£15,000 to £20,000	New micro-campers, nearly new coachbuilts and good quality van conversions. Elderly, but well-maintained Auto Sleepers monococques.	New or nearly new compact two-berths are a realistic possibility for this money, but you'll get significantly more for your money on the used market and somebody else will have paid the early depreciation.

PRICE	VEHICLE TYPE	COMMENTS
£20,000 to £25,000	Enormous choice of used vehicles from quality used coachbuilts and low profiles to elderly but well-maintained A-classes. High quality, low mileage van conversions. Poverty-spec new overcab coachbuilts.	Here's where the new versus used dilemma starts to rear its head. For this money, you could buy new or nearly new, but buying used still gets more bangs for bucks. Low mileages are common on under-used motorhomes, but check mileage records of older vehicles with obvious signs of wear and tear. Expect good service histories on private sales and warranties from dealers.
£25,000 to £30,000	Realistic entry level for economy class overcab coachbuilts and basic van conversions and campers. Huge amount of quality used coachbuilts and the odd LHD A-class.	You'll still get a lot more for your money in the used market, but if the reassurance of a manufacturer's warranty is an important factor, buying new is an option. The choice of new vehicles remains limited however. Look for full service histories and consistent habitation checks on used vans. Check for signs of water ingress or accident repairs.
£30,000 to £40,000	Fabulous choice of desirable, high spec used vehicles – A-classes, big US RVs, TAG-axle multiberths. New coachbuilts, low-profiles and compact A-classes – but few extras for this money.	Buying new is a serious prospect in this territory and there's a huge choice of layouts and construction styles, but don't expect too many optional extras at this money. A well-specced three-year-old van will have more toys – but think hard about the huge difference in the driveability of older base vehicles like the old Ducato and Transit compared with new models.
£40,000 to £50,000	We're running out of used options here – but this price range includes high end van conversions, well-specced low-profiles and coachbuilts with more refined engines and entry level A-classes.	Bear in mind that while the smaller converters may offer a bespoke personal service, the large operations will have more extensive dealer networks. Demand first class service if buying new from a dealer. When considering used upmarket vans, look for comprehensive service histories and a genuine reason for sale.
£50,000 to £60,000	This sort of money used to secure a decent new A-class, but the weakness of Sterling has put paid to that. Upmarket UK coachbuilts currently represent better value.	The value of Sterling has a huge bearing on the affordability of imported motorhomes and recent market turmoil has played havoc with pricing. This puts UK manufacturers like Swift and Auto-Trail at a distinct advantage at this end of the market.
£60,000 to £70,000	Top of the range coachbuilts and brand new A-classes – but you may be surprised by the standard level of spec. Huge US RVs.	While UK manufacturers tend to throw in a generous level of specification as standard for this sort of money, some German brands can still be surprisingly mean – charging extra for everything from metallic paint to a cab door on the right side.
£70,000 Plus	Prestige German A-classes and truck-based coachbuilts with all the bells and whistles.	You'll need to check your eligibility to drive vehicles of over 7.5-tonnes then work out where you're going to store it.

New or used?

IT'S the motorhomer's eternal dilemma and subject of countless dinner table discussions – do we buy new or look for something bigger and better equipped on the used market?

You can actually buy a new motorhome in the UK for a little over £20,000, but it will be a pretty small and Spartan affair and imagine how much further that money would go if it were spent on the used market.

Now motorhomes don't lose money as quickly as cars, but it's an inescapable fact of life that the steepest part of the depreciation curve is in the first year or two of a motorhome's life.

For those who are lucky enough to have the money, buying new seems like the logical solution, but once you've settled on a budget and chosen your dream van, you'll be about to sign on the dotted line when someone points out that, for the same money, you could afford an immaculate three-year-old A-class with a fixed bed and a fancy end washroom.

The table on page 46 gives a rough illustration of how far your money goes on the new and used markets – illustrating just how tricky the decision can be – and it's the sheer number of variables involved in the decision that often pushes the actual cost of the vehicle right down the priority list!

Like so many decisions relating to the size and style of motorhome, there's a huge amount of choice and variation out there, so we can only offer a few pointers: the big decision has to be made by the individual. As ever, do your homework first, look at as many different makes and models as possible and shop around.

BUYING NEW

There's nothing quite like picking up a new vehicle from the dealers and the experience is probably still more exciting when the vehicle in question is a motorhome. Collecting your brand new van marks the culmination of months of contemplation, elimination and anticipation and it's always going to be an exciting experience – particularly if you're planning to head off on your first adventure straight from the dealer's showroom.

However, simply driving it off the forecourt usually equates to a paper loss of several thousand pounds – although that's probably not a very positive way of looking at your brand new pride and joy.

There are some very good reasons for a buying a motor home new, however. Perhaps the biggest advantage given the vast range of choice out there, is the ability to specify the exact layout, level of equipment and engine spec you want. Finding the perfect combination on the used market is always going to be more hit and miss.

Opt to purchase from a smaller converter and you may even be able to choose the base vehicle and specify some very individualised options into the bargain.

Motorhomes are complex beasts, much more so than even the most luxurious passenger car and it's reassuring to know that if something does go wrong, you should have immediate expert back-up from your dealer – and in some cases – direct from the manufacturer.

The vehicle upon which the motorhome is based should be covered by a two- or three-year manufacturer's warranty and the bigger converters usually include a longer warranty to cover the integrity of the body. Smaller converters also usually offer some sort of warranty – although the customer is likely to have developed a strong personal relationship with the converter during the specification and build process and any issues that do arise subsequently are likely to be dealt with promptly.

Once you've swallowed the initial depreciation hit, the van should still be worth a substantial proportion of the purchase price when you come to trade it in as there's a ready market for well looked after three-to-five year old motorhomes.

Timing of the purchase is also an important factor – both for the dealer and the customer. Pick the right time of year to buy and you may be able to negotiate a substantial discount, particularly on 'nearly new' vehicles which have been used as

BUS II
85
FIAT

demonstrators. Dealers traditionally start looking to offload stock in September, so a ring-round then may yield some surprising results, as long as you are prepared to be flexible over layout and specification.

September is also a good time to start thinking about ordering a brand new motorhome for the following year, leave it until spring and the lead times many manufacturers operate on could mean you don't take delivery until the following autumn if demand is high.

The biggest risk facing prospective buyers of new motorhomes is realising after just a few months' ownership, that they have brought the wrong layout. Experienced motorhomers are less likely to suffer this problem, but first time buyers should be satisfied that they've done their homework on the right layout for them or risk losing a lot of money when they are forced to trade it in for a motorhome with a more appropriate layout.

BUYING NEW: PROS & CONS

PROS

- Ability to specify exact layout, trim and engine options
- Base vehicle and manufacturer warranties
- Ongoing dealer support
- Latest technology, better fuel efficiency lower emissions
- More refined to drive

CONS

- Steep initial depreciation
- Long lead times between order and delivery
- A used van which meets your needs more closely may represent better value
- Trading in a new van with the 'wrong' layout could prove costly

Buying second-hand can offer much better value

BUYING USED

Motorhomes are based on panel vans which are designed to withstand a fair amount of abuse during their working lives. It's not unusual for commercial fleets to expect their vehicles to cover 50,000 miles a year and they'll often be subject to an unpredictable combination of high motorway speeds and stop-start city traffic with variable loads over the course of their relatively short working lives.

Motorhomes, by comparison, have it relatively easy. Many clock up only a few thousand miles a year and never carry anything approaching their maximum payload. Their owners generally cherish and look after their vehicles and treat them rather like pampered pets.

So buying a second-hand motorhome with a mileage that in commercial vehicle terms would be viewed as only just run-in, can make a great deal of sense.

However, motorhomes are complicated vehicles and there's an awful lot which can potentially go wrong, so it's even more important to do your homework prior to making a purchase.

Check the classified sections of the established motorhome magazines such as MMM to get an idea of current prices and bear in mind that asking prices are likely to be inflated to leave room for haggling.

If you have a specific make and model in mind, find out as much as you can about that vehicle so you can recognise the various layout options and trim levels.

Irrespective of whether you are buying privately or from a dealer, be prepared to ask lots of direct questions (see page 67) and to get the best possible deal, you should also be happy to haggle, or walk away when you know the price is too high.

Above all, make sure you know exactly what you are buying and don't, whatever you do, get attached to the vehicle and start planning your first trip away, BEFORE you've agreed on a price.

HERE'S THE DEAL

PROS

- More motorhome for your money
- Large numbers of low-mileage vans in good condition for sale
- Slower depreciation
- Wider choice of makes and models
- Chance of finding a real bargain in the private ads

CONS

- Unlikely to find the perfect layout, trim and engine combination
- Interiors can date very quickly
- Unwanted modifications from previous owners
- Hidden mechanical or habitation problems
- Older base vehicles are significantly less refined to drive
- Big margins if buying through a dealer
- No warranty support if buying privately

DEALER OR PRIVATE SALE?

While you'll almost certainly get a sharper price from a private vendor, buying from a reputable dealer should offer a little more reassurance in the form of a warranty and hopefully some sort of after-sales service – particularly if you are spending upwards of £20,000.

Only you can decide what constitutes a 'reputable' dealer, but if you get evasive or ambiguous answers to the key questions on page 67, our advice is to exercise extreme caution before proceeding with a purchase.

There's nothing wrong with buying a motorhome which has a 'history' – repaired accident damage or mechanical issues, but an honest dealer will be upfront about this and it should be reflected in the price. View any attempts to cover up issues such as water ingress, excessive wear and tear for the mileage or major accident damage as a good reason for walking away from the deal.

Remember that size doesn't always equate to strength when it comes to customer service and the slick salesman in the glass and steel showroom may be much less enthusiastic about rectifying a broken gearbox than the small family-owned outfit on the industrial estate and vice versa.

It's also worth bearing in mind that if you travel a couple of hundred miles to get a 'never to be repeated' deal on a used van, you might have to repeat that journey every time it needs servicing.

If you can find a dealer you trust within an hour of where you live who has a good turnover of quality used stock and their own workshop, it will save an awful lot of to-ing and fro-ing – with possible overnight stops – for servicing and repair.

Private sales usually involve a lot more telephone calls and legwork, but the rewards can be handsome. Regrettably, many motorhomers are forced to 'retire' from the scene through illness or infirmity, and dealers will be unwilling to pay a realistic price for their vans unless they're going to replace it with another motorhome.

People in this situation are genuinely reluctant vendors and whilst it may seem opportunistic to capitalise on their particular predicament, offering a fair price for the vehicle will probably exceed what they would get from a dealer.

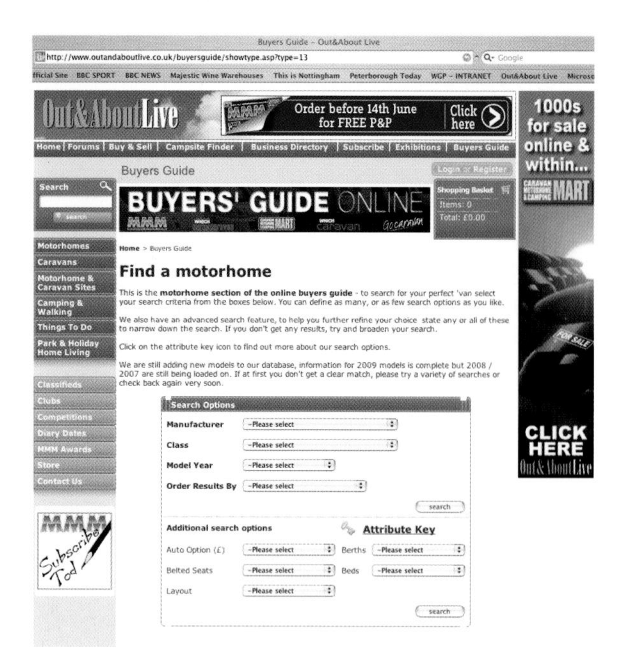

There are hundreds of motorhomes at outandaboutlive.co.uk

Again, make sure you ask the right questions, preferably over the phone before travelling any significant distance to view a van and don't get involved if any of the responses seem questionable.

Try to build up a picture of the vendor's pattern of usage and look for evidence of regular base vehicle servicing, habitation checks and gas and electrical tests and, of course, MOTs. Membership of an owners' club is often a positive indication of genuine enthusiasm for the brand and usually signifies that the van has been well looked after.

Check for wear and tear inside and out, especially around the seals and joins, and be especially alert for signs of damp or mould. Amateur improvements and modifications, especially if they involve cutting or screwing into the bodywork, should be treated with an element of caution.

Always ask to see the motorhome at the seller's house if possible (check the address on the vehicle registration document). Be wary if it is at a storage site and never, ever arrange to meet the seller in a car park. Avoid viewing the vehicle either after dark or in the rain, as dents and scrapes are more easily concealed. Try to take a friend for advice and moral support.

Just as if you were buying a car, always insist on seeing full documentation and proof of ownership, along with the chassis and engine number. Both the AA and the RAC offer online history checks and you can book a full inspection and road test.

Insist on a test drive and a demonstration of all the equipment, including everything that operates from a mains hook-up. Thoroughly check the condition of all seals, both external and internal, as it can be a very time-consuming operation to replace them.

Private vendors won't offer you a warranty, but most vehicles under seven years old will qualify for an insured warranty from a specialist provider if you want additional peace of mind.

EBAY

THERE are literally thousands of motorhomes available at any one time on auction website eBay and many motorhomers who have purchased using this avenue report positive experiences.

More and more motorhome dealers are offering vehicles with 'Buy it Now' prices or using eBay's classified adverts as a route to market.

If you're internet-literate, it's definitely worth factoring eBay into the equation, but we'd suggest the following precautions:

- Don't bid without inspecting the vehicle – always arrange a viewing and avoid any vendor who tells you it breaks eBay's auction rules.
- Ask the vendor to answer the questions on our buyer's checklist (see P65).
- Ask for a test drive. If it's refused, think very carefully whether you are comfortable buying a vehicle you have never driven.
- Know what you're dealing with – establish the exact make and model before making any sort of bid.
- When considering an eBay purchase from a dealer – check their customer feedback – it's in the top right hand corner of the page.
- If buying privately, also take feedback into account. Be wary about buying from anyone with zero feedback or any negative feedback.

Buying at auctions can bag you a bargain, but only if you know exactly what you want and how much you are prepared to pay

- Establish a reasonable price and stick to it – don't get into a competitive bidding war which is one of the reason's why eBay's is so popular with vendors!

- Think about how you are going to arrange payment if you 'win' the item – some vendors insist on conducting transactions through the Paypal online payment system.

AUCTIONS

SOME of the big car auction houses hold occasional caravan and motorhome auctions where the odd bargain may pop up.

Many of the vehicles up for auction are likely to be relatively new and some may be finance company repossessions, so these auctions usually attract a healthy attendance of professional traders who can spot a lemon – or a genuine bargain – from 100 yards away.

If you're confident you know exactly what you are looking for and happy to bid against the pros, then get to the auction early and check out every motorhome that may be of interest before they go under the hammer.

Our advice is to go along to at least one auction to get the feel for how it works, but don't take any form of payment in case you are tempted!

When you are ready to buy, you'll need to be prepared to pay within a couple of days of purchase, or you'll lose the deal.

For details of British Car Auctions' specialist sales at Measham, Nottingham and Tewkesbury, log onto www.british-car-auctions.co.uk

PRIVATE IMPORTS

Not so long ago, buying a motorhome on the continent was a pretty smart move. The strength of the Pound meant there were significant savings to be made by buying new or used in France, Germany or Holland.

Big European motorhome dealers were only too happy to receive enquiries from the UK and many couples combined a visit to the dealer with a short break over the Channel.

Some people made savings of up to 20 per cent – several thousand of pounds – on the equivalent model in the UK and most were able to overcome any issues with servicing and warranties with surprisingly little fuss.

The majority of people who opted to buy in Europe reported a positive experience, with helpful, English-speaking dealers who were very amenable to UK customers.

As long as you were prepared to settle for a left hand drive model, buying used overseas also made a lot of sense with the potential for sizable savings to be made.

The recent turmoil in the global economy and massive fluctuations in the foreign currency markets have all but cancelled out the advantages of hopping across to the continent in search of big savings and unless Sterling makes a strong recovery against the Euro – this state of affairs looks set to prevail for some time.

However, if you want a wider choice of layouts and vehicle specifications or a specific layout which is unavailable in the UK for example a large family-orientated multi-berth motorhome, a trip to Europe may still be an option, although it's unlikely to be any cheaper than a similar model in Britain.

The other complications you may encounter are getting hit for two lots of VAT – in the country where you buy it and again upon import into the UK – and difficulties obtaining insurance for the journey from the supplying dealer into the UK. Some insurance companies are now insisting that the vehicle is UK-registered BEFORE they will cover it.

To research the potential for savings or pinpoint a specific model, the following sites are worth a look, but with the exception of Bundesvan, you'll need a basic grasp of German to navigate them!

www.bundesvan.co.uk
www.dhd24auto.com
www.mobile.de

Hopping over to the continent for a bargain is a thing of the past but it may still be worth it if you want a wider choice of layouts

Grey imports from the Far East and converted in the UK look good value and are gaining in popularity

JAPANESE IMPORT CAMPERS

IF you're in the market for a compact campervan, the growing number of specialist converters of Japanese import vehicles are worth considering.

Draconian Japanese pollution legislation means motorists over there trade in their RHD cars much more frequently than we do, ensuring a steady supply of high quality, low-mileage vehicles in very good condition. They also tend to be almost universally well specced, although the detail finish and styling aren't always to European tastes.

Basically, the converter imports lightly used MPVs from the Far East and converts them into campers in the UK. Compared with European campers of a similar vintage, the prices are attractive and, being Japanese, build quality and reliability are usually excellent. Perhaps the biggest hurdle to overcome is learning to live with something called a Bongo!

For more information on these increasingly popular vehicles, visit: www.wellhouseleisure.com or www.imperialcar.co.uk

HPI CHECKS

If you're about to invest several thousand pounds in a used motorhome, it's important to know that the vehicle doesn't have a hidden history. If it's been stolen, written off or there are outstanding finance payments on it, you could end up losing money, the motorhome or both. In 2001, the UK Motorhome Industry and HPI joined forces to create MINDER, a vehicle security and asset registration system to help protect against theft and fraud.

Motorhomes sold since 2001 carry a unique Motorhome Identification Number (MIN), a Vehicle Identification Number (VIN) and their Vehicle Registration Mark (VRM). This gives a greater all-round level of security to owners and enables future buyers to identify the vehicle and check its history with confidence. In addition, to ensure accurate identification, each motorhome has a hidden electronic tag and visible etching of the MIN number, as well as a permanent warning sticker.

For more information about this service, which is available for a small fee, log onto www.hpicheck.com or contact MINDER on 01722 435478 or email minder.uk@hpi.co.uk.

Left or right hand drive?

A left hand drive motorhome could be a good bet if you plan to take extended trips abroad

THIS may seem like an obvious question, but arrive at the right answer and you could save yourself a significant amount of money.

If you're likely to be covering most of your motorhoming miles in the UK, then obviously, a right hand drive model is the logical answer.

If, however, you are planning to explore the continent for extended periods, then would a 'left hooker' be a better bet?

For someone who has never driven a left hand drive vehicle, the prospect may seem a little intimidating, but it's surprising how quickly people acclimatise. Like learning any new skill, it just takes a little practice and don't worry if you attempt to change gear with the door handle a few times before getting into the swing of it!

Driving a left hand drive van in the UK requires a little bit more circumspection, but if there are usually two of you on board, a little teamwork is all that's needed to check the traffic at junctions and when pulling out and let's face it, you are unlikely to be doing an awful lot of overtaking in a big motorhome.

Another unexpected dividend of driving a left hooker in the UK is the ability to better judge how much room you have to pull onto the verge on narrow country lanes to avoid oncoming vehicles.

On our first (solo) trip in a big left hand drive Carthago, involving some 1,200 miles on a variety of British roads, ranging from motorways to tiny unclassified back roads, after a great deal of initial apprehension, we were completely at home within 36 hours.

On the continent is where a left hand drive motorhome really comes into its own and it's arguably safer than piloting a right hand drive vehicle.

The downside if buying new is that dealers and private punters will be more wary of a left hooker when it comes to trade-in time, which usually translates to lower resale values. The upside of this for the used buyer is that there are some real bargains out there for folk who are prepared to drive a left hooker, but bear in mind that some of the up front savings on the purchase price will be offset by a lower resale value when you come to trade it in.

It's also worth remembering that some continental motorhomes simply aren't available in right hand drive, so if you want a particular layout which isn't available in the UK, the left drive option may be the only one open to you.

The other issue to bear in mind is that a left drive motorhome may be more difficult – and expensive – to insure.

Try before you buy

Trying before you buy is a good way of deciding what suits you before parting with your money – this one is from Campervans.com

AS we've mentioned at several points in the previous chapters, if you're new to motorhoming, sampling the motorhome lifestyle is highly recommended before committing to actually buying your first van.

If you have motorhoming friends, you may be lucky enough to be able to borrow a vehicle, but if this isn't an option, we'd strongly suggest renting a motorhome for at least a weekend to try before you buy. It's a sizable sum of money to spend only to discover that you've bought a completely inappropriate vehicle or, worse still, you conclude that the lifestyle isn't for you.

It's only once you've cooked, slept, washed and generally lounged around in a motorhome that you're in a position to make an informed choice as to what works for you.

Campervan hire from Wellhouse Hire

Even an extended test drive simply won't reveal all the niggles and idiosyncrasies which most motorhomes exhibit, but spending at least 48 hours with a van offers a more meaningful insight into its positive and negative attributes.

Motorhomes inevitably involve compromises: if you want a big fixed bed in a compact coachbuilt, you're unlikely to have a lounge in which you can sprawl around. And if a big garage is more important to you, don't expect to find a large end washroom as well.

Living with a van for a couple of days will allow you to learn which compromises you can live with and which you can't and could save you much more than the rental fee if it helps you make a better choice of vehicle when you are ready to buy.

Motorhome hire isn't as well established in the UK as it is in the States or continental Europe, but it is catching on with well over a hundred rental operators in business in Britain.

Some motorhome dealers offer a rental service and as well as going through a full hand-over of the vehicle, which should include a 'walk-through' demonstrating how the key habitation services work, will even help find you a pitch on a nearby

site. Many will also offer full technical back-up in the event of a breakdown or equipment failure.

If you do hire through a dealer, some will offer a deal whereby they refund the cost of the hire if you subsequently decide to buy a van from them after an enjoyable taster session.

Counterintuitive though it may seem, the best time to hire a motorhome is during the winter months. Hire fees are likely to be much lower and the colder temperatures and shorter days will provide an ideal opportunity to get to grips with important equipment like heating and lighting systems which you may not even use during the summer months.

An alternative, although potentially riskier approach, is to buy a bit of a banger which seems

MOTORHOME RENTAL SPECIALISTS

A1 Motorhome Hire
Tel: 01733 233552

Alnwick Motorhome Hire
Tel: 01665 572632

Amber Leisure (Luton)
Tel: 01582 490079

Atlas Motorhomes
Tel: 01924 862599

Blucamp - Prestige Motorhomes
Tel: 0870 7601400

Blue Sky Motorhome
Tel: 01656 650535

Campervans.com
Tel: 0800 9174347

Danum Motor Company Ltd
Tel: 01302 708566

Easirent Preston
Tel: 01772 886888

East Coast Leisure
Tel: 01268 272227

Emm-Bee Caravans
Tel: 0161 7972988

Escape Motorhome Hire
Tel: 01293 824400

First Class Motorhomes
Tel: 01355 261800

Freedom To Go
Tel: 01697 344759

Go Motorhome
Tel: 0845 686 4473

Hebridean Campervan Holidays
Tel: 01851 704578

Hemmingways
Tel: 0870 7422673

Highland Classic Campers
Tel: 01349 831005

Hirebuddies
Tel: 01623 553988

Johns Cross Motorcaravan Centre
Tel: 01580 881288

Just go
Tel: 0870 2401918

Leisure Hire UK
Tel: 01270 290453

Leisure Time Hire
Tel: 01455 824590

Lincoln Motorhome Hire
Tel: 08454 666667

Meridian Motorhomes
Tel: 02392 467924

Midland Motorcaravan Hire
Tel: 01386 792434

PJB Motorhome Hire
Tel: 01675 481425

Motorhome Ireland
Tel: 02840 621800

North Western Motorhomes
Tel: 0161 4866055

Prestige Motorhomes Ltd
Tel: 0870 7601488

RDH Motorhome Centre
Tel: 0870 7585050

Sharps Vehicle Rental
Tel: 01463 236684

South Coast Campers
Tel: 07989 449393

South West Camper Hire
Tel: 01392 811931

Stewart Mouland Motorcaravans
Tel: 0800 9809462

Sussex Motorhomes
Tel: 07738 914280

Wellhouse Leisure Ltd
Tel: 01484 600416

West Country Motorhomes
Tel: 01934 732503

West Highland Motorhome Rental
Tel: 01631 563638

like good value and spend a couple of months picking up the basics and learning what you like and don't like.

After a few trips, you'll have acquired a surprising amount of knowledge and be in a much stronger position to make an informed decision on the sort of motorhome you really want to commit your nest egg to.

At this point, you could sell the vehicle privately and pay cash for your ideal van or trade it in against the dream machine. With a bit of luck the depreciation on the 'banger' over a period of just a few months will be less than the cost of hiring a van for a taster session. The risk, of course, is that you buy a lemon, which then breaks down and costs an arm and a leg to return to roadworthiness.

Motorhome shows

SHOWS have an important role to play in the motorhome sales process and are popular with both dealers and potential customers.

Unlike car dealerships, motorhome dealers aren't as widely distributed across the country, so it can be difficult to compare competing models from different manufacturers without driving significant distances.

At a show however, all the main manufacturers, importers and converters assemble together in once place, allowing potential buyers to compare the relative merits of their shortlisted vans.

Shows are also a great place to negotiate attractive discounts as the dealers are all keen to beat each others' deals to secure a sale. Indeed, the atmosphere on the last day of some of the outdoor shows can reach fever pitch when dealers are busy trying to clinch deals with tempting incentives.

Under such circumstances, it's easy to get carried away and lose the objectivity and detachment required to make a wise buying decision, so it's important to attend a couple of shows to get a feel for the deals on offer before taking the plunge.

Even then, it's a good idea to stick to a preordained gameplan. Draw up a shortlist of vehicles based on your specific requirements and try not to be seduced by 'never to be repeated' offers on attractive-looking motorhomes which may turn out to be wholly unsuited to your specific needs. Also take into account the practicalities of buying from a dealer at a show who is located a long way from your home such as servicing and repair considerations and the other important aspects of the after sales experience.

British motorhome shows fall broadly into two categories: indoor and outdoor events. The former take place at big venues such as the National Exhibition Centre where the big manufacturers, importers and dealers spend thousands on lavish stands from which to promote their latest models. The latter are often less formal affairs held on showgrounds around the country and while the sales and marketing activity is an important aspect of these shows, they also attract thousands of motorhomers to stay for the weekend on the adjacent rally fields. There's often entertainment in the evenings and, as long as the sun's out, a bit of a festival atmosphere.

The outdoor shows are a fantastic opportunity to compare hundreds of motorhomes in one place, but they're also a great place to meet motorhome enthusiasts and swap tales and experiences – good and bad. Newcomers are usually welcomed into the fold and help and advice is usually readily on offer, so it's an ideal opportunity to get a real flavour of the realities of the motorhome lifestyle.

For the price of a couple of rounds of drinks, you'll get no-nonsense advice from a friendly bunch of folk who know their stuff but don't have an axe to grind.

• *Many of the outdoor shows are organised by Warners Group Publications – publishers of the best-selling MMM Magazine and this guide. For more information about Warners shows, log onto www.outandaboutlive.co.uk/exhibitions*

INDOOR SHOWS

CARAVAN AND MOTORHOME 2009
NEC Birmingham, October 13 – 18
www.caravanshows.com

The biggest indoor caravan and motorhome show in the UK. The NEC this October is the

DIRECTOR'S CUT
EPIC
ERIBA
ERIBA
£72,290
£64,9
£15,18
SPRIT
DETHLEFF
FIAMMA CARE
0870 777 85 86

place to see all the brand new 2010 models from both UK and international manufacturers plus lots more. See caravans, motorhomes, trailer tents, awnings, holiday homes and accessories.

CARAVAN AND MOTORHOME 2010
Manchester Central, January 21 – 24
www.caravanshows.com

Manchester Central (the new name for G-Mex) offers the widest choice of caravans and a wide selection of motorhomes and holiday homes from leading UK and overseas manufacturers.

WELSH CARAVAN MOTORHOME AND OUTDOOR LEISURE SHOW 2010
Cardiff International Arena, January 15 – 17
www.welshcaravanshow.co.uk

Regional caravan and motorhome show for enthusiasts and potential newcomers in the Principality. A mix of big manufacturers and local dealers represented.

SCOTTISH CARAVAN AND OUTDOOR LEISURE SHOW 2010
SECC Glasgow, February 4 – 7
www.caravanshows.com

Big regional caravan and motorhome show for enthusiasts and potential newcomers based north of the border. A good mix of big manufacturers and local dealers represented.

NATIONAL BOAT CARAVAN AND OUTDOOR SHOW 2010
NEC Birmingham, February 23 – 28
www.boatandcaravan.co.uk

A big spring show dominated by caravan and motorhome manufacturers, but also featuring other outdoor activities. Ideal location and a great show for families to visit during the half-term holiday

OUTDOOR SHOWS

THE NATIONAL MOTORHOME SHOW
East of England Showground, Peterborough, April 2010
www.outandaboutlive.co.uk/exhibitions

Curtain-raiser for the new season attracting thousands of visitors emerging from winter hibernation and meeting up with motorhoming friends, many of whom will have spent winter months in sunnier climes in southern Europe or even further afield.

Excellent selection of new and used vehicles for sale, good evening entertainment and plenty of accessories stands and opportunities to chat to friendly enthusiasts. The biggest outdoor show of the year.

THE SOUTHERN MOTORCARAVAN SHOW
Newbury Showground, Berkshire, May 2010
www.outandaboutlive.co.uk/exhibitions

Smaller regional outdoor show which attracts a big attendance of enthusiasts and good representation from manufacturers and local dealers in a pretty setting.

THE NORTHERN MOTORCARAVAN SHOW
Pickering Showground, North Yorkshire, July 2010
www.outandaboutlive.co.uk/exhibitions

Midsummer Show following the usual format which combines motorhome dealer stands and accessories vendors with a big rally.

THE WESTERN MOTORHOME SHOW
Three Counties Showground, Great Malvern, Worcestershire, August 2010
www.outandaboutlive.co.uk/exhibitions

Laid-back summer show with the usual mixture of motorhomes, accessory and specialist stands and evening entertainment with a strong country and western flavour. Don't forget your stetson and line-dancing boots!

MOTORHOME AND US RV SHOW
Royal Bath & West Showground, Shepton Mallet, Somerset, Mid September 2010
www.stoneleisure.com

As well as being an exhibition of motorhomes and accessories it is also a huge gathering for all the major motorhome clubs and an interesting weekend even for the casual motorhomer. There's also potential for an early preview of next season's new models

THE MOTORHOME SHOW, SEASON FINALE
Lincolnshire Showground, Lincoln, September 2010
www.outandaboutlive.co.uk/exhibitions

Another huge outdoor show with a massive attendance of ralliers and over 250 specialist outdoor traders exhibiting the best there is to see in the outdoor leisure market. This is the show for serious bargain-hunters as dealers begin to clear slow-moving new and used stock to make way for the new season's models. Over 50 dealers will be showcasing both new and used British, European and American motorhomes.

The Motorhome Show at the Lincolnshire Showground

Driving licence restrictions

YOUR age and the date when you passed your driving test both have a major bearing on the size of motorhome you can drive on your existing licence together with any trailers you may want to tow.

Changes to the driving licence system which came into force on January 1, 1997 could potentially restrict the weight of vehicles which you are entitled to drive.

So if you passed your test after the above date or are approaching your 70th birthday, read on.

Basically, what you are allowed to drive depends on the category of licence – B, C1 or C – you are in possession of together with when you passed your test. You can establish which category (or categories) of licence you have by checking the letters in the entitlements section on your photocard or licence paperwork.

If you have C or C1 entitlements, and passed the driving test before January 1, 1997, but are under the age of 70 you can drive anything up to 7500kg and tow a trailer weighing up to a further 750kg as long as the Gross Train Weight doesn't exceed 8250kg. If you need to tow a heavier trailer – for example a small car – if the combined weight of the motorhome and trailer exceed 8250kg, you'll need to take a separate test to gain a Light Goods Vehicle licence.

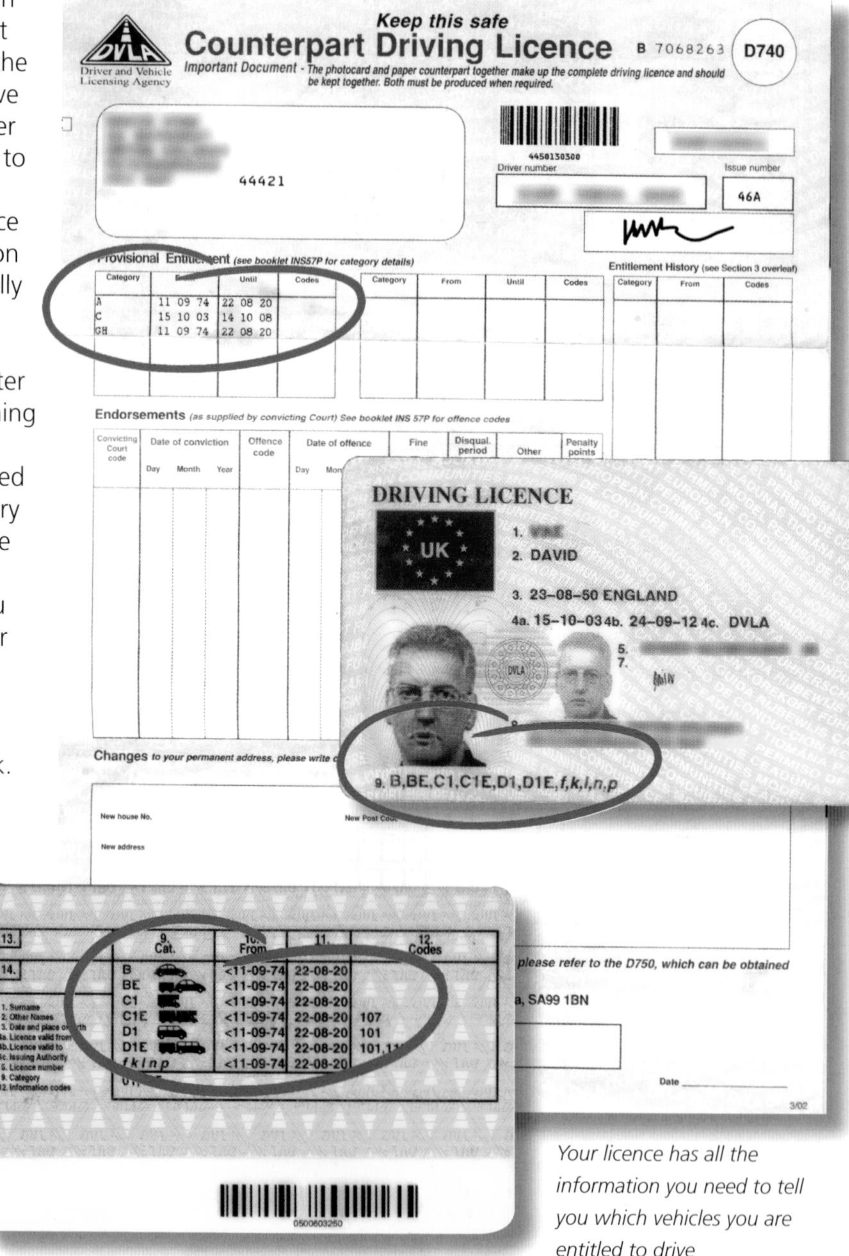

Your licence has all the information you need to tell you which vehicles you are entitled to drive

Those who gained their full licence after January 1, 1997 are fine to drive motorhomes up to 3500kg and tow a trailer of up to 750kg as long as the Gross Train Weight doesn't exceed 4250kg.

People who passed their test after January 1, 1997 who want to drive a motorhome of more than 3500kg need to take a Light Goods Vehicle test and if they want to tow a bigger trailer

Before driving off in a big tag axle beauty like this, make sure you are eligible to drive it!

(such as one with a small car mounted) behind a motorhome of 3500kg or more, then they'll need to take both Category E and C1 tests.

On reaching their 70th birthday, as long as they passed their test before January 1, 1997, drivers of vehicles weighing less than 3500kg should retain their driving entitlements. But if the motorhome's MTPLM exceeds 3500kg, when they reapply for their licence, they'll also need to ask their GP to complete a medical assessment form, including an eyesight test.

Those over 70 who passed their test after January 1997 are still legal to drive motorhomes of under 3500kg, but if their vehicle exceeds this, they'll need to take a C1 test. If the motorhome in question exceeds 7500kg, a further C test is required.

Basically, as long as you restrict yourself to motorhomes with MTPLMs under 3500kg, there shouldn't be any difficulties, but if you want something bigger and/or need to tow a heavy trailer, make sure you know your entitlements before committing to spend any money.

The 3500kg point is also widely used as a threshold on the continent where the normal rules of the road no longer apply. Motorhomes weighing more than this may be subject to different speed limits and pay additional road tolls, so again, do your homework before travelling to unfamiliar countries with a heavy van and bear in mind that some breakdown and recovery organisations will not repatriate a vehicle exceeding 3500kg

If all this still sounds complicated, it's because it is. For chapter and verse on the finer detail, log onto www.dvla.gov.uk or consult the DVLA Booklet D100.

REPLATING

In the case of motorhomes which are only marginally over 3500kg, the simplest course of action may be simply to get them replated to under the threshold weight. This basically means reducing the vehicles' payload, which you'll then need to stick to. For further information on this relatively simple undertaking, contact VOSA for a VTG10 form. Tel: 0300 123 9000. www.vosa.gov.uk

The MTPLM plate

Motorhome magazines

MOTORHOME enthusiasts are blessed with a wide range of magazines – and increasingly websites – which offer a wealth of information on every aspect of buying, maintaining and making the most of your van.

These magazines are a useful starting point for researching the type of motorhome which will suit your needs and are packed with advice on everything from repairing or modifying your van to planning a six-month tour of Europe.

Most magazines devote several pages each month to new motorhomes, often with in-depth reviews and live-in tests, and some cover the used market well, with guidance on what to pay and what to look out for when buying second-hand.

The magazine's classified sections are also a useful indicator of what's available on the used market and how much you can expect to pay for a given vehicle – although the asking prices advertised are usually above the actual transaction price.

There are also a growing number of motorhome forums online, where enthusiasts congregate to chat and pass on handy tips and practical advice together with the odd scurrilous rumour. As with most things on the internet however, these forums are only as good as their participants and the quality and credibility of the debate and information imparted does vary, so it's worth exercising a little discretion until you can discern which sites you can trust and which need to be taken with a healthy dose of scepticism.

MAGAZINES

Motorcaravan Motorhome Monthly

Britain's favourite motorhome magazine. *MMM* is the longest established and highest circulation motorhome magazine, selling some 40,000 copies every month. Technical, travel and product features, plus practical advice and a lively letters page. Much of the editorial is submitted by readers who are incredibly passionate about all things motorhoming. The publishers also organise several outdoor shows and rallies throughout the year and operate the Out and About Live website.

PUBLISHER

Warners Group Publications
The Maltings
Manor Lane
Bourne
Lincolnshire
PE10 9PH

Tel: 01778 391153
Web: www.outandaboutlive.co.uk

Which Motorcaravan

Another magazine from the Warners' stable, but as the name implies, *Which Motorcaravan* focuses almost exclusively on the choosing and buying process. The magazine specialises in detailed, independent motorhome tests and is full of information on forthcoming new models from both British and European manufacturers. Monthly three or four motorhome comparison tests and some useful coverage of the used market.

PUBLISHER

Warners Group Publications
The Maltings
Manor Lane
Bourne
Lincolnshire
PE10 9PH

Tel: 01778 391153
Web: www.outandaboutlive.co.uk

Practical Motorhome

Well-produced lifestyle magazine from the publishers of *What Car?* Magazine. Inspirational travel articles and some good product coverage with a sprinkling of practical advice thrown in for good measure. The magazine always looks great and the articles are presented in a fashion which newcomers will find easily accessible.

PUBLISHER

Haymarket Motoring Publications
60 Waldegrave Road, Teddington TW11 8LG

Tel: 01795 414812
Web: www.practicalmotorhome.com

Motor Caravan Magazine

Lively monthly magazine from publishing giant IPC. Enjoyable, easy-to-read travel articles and some good new products coverage. Private classified ads are free, so it's a good place to find affordable second-hand bargains.

PUBLISHER

IPC Focus
Leon House, 233 High Street
Croydon CR9 1HZ

Tel: 0208 726 8221
Web: www.motorcaravanmagazine.co.uk

Motorhome Monthly

Monthly magazine distributed through selected motorhome dealerships. Usual blend of travel and product articles and a growing website presence. The publishers also organise two popular outdoor motorhome shows at Shepton Mallet and Stratford.

PUBLISHER

Stone Leisure Ltd
Andrew House, 2a Granville Road
Sidcup, Kent DA14 4BN

Tel: 0208 302 6069
Web: www.stoneleisure.com

Caravan, Motorhome & Camping Mart

Dedicated to buying and selling used motorhomes and caravans, *Caravan, Motorhome & Camping Mart* is packed with classified and dealer adverts, but also has some useful articles on the used market. Well worth buying on a regular basis if you're in the market for a used van.

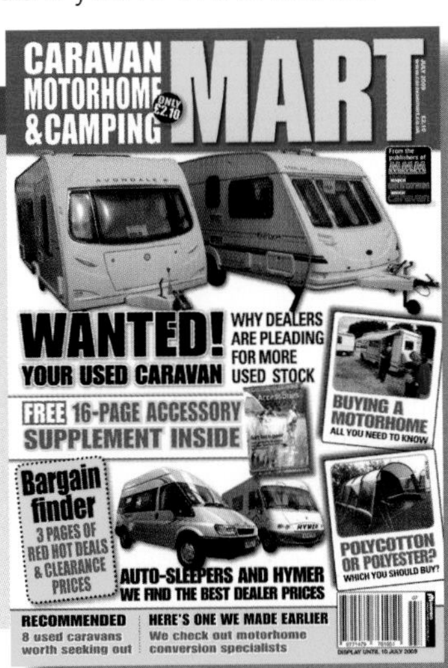

PUBLISHER

Warners Group
Publications
The Maltings
Manor Lane
Bourne
Lincolnshire
PE10 9PH

Tel: 01778 391153
Web: www.

Motorhome & Caravan Trader

Advertising sheet packed with dealer and private ads, but virtually free of editorial. Worth a look if you're seriously in the market for a new, nearly new or used motorhome.

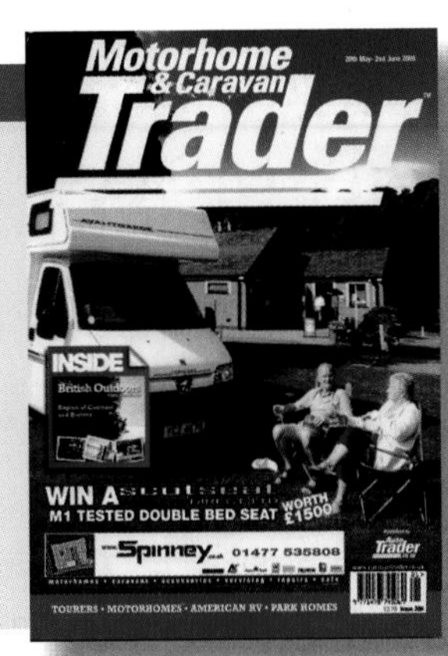

PUBLISHER

Trader Publishing Ltd.
Optimum House Clippers Quay
Salford Quays
Salford
MS0 3XP

Tel: 0161 877 6318
Web:
www.caravantrader.co.uk

WEBSITES

www.outandaboutlive.co.uk

Companion site to Warners Group Publications' portfolio of motorhome, caravan and outdoor titles. A wealth of information available for free and some lively and well patronised forums attracting a friendly crowd of knowledgeable motorhome enthusiasts. Dedicated forums focusing on handy tips, practical advice, travel and technical issues.

www.motorhomefacts.com

There's a lively online community of enthusiasts on this popular forum and newcomers are usually made very welcome.

www.motorhomefun.co.uk

Relatively recent addition to the online motorhoming community – forums are quite busy and the banter remains pretty light-hearted most of the time.

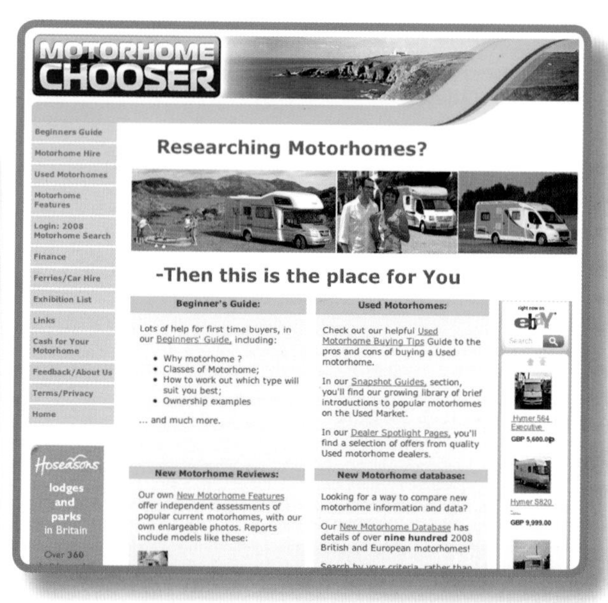

www.motorhome-chooser.com

Interesting site dedicated to the choosing and buying process. Still developing, but some good advice for folk considering their first motorhome purchase.

Motorhome chooser checklist

MOST first time buyers use a process of elimination to narrow down the vast range of motorhomes on the British market to a manageable shortlist of a dozen or so vehicles which fit the bill.

Answer the following series of questions carefully and you should arrive at the ideal specification for your perfect motorhome. The questions get progressively more detailed so you may not need to go right to the end of the list to arrive at a manageable shortlist, but you may want to add some questions of your own if you have any very specific needs.

It's then simply a case of finding a vehicle which fits the bill. Study the magazine reviews, get as many brochures as you can, visit the shows and pore over the small ads and sooner or later, you should find your ideal motorhome at a price you can afford.

Happy hunting!

How many berths do you need?

1☐ 2☐ 3☐ 4☐ 5☐ 6☐ 6+☐

How many travel seats do you need?

1☐ 2☐ 3☐ 4☐ 5☐ 6+☐

What sort of layout?

- ☐ Rear lounge
- ☐ Front lounge
- ☐ Fixed bed: French bed
- ☐ Fixed bed: Island
- ☐ Fixed bed: Twins
- ☐ End washroom
- ☐ Garage
- ☐ Bunks

What cab specification do you need?

- ☐ Electric windows
- ☐ Electric mirrors
- ☐ Stereo
- ☐ CD player
- ☐ Air conditioning
- ☐ Driver and passenger airbags
- ☐ Cab blinds
- ☐ Cruise control
- ☐ Sat Nav
- ☐ Reversing camera

What kitchen equipment do you need?

- ☐ Small stove
- ☐ Hob
- ☐ Grill
- ☐ Oven
- ☐ Microwave
- ☐ Fridge
- ☐ Fridge Freezer

What washroom equipment do you expect?

- ☐ Portable chemical toilet
- ☐ Cassette toilet with flush
- ☐ Hot and cold running water
- ☐ Sink
- ☐ Shower
- ☐ Vanity unit

What sort of heating do you need?

- ☐ None
- ☐ Simple space heater
- ☐ Blown air system
- ☐ Radiators
- ☐ Air conditioning

Do you know what class of motorhome are you looking for?

- ☐ Microvan
- ☐ Camper Van
- ☐ Van Conversion
- ☐ Low Profile
- ☐ Coachbuilt
- ☐ Overcab
- ☐ A-Class
- ☐ US RV

What is the maximum vehicle weight your licence permits you to drive?

- ☐ 3500kg or under
- ☐ 3500kg – 7500kg
- ☐ More than 7500kg

Which base vehicle would you prefer?

- ☐ Fiat Scudo
- ☐ Fiat Ducato/Peugeot Boxer
- ☐ Ford Transit
- ☐ Volkswagen Caddy
- ☐ Volkswagen Transporter
- ☐ Mercedes Sprinter
- ☐ Other

What sort of engine would you prefer?

(We'd recommend at least 35bhp per tonne)

- ☐ Under 100bhp
- ☐ 100 – 130bhp
- ☐ 130 – 160 bhp
- ☐ More than 160bhp

What sort of transmission?

☐ Manual 5-sp ☐ Manual 6-sp ☐ Automatic

Driven wheels?

☐ Front ☐ Rear

What length of vehicle?

☐ Under 6m ☐ 6m to 7m ☐ 7m to 8m
☐ 8m to 9m ☐ Over 9m

How much payload do you need?

☐ Under 250kg ☐ 250 – 500kg
☐ 500 – 750kg ☐ 750kg – 1000kg
☐ More than 1000kg

How much water and waste water capacity do you need?

- ☐ Under 100 litres
- ☐ 100-200 litres
- ☐ 200 litres +

How much gas capacity do you need?

☐ Under 5kg ☐ 5-10kg ☐ 10 – 15kg
☐ 15-20kg ☐ 20kg +

Is there sufficient storage space to fully utilise the payload?

☐ Yes ☐ No

Would you consider a left hand drive motorhome?

☐ Yes ☐ No

Do you need external access to storage lockers?

☐ Yes ☐ No

Do you want a factory-fitted bicycle rack?

☐ Yes ☐ No

Do you want to tow a small car behind your motorhome?

☐ Yes ☐ No

Do you need solar panels to top up the battery?

☐ Yes ☐ No

How many mains sockets do you need?

☐ 0 ☐ 1-3 ☐ 3-5 ☐ 5+

What sort of carpets?

☐ None ☐ Fitted ☐ Removable (Looselay)

Second hand checklist

GOOD QUESTIONS TO ASK THE VENDOR

COMBINING the list of your own individual needs in a motorcaravan with a list of standard questions to put to the vendor can save you an awful lot of miles when you're trying to locate your ideal van.

Many of these questions can be asked over the phone and we'd recommend you go right through this list - together with any questions about your individual preferences - before even considering driving a significant distance to view a van.

If any of the responses seem ambiguous or unconvincing, thing very carefully about whether your journey is going to be worth it.

Most private sellers will be only too happy to give chapter and verse about their van's exploits probably interlaced with some funny anecdotes and a few happy memories, but it's surprising how many people don't appear to know the specific make and model of their motorhome – so it's important to be very precise to establish exactly what you are dealing with.

These questions are equally applicable to private and trade sellers, and while a trade vendor is less likely to be able to give immediate answers to the more detailed enquiries, if a trader doesn't appear to know anything at all about the vehicle's ownership history, we'd advise caution.

If, after going through this checklist over the phone, you decide you'd like to view the vehicle, always arrange to meet the vendors at their home address – never in a car park or motorway service station – and insist on taking a test drive.

▶ Do you have the logbook (V5C)?

▶ What sort of van is the motorhome based on?

▶ Who converted it into a motorhome?

▶ Do you know the van's MRO, MTPLM and User Payload?

▶ Do you know the engine capacity?

▶ How long is it?

▶ How many berths does it have? Where are they located?

▶ Can you describe the layout to me?

▶ What's the bathroom like?

▶ What's the kitchen like?

▶ How does the heating work?

▶ What size water tanks are fitted? Where are they?

▶ Are any extras fitted to it such as a bike rack or solar panels?

▶ Who fitted these?

▶ Have you made any modifications or improvements to the interior or exterior?

▶ Who carried out these improvements?

▶ Has the vehicle suffered any accident damage and if so, what was the extent and how was it repaired?

▶ Does the van have a full mechanical service history? (ask to see relevant documents)

▶ Has the habitation been regularly serviced? (ask to see relevant documents)

▶ Has the van had a damp test recently?

▶ When did the van have its last MOT test?

▶ How long have you owned the van?

▶ How many miles have you covered in it?

▶ How often do you use it?

▶ Why are you selling it?

Jargon buster

DON'T get bamboozled by the abbreviations, acronyms and general jargon which is bandied about by the cognoscenti. Consult our simple glossary and you'll be fluent in motorhome parlance sooner than you can say: 'Maximum Technically Permissible Laden Mass!'

A-CLASS: upmarket coachbuilt motorhome in which the cab is integrated into the habitation area

A-FRAME: a towing frame which is attached to small cars for towing behind motorhomes

AIRES DE SERVICE: enhanced laybys with facilities for campers – rare in the UK, but commonplace on the continent

AL-KO: German chassis manufacturer which makes specially adapted chassis for motorhomes

AWNING: a fabric canopy which extends from the side of the van to provide additional shelter from the sun. Standalone versions can be attached to the van and provide additional living space

BASE VEHICLE: the make and model of commercial vehicle which underpins a motorhome

BP GAS LIGHT: Lighter, plastic and composite gas cylinder containing propane, Requires special regulator fitting

BUTANE: Most common form of gas for motorcaravans. Cylinders widely available throughout the UK – but trickier to get hold of in Europe

CALOR GAS: The UK's biggest supplier of gas cylinders for leisure use. Both butane and propane available

CAMPER: Compact van-based motorcaravan – usually with a very simple two-berth layout and only basic camping facilities.

CAMPINGAZ: Butane (usually mixed with a bit of propane) which is widely available throughout continental Europe (except Scandinavia). Requires special regulator fitting

CASSETTE TOILET: Chemical toilet with removable container which seals itself before removal for emptying

COACHBUILT MOTORHOME: a motorhome whose habitation section has been purpose-fabricated by a specialist converter and then attached to a commercial vehicle cab and chassis

DISMOUNTABLE BODY: standalone habitation compartment which can be physically removed from a flatbed or pick-up style vehicle

FIFTH-WHEELER: has a towable habitation compartment which is attached to a pick-up van using an articulated attachment or 'Fifth Wheel'

GTW: Gross Train Weight – the combined weight of a motorhome and trailer and their respective payloads

HABITATION: Everything apart from the cab – i.e. the compartment where you live.

INVERTER: An electrical device which turns an 12-volt DC electrical supply (from a battery) into a 230-volt AC supply to power mains equipment

LCV: Light Commercial Vehicle – the posh term for van

LED: Light Emitting Diode –new type of lightbulb which is popular with motorhomers because of its tiny electrical demands and low heat output

LEFT HOOKER: no, not a socialist lady of the night, but a left hand drive motorhome

LEZ: London's Low Emissions Zone roughly sits inside the M25 and means some older motorhomes have to pay a steep charge to venture inside the M25

LPG: Liquid Petroleum Gas – the catch-all term for the gas which motorhomers use for heating and cooking. Some large petrol-powered motorhomes' engines may also have been converted to run on LPG

MAM: Maximum Authorised Mass – the DVLA's term for MTPLM

MRO: Mass in Running Order – the weight of the motorhome minus its payload, but some manufacturers also include the weight of 90 per cent full fuel and water tanks and gas cylinders, plus 75kg for the driver

MTPLM: Maximum Technically Permissible Laden Mass – the fully laden weight of the vehicle including passengers and payload. Every motorhome has a defined MTPLM which must not be exceeded

PROPANE: Preferred type of gas for winter heating and cooking use. Widely available in the UK, but less easy to get hold of in cylinders in Europe

REPLATING: A means of increasing or decreasing the MTPLM of a motorhome. Largely a paper exercise, but some technical modifications to brakes or suspension may be required to increase the MTPLM

SOG TOILETS: Cassette toilet with mini extractor fan fitted to contain odours allowing toilet chemicals to be dispensed with

TRAVEL SEATS: Forward-facing rear seats with lap and diagonal seatbelts. Future legislation may make these mandatory for carrying passengers

USER PAYLOAD: The difference between the MRO and the MTPLM

US RV: Stands for United States Recreational Vehicle – big, usually multi-berth American motorhomes

VAN CONVERSION: Motorhome which retains the panel van exterior, but has habitation equipment fitted inside

Manufacturers and importers

Adaptacar
Tel: 01769 572785
www.adaptacar.co.uk

Adria United Kingdom
Tel: 0870 7740007
www.adriaconcessionaires.co.uk

Apollo Motorhomes
Tel: 01706 378045
www.agm-apollo.co.uk

Autocruise Motorhomes Ltd
Tel: 01709 571411
www.autocruise.co.uk

Auto-Sleepers Ltd
Tel: 01386 853338
www.auto-sleepers.co.uk

Autovan Services Ltd
Tel: 01202 848414
www.autovan.co.uk

Auto-Trail VR Ltd
Tel: 01472 571000
www.auto-trail.co.uk

Awaydays
Tel: 01978 761863
www.awaydaysuk.co.uk

Aztec Motorhomes
Tel: 01792 586715
www.azteccampers.co.uk

Bavaria
Tel: 00 33 240 321600
www.bavaria-camping-car.com

Bessacarr Motorhomes
Tel: 01482 847332
www.swiftgroup.co.uk

Bilbo's Design
Tel: 01342 892499
www.bilbos.com

Bürstner UK
Tel: 01388 537960
www.buerstner.com/uk/motorhomes

Carado
Tel: 01772 / 684619
www.carado.de

Carthago
Tel: 0845 0552179
www.lowdhamleisure.com

Chausson Camping Cars
Tel: 00 33 475 075500
www.chausson.co.uk

Ci Motorhomes
Tel: 01472 571075
www.ci-motorhomes.co.uk

City Van
Tel: 00 33 240 321600
www.hayesleisure.co.uk

Compass Motorhomes
Tel: 01207 699000
www.explorer-group.co.uk

Concept Multi-Car Ltd
Tel: 01303 261062
www.conceptmulti-car.co.uk

Danbury Motorcaravans
Tel: 01454 310000
www.danburymotorcaravans.com

Dethleffs UK
Tel: 01472 605001
www.dethleffs.co.uk

Devon Conversions Ltd
Tel: 01740 655700
www.devonconversions.com

Drivelodge Motorhomes
Tel: 01535 637777
www.drivelodge.co.uk

East Neuk Campervans
Tel: 01333 310440
www.encmotorco.fsnet.co.uk

Elddis Motorhomes
Tel: 01207 699000
www.explorer-group.co.uk

Eriba
Tel: 0845 055 2179
www.eriba.eu

Euramobil
Tel: 01277 222555
www.euramobil.de

Event Homes Ltd
Tel: 01724 847744
www.eventhomesuk.com

Excel
Tel: 01472 571000
www.excelmotorhomes.co.uk

Free Country Conversions Ltd
Tel: 0161 6841166
www.freecountryconversions.co.uk

Freedom Motorhomes
Tel: 01452 730545
www.freedom-motorhomes.co.uk

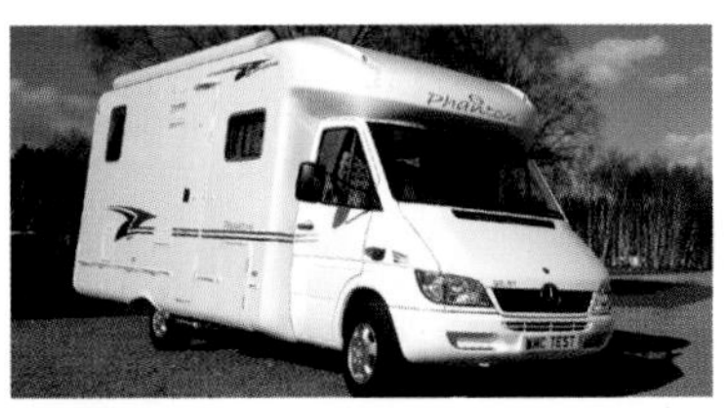

Geist Vehicle Leisure
Tel: 0191 415 9455
www.geistforlife.com

Hobby Motorhomes
Tel: 01773 853900
www.hobbycaravansuk.co.uk

Horizons Unlimited
Tel: 0118 9785079
www.horizons-unlimited.co.uk

Hymer UK
Tel: 01772 684619
www.hymeruk.com

IH Motor Campers Ltd
Tel: 01977 677118
www.ihmotorhomes.com

J C Leisure
Tel: 01797 227337
www.jcleisure.co.uk

Karmann
Tel: 01332 781562
www.karmannmobil.com

Laika Motorhomes
Tel: 02392 674823
www.southdowns motorcaravans.co.uk

Lifestyle Vehicle Developments
Tel: 07970 672915
www.lvdltd.co.uk

Lunar Motorcaravans Ltd
Tel: 01772 337628
www.lunarcaravans.com/motorhomes

Maesss
Tel: 01526 345000
www.maesss.be

Magnum Motorhomes & Caravan Supplies
Tel: 0870 8796051
www.magnummotorhomes.co.uk

MCL Motorhomes
Tel: 01766 770011
www.mcl-motorhomes.org

Mooveo
Tel: 0121 526 3433
www.groupepilotemooveo.info

Murvi Motorcaravans Ltd
Tel: 01752 892200
www.murvi.co.uk

Nene Overland
Tel: 01733 380687
www.neneoverland.co.uk

Niche Marketing
Tel: 01507 327172
www.niche-marketing.net

Nu Venture Motorhomes
Tel: 01942 494090
www.nuventure.co.uk

Oakwell Motorhomes
Tel: 01226 293300
ow.brlive.co.uk

O'Leary Motor Homes
Tel: 01482 868632
www.olearymotorhomes.co.uk

Orian Motorhomes
Tel: 07000 074473
www.orianmotorhomes.co.uk

Pilote UK
Tel: 0121 526 3433
www.pilote.co.uk

PJB Motorhomes
Tel: 0121 248 2860
www.pjbmotorhomes.co.uk

Premier Creations
Tel: 0161 7996634
www.premier-creations.co.uak

Rainbow Conversions Limited
Tel: 01945 585931
www.rainbowconversions.co.uk

Rapido
Tel: 0118 979 1023
www.rapido.fr

Rimor
Tel: 02392 674823
www.southdownsmotorcaravans.co.uk

Roller Team
Tel: 01472 571075
www.rollerteammotorhomes.co.uk

Romahome Ltd
Tel: 01983 292451
www.romahome.com

RS Motorhomes
Tel: 01709 891297
www.rsmotorhomes.com

SC Sporthomes
Tel: 01633 862419
www.scsporthomes.com

South West Camper Conversions
Tel: 01237 423399
www.swcampers.co.uk

South West Sportshomes
Tel: 01392 832356
www.swsportshomes.co.uk

Stimson Designs
Tel: 07710 439907
www.stimsondesigns.com

Swift Motorhomes
Tel: 01482 847332
www.swiftgroup.co.uk

The Imperial Car Company
Tel: 01202 631500
www.imperialcar.co.uk

Torbay Camper Conversions
Tel: 01803 323231
www.camperconversions.com

Timberland Motorhomes
Tel: 0845 0099998
www.timberlandmotorhomes.com

Trigano Motorhomes (Tribute)
Tel: 01472 571075
www.tributemotorhomes.co.uk

Volkswagen Group UK Ltd
Tel: 0800 333 666
www.volkswagen-vans.co.uk

Wandahome (South Cave) Ltd
Tel: 01430 424342
www.caravanbuys.com

Wellhouse Leisure Ltd
Tel: 01484 600416
www.wellhouseleisure.com

Wentworth Motor Caravans
Tel: 01784 433081
www.wentworthmc.co.uk

Westfalia
Tel: 0118 9785079
www.westfalia-ford.co.uk

Willow Motorhomes
Tel: 01964 563127
www.willowmotorhomes.co.uk

Wyvern Accessories Ltd
Tel: 01749 346063
www.wyvernaccessories.co.uk

Young Conversions
Tel: 01908 639936
www.youngconversions.com

IMPORTERS

Lowdham Leisureworld (Nottm)
Tel: 0845 0552179
www.lowdhamleisure.com

Signature Motorhomes
Tel: 01902 725394
www.signaturemotorhomes.com

Southdowns Motorcaravans Ltd
Tel: 02392 401821
www.southdownsmotorcaravans.co.uk

Spinney Motorcaravans
Tel: 01477 535808
www.spinney.co.uk

Travelworld RV
Tel: 0845 2305033
www.travelworldrv.co.uk

Wokingham Motor Homes
Tel: 0118 9791023
www.wokinghammotorhomes.com

Section 2: Using your Motorhome

So you've taken the plunge and invested a substantial slice of your nest egg in a home on wheels. What now?

Well, the adventure is only just beginning. A huge vista of almost boundless opportunities is about to open up in front of you.

This section of the book will take you through the first steps of motorhome ownership and show you how to get the basics right before spreading your wings and hitting the open road – either in the UK or further afield in continental Europe.

Driving tips

DRIVING off the dealer's forecourt in a shiny new motorhome can be a surprisingly nerve-wracking experience, especially if you've had only limited experience of driving such a large vehicle.

The good news is that the vans upon which motorhomes are based have been getting progressively more car-like in recent years – to the extent that the latest Fiat Ducato, Ford Transit and Renault Trafic derived motorhomes are intuitively easy to drive.

The driving position, although elevated, is very car-like, as is the steering wheel, gearshift and clutch. The main difference between a van and a car is simply a matter of size and once you've become accustomed to the dimensions of your new van, most modern motorhomes are actually very pleasant and relaxing to drive.

The elevated seating position offers a commanding view of the road, allowing you to anticipate the traffic flow much better and there's something quietly satisfying about looking down on your fellow motorists, unless they're at the wheel of a big articulated truck.

For the first few hundred miles, there's a simple golden rule to becoming safely acquainted with your new steed:

SLOW DOWN!

While modern motorhomes are capable of matching the speed of a typical family car and the typical 'white van man' seems intent on proving it, they're not really designed to be thrown about like a sports car on a race-track.

Approach the process of familiarisation as if you're effectively learning to drive all over again and hopefully you won't develop any bad habits. It will also pay dividends at the pumps because while modern vans will return quite respectable fuel consumption if driven carefully, stand too heavily on the loud pedal, especially when fully laden and fuel economy deteriorates alarmingly.

If you've opted for a fairly compact sub-3050kg (unladen weight) camper-type van, the driving experience really won't be dramatically different to that of a family car and it's unlikely that you'll need to markedly adjust your driving style.

Drivers of larger 3050kg-plus van conversions will need to adapt not only to different dimensions and driving characteristics, but also to the revised speed limits which apply to larger vehicles. The main difference is that motorhomes which fall into this category – and it includes the vast majority of coachbuilts – are limited to 50mph instead of 60mph on single carriageways and 60mph instead of 70mph on dual carriageways.

BE AWARE

SPEED LIMITS FOR MOTORHOMES OF OVER 3050KG

Motorways:	70mph
Dual carriageways:	60mph
Single carriageways:	50mph
Built-up areas:	30mph

The other considerations to bear in mind when familiarising yourself with the motorhome are pretty straightforward. It's bigger, heavier and slower to stop, so scale up the 'safety zone' all drivers should attempt to maintain around their vehicle and adjust your stopping distances accordingly – particularly when fully laden.

Most motorhomes have a higher centre of gravity than cars, especially coachbuilt vans with overcab beds. Consequently, these are much more prone to body roll under cornering, so break earlier when approaching corners and try to maintain steady progress through the bend. Body roll can be especially pronounced on roundabouts, so brake early and consider changing down to second gear to negotiate them, remembering to leave enough room on the inside for the rear wheels to follow the front without cutting the corner.

Similarly, six-metre-plus motorhomes with lengthy overhangs sometimes exhibit quite a pronounced pitching motion, especially when fully laden, so it pays to accelerate smoothly and brake early and gently.

Like a lot of cars, most motorhomes have blind spots, but they tend to be bigger, so it's vitally important that you are aware of their extents and to exercise caution when pulling out into traffic or overtaking other vehicles.

While there are some exceptions to this general rule, on the whole, you'll have minimal to zero vision in the rear-view mirror and you'll gradually learn to rely almost totally on your wing mirrors. Various forms of electronic wizardry such as parking sensors or rear view cameras are available to assist the driver for close quarters manoeuvring, but under general driving conditions, it pays to learn how to use your wing mirrors properly.

LEARN TO LOVE YOUR MIRRORS

Look at the wing mirrors fitted to the typical articulated truck or bus and you'll notice that they're absolutely huge and for good reason. Drivers of these vehicles are almost wholly reliant on the view afforded by these mirrors to tell them what's going on alongside and immediately behind them.

Van manufacturers and motorhome converters are adopting similar strategies when it comes to the size and quality of the wing mirrors they fit to their products and certainly, many posh A-class motorhomes now come complete with huge reflectors which wouldn't look out of place on a luxury coach.

Even the mirrors fitted to fairly modest motorhomes often have wide angle primary mirrors to minimise any blind spot and smaller secondary mirrors designed to assist low-speed parking manoeuvres.

Make sure you set them up to offer a good view down the side of the van and as clear an indication as possible of the extremities of the vehicle. Secondary mirrors should be adjusted to give a clear view of the wheels and kerbs to assist reversing and parking manoeuvres.

If you have an older vehicle whose mirrors feel inadequate, you may be able to buy better units on the after-market or at least add some secondary mirrors to improve all-round vision.

Get into the habit of checking the mirrors alternately every 15 seconds or so and you'll build up an accurate picture of what's going on around you.

The best exercise to build confidence in the mirrors for low speed manoeuvring is to find a

Characteristically large mirrors on a Dethleffs Advantage A-class (left) and a standard Transit-based mirror on a Ci Cusona

quiet car park, and place a traffic cone (or some other obstacle) 15 yards or so behind the van and practice reversing either side of it. Simply start with the cone visible in the mirror on one side of the van and then slowly reverse and street until it appears in the other mirror.

Attend a motorhome manoeuvring course (see below) and you'll repeat this exercise over and over again until you're confident enough to undertake it without even the sneakiest glimpse over your shoulder!

WORK AS A TEAM

It's highly likely that most of the journeys undertaken in the new van will be in the company of your partner, so when it comes to low-speed manoeuvres in tight spots, enlist the help of your significant other.

To minimise the potential for blazing rows in congested car parks and on busy campsites, do make sure you understand one another's signals.

Wind down both windows, so you have an even chance of actually hearing verbal instructions and agree a series of simple hand signals for 'Left', 'Right', 'Reverse', 'Pull forward' and 'Stop'.

Bear in mind that 'left hand down a bit' and 'come on, you're allright' may mean different things to different drivers, so stick to the agreed signals.

Make sure you can clearly see your partner either in the mirrors or by looking over your shoulder and impress upon them the importance of their remaining visible until you are safely parked up.

GENERAL DO'S AND DON'TS

- Do know the exact height, width and length of your van by heart
- Don't try to park in a multi-storey unless you're sure of the maximum height restrictions
- Do know the speed limits which relate to your vehicle
- Don't rely on sat-nav to pilot you safely through unfamiliar territory
- Avoid single-track roads unless you're sure there's somewhere to turn round
- Do consider alternative modes of transport such as bikes and buses to explore your surroundings
- Don't drive into busy car parks unless you're sure you can get back out again
- Do send your partner to recce the dimensions of potential parking places
- Don't drive onto a petrol forecourt without checking the height of the canopy
- Do know which side of the vehicle the fuel filler cap is on

MOTORHOME MANOEUVRING COURSES

If you're completely new to motorhoming, then completing a motorhome manoeuvring course is highly recommended. Both the Caravan Club and the Camping and Caravanning Club run regular courses at locations nationwide where novices can learn the ropes in a relaxed and friendly environment.

Participants use their own vehicles to learn the basics in small, informal groups and the courses include sessions in a private car park off the highway as well as practical road work.

For further details contact:
The Camping and Caravanning Club
at www.campingandcaravanningclub.co.uk/manoeuvringcourses or call 0845 130 7412

The Caravan Club
at www.caravanclub.co.uk/Practical+advice or call 01342 336 808

If you are unsure about driving a motorhome, a motorhome manoeuvring course like those run by the Caravan Club and the Camping and Caravanning Club will boost your confidence.

First steps

COLLECTING your new motorhome is a bit like bringing your first child back from the hospital. It's the start of a whole new way of life and while it's a hugely exciting experience, there's a steep initial learning curve which can lead to some anxieties. What if we break something? What if we get stuck? How does the gas work? Is it safe?

Motorhomes are pretty complicated machines, combining all the mechanical components of a car with the domestic appliances of home and gas, electrical and water systems to feed them. So where on earth do you start?

Relax, the big difference between a motorhome and a new baby is that the motorhome comes with instruction manuals – lots of instruction manuals.

Coping with this volume of information may seem daunting, but take it step by step and you'll soon absorb all the important bits.

HANDOVER

If you're buying from a dealer, you should expect to receive a comprehensive handover lasting as much as half a day for the most complex motorhomes, about which more later.

Private sales

If you're buying privately, get the owners to take you on a comprehensive guided tour of the van before you drive it away. Chances are, you'll have established a good rapport with the vendors and they'll be only too happy to show you how all the systems work, together with any quirks which are particular to their make and model.

If you have driven some distance to collect the van, it may make sense to stay locally overnight so that the vendors are close at hand if something does go wrong. Ask the vendors if they know of a site near to them where you can pitch up and go through all the services – it's possible they'll accompany you and 'walk you through' the process.

If so, take a notebook and make extensive notes on getting all the systems up and running. Many newcomers type these notes up and keep them in the van as a handy reference guide to consult for the first few trips.

If time allows, it's also important to familiarise yourself with the manuals that accompany all the various systems and appliances. In the typical coachbuilt motorhome, you should have comprehensive manuals from the converter and the base vehicle manufacturer, plus separate manuals for the heating systems (blown air and hot water), water pump, fridge, hob, grill, oven, microwave (if it has one), toilet and any entertainment systems (that's the wireless to you and me).

In recent years, these items have become progressively more user-friendly, but they don't always function in exactly the same way as their domestic equivalents, so it pays to note the basic operating instructions and maybe incorporate these points into the crib sheet mentioned earlier.

You should expect a comprehensive handover at a dealers

Collection from a dealer

While, to a certain extent, buyers are relying on the goodwill of a private seller to show them the ins and outs of using their new van, if you buy from a dealer, you should legitimately expect a comprehensive handover.

This should last at least an hour or two and cover every aspect of the motorhome's safe operation and include instructions on how each

AUTO-SLEEPER
Dealer Finance
BANK OF SCOTLAND
£39060
2632
Ford
TDCi
MARQUIS

Club Brownhills overnight pitches

appliance works. The person doing the handover should also be happy to answer specific questions and if he doesn't have the immediate answer, be capable of finding out pretty quickly.

Some of the bigger dealers take this process even further and throw in the first night's accommodation – either on a local site or on purpose-built motorhome pitches on the premises – as part of the service.

It's a reassuring option for newcomers as the handover should incorporate details on getting the van set up on pitch and, in the event of a problem, the dealer's technicians are close at hand to resolve it.

It may not be the most idyllic setting for your first night in the van, but if this option is available, we'd recommend taking it, asking lots of questions and making copious notes during the handover.

From your notes, you could draw up something like the checklist on the right:

Pitching up checklist

1 Park on pitch. Level up. Chocks. Spirit level. Switch off ignition

2 Check master power switch is in off position and all appliances are switched off. Connect lead to van then plug into mains hook up pillar

3 Switch master switch to 'on' — check battery level

4 Check 240-volt lights work

5 Switch on electrical heater if required (flick fuse switch to 'on' and select desired power output on control dial)

6 Switch fridge to mains power

7 Turn gas cylinder valve and regulator valve to 'on' position

8 Check gas supply (turn on one of the hobs briefly to check pressure)

9 Turn on gas heating if required (check pilot light is lit through inspection window, depress control switch, turn and wait for ignition before releasing)

10 Check fresh water tank level. Activate water pump and check flow at taps

11 Remove protective cowl from water heater exhaust

12 Check emergency draining switch is in 'closed' position

13 Switch on water heater (flick fuse switch to 'on' and turn control dial to required heat output. Light in control dial should remain green, if it turns red, check the exhaust cowl has been removed and there's water in the heater)

14 Put the kettle on!

FILLING UP

Fuel

Unlike a conventional van, a motorhome has several tanks and it's very important you quickly grasp which is which.

On many models, the most obvious external filler cap actually leads to the freshwater tank and depositing a hundred pounds worth of diesel in here could prove to be an extremely costly exercise. Not only will you probably lose the £100 worth of fuel, but you'll also need to replace the water tank as even a small amount of diesel will contaminate it beyond repair.

It is important to know which side of the van your filler cap is

Some manufacturers and converters seem to go out of their way to hide the fuelling point, so do check the exact location with the vendor and make sure you are in possession of the relevant key if it's of the locking variety. It's even worth placing a sticker at the bottom of the windscreen to indicate which side the filler cap is on, as a petrol station isn't the ideal environment to begin practicing your close-quarters manoeuvring skills if you pull up on the wrong side of the pump.

While most modern petrol forecourts will comfortably accommodate a motorhome, if you're driving a tall overcab model, do check the height of the canopy over the pumps before pulling in.

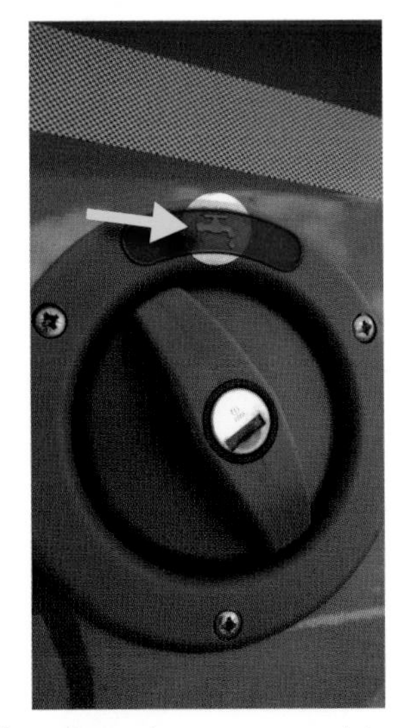

Looks like a filler cap...but on closer inspection you can see it is actually a water filling point.

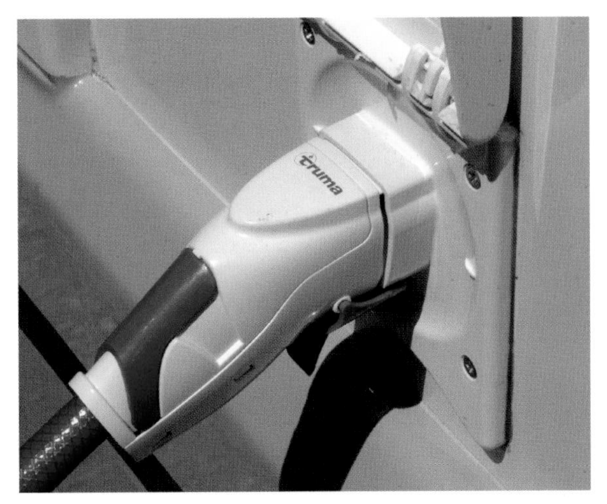

On some models this clip on water filler replaces the hose pipe

Water

Filling the water tank is a straightforward exercise, but keeping it full and deciding when to drain it can be surprisingly complex undertakings.

It's important that you carry a 'food quality' length of hosepipe with similar quality fittings to fill the tank from whatever sources are available.

The vast majority of sites will have at least a basic mains water tap somewhere and an increasing number pipe mains water to every pitch, but it may not be possible to park up immediately adjacent to the only available tap, so we advise that you carry at least 25 metres of hose to cope with every eventuality.

A growing number of sites now have dedicated Motorhome Service Points (MSPs) which usually incorporate a mains water supply plus large drainage grills for emptying waste water tanks.

Filling the tank brimful is the best policy if you plan to stay on site for several days, but if you are off again in the morning, do you want to travel with 80 per cent full tanks or have the hassle of waiting for a slot at the Motorhome Service Point to offload most of what you put in the previous evening?

Many motorhomers are happy to travel with full water tanks, but this practice has its disadvantages. Water is heavy stuff: every litre of it weighs a kilogram, so a full water tank can have a significant impact of the van's performance, stability and fuel consumption. Furthermore, if your motorhome is approaching its maximum

Waste water drain at a typical motorhome service point

payload, emptying the empty water tank before travelling should keep you well underneath it.

The Caravan Club now recommends travelling with empty water tanks as far as it is practicably possible, but there are obvious exceptions to this guidance. If you are wild camping well away from centres of population, it's vitally important that you have enough water to get you through, so you must adapt your water management strategy to the circumstances in which you find yourself.

Taken to its logical extremes, a 'dry tanks' approach should also include the water heater (10 litres), toilet cassette, (17 litres) and toilet flush (7 litres) – saving a further 30 or so kilos of weight.

Waste water

While its sometimes important to hoard fresh water, there's little point in lugging waste water around with you, so our advice is to dump it at every opportunity.

Grey water tanks are usually slightly smaller than the freshwater tanks fitted to the van and will thus reach capacity before you've completely exhausted the contents of the fresh tank.

You'll need to find a proper Motorhome Service Point which you can drive the van onto and open the waste water drain-down valve to release the contents directly into a specially positioned drain.

But bear in mind that not every site, despite being very well equipped in most other respects, will automatically have an MSP, so it's a good idea to carry an old bucket to drain the grey water into before manually disposing of it into the designated grey water drains. It's a laborious, but necessary task, and care must be taken not to contaminate any drinking water dispensing areas – which are often immediately adjacent to the grey water disposal area.

While there are a minority of irresponsible motorhomer owners who will surreptitiously drain their grey water on a backroad when they think no-one is looking, this is tantamount to fly-tipping and, if caught, they could face the full force of the law. Grey water can contain a cocktail of pollutants which, if a farmer was caught discharging them into a watercourse, would earn him a hefty fine. So don't be tempted to do it – even in extremis.

Gas

Many used motorhomes are usually sold with at least one gas bottle included in the price, so unless you buy second-hand and the bottle is all but empty, you should be OK for a couple of nights away, but sooner or later you will need to exchange an empty cylinder for a full one or – in the case of refillable systems – replenish the fixed cylinders.

The size of your gas locker will dictate the size of the cylinders you can use – ranging from tiny 2.72kg Campingaz cylinders used in small camper vans to large 15kg cylinders for big A-class motorhomes and above, although the 11kg variety are probably the most popular.

If Calor Gas cylinders are supplied with your van, then exchanging these at a Calor Gas oulet is the simplest solution. The fittings, valves and regulators are standardised, so it's just a case of

A Calor lite cylinder

BP's Gaslight

returning the empty cylinder and paying out for a full one.

If you're buying new however, or you want to switch to BP's lighter Gas Light cylinders, then you'll also need to buy some new fixtures and fittings, as the valves aren't interchangeable.

Strictly speaking, you only hire the cylinder and it remains the property of Calor, so after paying the initial hire charge, you are in effect only paying for the contents.

Some vans are retro-fitted with fixed, refillable cylinders and a fixed filling point mounted in the sidewall of the van. These can be refilled at petrol stations selling Autogas, which is substantially cheaper than either Calor, BP or Campingaz.

More detailed information on all the gas options available to motorcaravanners is contained in a dedicated chapter later in the book.

Toilet

Most motorhomes built within the last decade or so have some sort of cassette toilet with either a separate tank to hold the flushing fluid or a flushing system which draws water direct from the freshwater tank.

The advantage of the latter is that the flush tank doesn't need to be refilled manually, but nor can you add sweet-smelling toilet-cleaning chemicals to the flush water to help keep the bowl spick and span. Separate flush tanks hold around seven litres of water and are usually topped up via an additional filler cap above the cassette door.

Thetford's C-250 cassette toilet. Inside they look much like your toilet at home

The toilet cassette is accessed via an external hatch

The cassette itself is a plastic container with a capacity of around 17 litres which is sealed airtight when the 'blade' which covers the main aperture is closed by a lever attached to the toilet bowl. This blade must be in the closed position before the cassette can be removed.

To prepare for use, remove the cassette. Add a litre of water plus the required volume of chemical agent and gently shake to mix. Replace the cassette, make sure it clicks into the correct position and it's ready for use.

Smaller campers may dispense with the loo altogether or incorporate a small locker where a Porta Potti can be stored for use in emergencies.

Motorhome gas systems

Most motorhomes use gas for heating, cooking and operating the fridges, as it's convenient and easily controllable. Clive Mott-Gotobed explores the options for motorhomers

Gas is a fossil fuel and, as such, a lot of potential energy can be contained in a relatively small space and weight. Two types of gas are commonplace in the leisure vehicle world: Butane and Propane - both of which are derivatives of petroleum. Both Butane and Propane gas are stored in pressurised containers as a liquid. The calorific value of butane gas is slightly greater than that of Propane. On older motorhomes, before the advent of a common bulkhead pressure regulator in the gas bottle locker of caravans and motorhomes it was normal to fit a pressure-reducing regulator directly to the gas bottle. This had two advantages, firstly, the flexible pipe from the regulator only had gas at low pressure within it and secondly, as Propane and Butane gas bottles have different threaded fittings, it was automatic to have a different dedicated pressure regulator for each type of bottle. The blue Butane regulator would control the outgoing gas pressure to 28 millibars. The red Propane regulator would control the outgoing gas pressure to 37 millibars. These two different regulated pressures meant that the gas appliance would get equally hot with either gas supply as the pressures compensated for the difference in calorific value.

An old style gas bottle locker

More recent leisure vehicles have a different system, with a BSEN12864 bulkhead- fitted pressure regulator set at a compromise 30-millibar and a short length of high-pressure hose connecting it to the gas bottle. Different interchangeable high pressure hoses are used for different gas bottles. Modern gas appliances are designed to be tolerant to the differences in calorific value and meet specifications with either. Some continental motorhomes however, have a blue-coloured 30-millibar regulator for each gas bottle and have short solid adaptors to suit Propane bottles.

A gas regulator

Although one might initially believe that Butane was the gas to use, it does have one major disadvantage. When you want to use the gas the most, in the winter when it's freezing cold outside, then the Butane liquid gas in your bottle stays as a liquid as it stops evaporating when it gets cold. Result: no gas and no heating.

To compound this, when gas is being used from a bottle (Butane or Propane) the fact that the gas in the bottle is evaporating as you use it causes it to cool just like a refrigerator. The faster the gas is used the quicker the bottle temperature falls and the pressure drops. The temperature at which Propane stops evaporating is very low and for motorhome use, it will not stop evaporating. For this reason alone Propane is the chosen fuel for most. Both Butane and Propane gas bottles have left hand but differently formed threads so the regulators are not interchangeable.

GAS BOTTLES

There are several types of gas bottle on the market. Calor being the best known as a nationwide supplier of bottles, with lots of outlets where empty bottles can be exchanged. Other companies also offer a similar service. Different Butane bottles are likely to have different outlet fittings but Propane bottle fittings are mostly made to a common standard. Gas bottles come in a range of sizes and it makes sense to fit the largest bottles your gas locker will accept. Butane exchangeable bottles in the UK are available in 4.5 kg, 7 kg, 12 kg and 15-kg sizes and Propane exchangeable bottles in 3.9 kg, 6 kg, 9 kg, 13 kg and 47 kg sizes – although the latter are too big for use in leisure vehicles.

A Calor Lite 6Kg bottle

Small portable cooking appliances made by Campingaz have disposable Butane canisters, and other companies offer similar products with disposable Propane canisters.

Traditional gas bottles are made of thick, formed, steel plate and are relatively heavy but lightweight bottles are now available from Calor and BP. The Calor Lite 6 kg bottles - although still made of steel - are almost 50 per cent lighter than their traditional counterparts, saving nearly 4.5 kg of weight per 6 kg bottle. The Calor Lite 6 kg bottle includes a 'Gas track' indicator to warn when over half of the contents have been used. Against this, BP have their 5 kg and 10 kg gaslight bottles. These are a composite construction which means you can see the liquid gas inside so you know exactly how much gas you have at any one time, its weight again is about half that of a conventional steel bottle of similar size.

A BP Gas Lite bottle

When you 'buy' your first full cylinder, you effectively pay for the gas plus a deposit for the bottles. When it's empty, you exchange it for a full cylinder, only paying for the gas inside. Cylinder deposits and refill costs are quite variable, so it pays to find a cheap supplier locally and carry two bottles, making sure that one of them remains full at all times.

Both Butane and Propane are heavier than air so will always find the lowest point if allowed to escape (This is why gas can be so dangerous in boats). UK motorhomes have a vent in the floor positioned close to all gas pipe junctions where any leaking gas can escape outside the vehicle. These 'gas drops' are typically 50 - 100mm diameter holes in the floor with some fine mesh over them. A normal gas installation in a motorhome would be a solid copper pipe between the bulkhead fitted regulator connecting to a manifold, this being a collection of gas taps. Each gas tap would feed a gas appliance, such as water heater, space heater and fridge and an external BBQ outlet as well if fitted. All pipe runs should be securely fastened in position with no intermediate joints. The gas locker will have a gas drop in its base, the area where the manifold is located should have a local gas drop and if the appliances are far from this position they also should have one. Central European motorhomes don't necessarily follow this arrangement.

The only guaranteed supply of gas bottles that will fit your UK hose or regulator in continental Europe will be if you have chosen to use Campingaz. The limiting factor here is they are all Butane and relatively small and expensive if you require a plentiful supply of gas. Local areas in Europe have different gas bottle exchange schemes. But there is an alternative: refillable gas bottles.

The simplest refillable system is a pair of bottles that fit in the same space as the conventional exchange bottles. Gaslow supply refillable steel bottles that maximise the space in your gas locker. They include the normal outlet connector, a filling point connector which has a one-way non-return valve, and cut-off valve which limits

Gaslow bottles can be filled up at any petrol station selling LPG (Liquefied Petroleum Gas)

If you are set up for using LPG, filling your gas bottles at a filling station is as easy as this

filling to 80 per cent (to allow expansion space) plus a gauge to show the gas level once it has fallen to below half full. With this system, a filling point is added to the van sidewall or skirt and can be filled up at any fuel station selling LPG (Liquefied Petroleum Gas). LPG is mostly Propane in the UK. On the continent it may have a greater proportion of Butane, but all mixes do work. Simple adapters screw onto the UK LPG filler to suit continental fuel stations. Continental bulk gas tank installations have screw on adapters to fit UK pumps. If you have two gas bottles then automatic change-over valves exist to automatically switch the supply to the full cylinder when its counterpart is empty. Some gas regulators are fitted with 12-volt heaters, which can be turned on from inside the motorhome when camping in very cold climates to prevent the regulator freezing up.

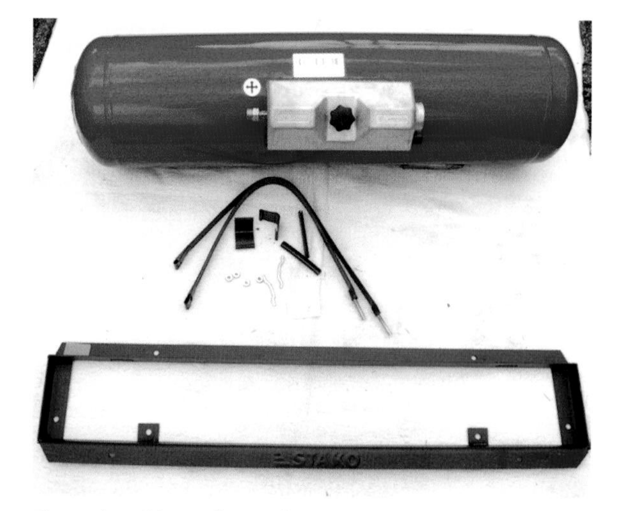

The tank and frame fittings for a bulk gas tank

The other alternative is to have a properly fitted bulk gas tank underneath your motorhome. This shares the same filler system as the Gaslow arrangement but would normally hold more gas, and would connect to a remote fuel gauge inside the motorhome which will indicate the level of LPG. A bulk gas tank will also leave you with a spare locker.

The cost of LPG at the pumps - including road fuel duty - is still less than half the cost of buying bottled gas and it's even cheaper on the continent, where some countries have lower rates of duty.

SAFETY PRECAUTIONS

It's important when replaceable gas bottles are exchanged that the bottles are turned OFF at the main tap on the bottle. There should be no naked lights, definitely no smoking and nothing to cause any sparks anywhere close by. Similar precautions apply equally when changing small disposable canisters on portable Campingaz or similar appliances.

If you have a refillable gas system, then the main bulk tank or Gaslow bottle outlet tap should be turned OFF well before filling commences. It is not unknown for the motorhome fridge to start up on gas whilst filling up is taking place and the timing couldn't be worse. When filling from an LPG pump, some gas is always lost when the filler nozzle is removed from the motorhome filling point. Turn the fridge OFF first!

When travelling on a ferry or using the Channel Tunnel, you must turn off your main gas tap – that's the one on the gas bottle or bulk tank outlet. If your motorhome has a remote switch for a Truma master gas valve, this is not sufficient for ferry or tunnel operators as it is on the low pressure side of the regulator.

FRIDGE

Most motorhomes have an absorption-type refrigerator made by either Dometic or Thetford that is capable of operating from three power sources, mains 230 volts AC, 12-volt DC from the vehicle alternator or gas. In all three cases the power source is used to heat a fluid within the refrigerant cycle. The 12-volt consumption is significant so is only used when the vehicle is in motion with the engine running. If parked up without a mains hook-up then the fridge normally runs on gas. Manual fridges need to be lit by hand with a push-button to enable the electronic ignition or piezo ignition. Should the flame in a gas fridge be extinguished for any reason then most will instantly run the electronic ignition (if fitted) to try to re-light. If unsuccessful they will automatically switch off the gas supply to the burner after a few seconds.

A few motorhomes have 12-volt compressor fridges. These give good cooling but they place huge demands on the 12-volt leisure battery. If your camping style does not include prolonged winter wild camping then perhaps a compressor fridge is the one for you? No gas needed for this!

COOKING

Most motorhomes have a gas hob, some also have a single electric hob plate as well, which only works with a mains hook-up taking full advantage of the hook-up and saving gas. Similarly a gas oven is the norm. A small number of motorhomes have the new Webasto diesel-fired hob for cooking saving even more gas, although hobs with ceramic tops (which include the latest diesel variants) do take quite a bit longer to bring a pan to the boil compared to a traditional gas flame hob.

WATER HEATING

Whilst on diesel fuel, Eberspacher and Webasto both make diesel-fuelled water heaters and warm air blowers. Combine these with a diesel hob and a compressor fridge and you could have a gasless motorhome. This could be important if you want to venture further afield to some of the North African countries when the only fuel likely to be found en route will be diesel. However most motorhomers still opt for gas because of its simplicity – plus it's half the price of diesel.

Older motorhomes have separate systems for water and space heating. The water heating could be a Carver Cascade or (more recently) a Truma water heater. These include a reservoir of water, which is heated by a gas burner. The gas burner is controlled electronically, the status of the flame being monitored at all times. If the flame has not lit within a second or so from when it should have, then the system has a couple of re-tries and if still unsuccessful shuts down, turns off the supply to the gas burner and displays a fault on its control panel.

Webasto's diesel powered Dual Top provide both hot air heating and hot water

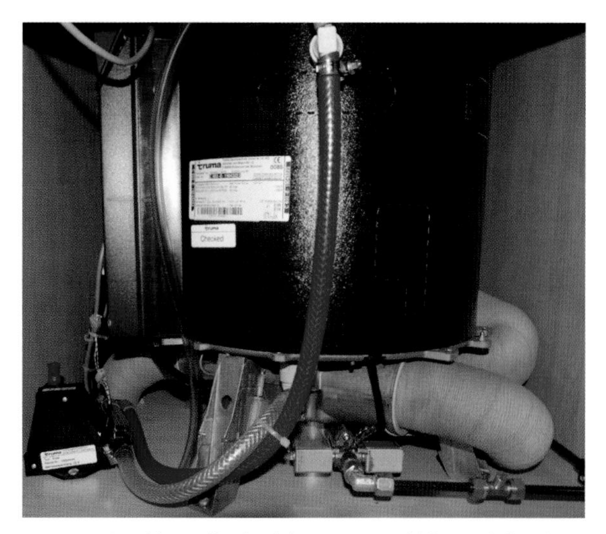

A Truma Combi supplies both hot water and blown air heating

An Alde heat exchanger

SPACE HEATING

Until recently, Carver and Truma both produced a simple convector heater with electronic ignition This provided warm air direct from the heater and via a circulating fan, warm air could also be blown to distant parts of the motorhome via concealed ducting.

More recent motorhomes are usually fitted with a Truma system, which includes a water jacket to supply hot water and an outlet for blown warm air, which is ducted around the vehicle. These are frequently fitted with a supplementary mains-powered electric heating element as well. Because this system contains water, Truma have built in a temperature sensor to protect the unit from freezing. When the temperature of the water is close to freezing, a valve in the base of the water vessel opens and dumps the water beneath the motorhome. If you happen to be inside the motorhome at the time and the motorhome electrics are turned on you'll hear the water pump start up and run until the contents of the water tank have been pumped through the heater and onto the ground beneath the van. To re-set the safety valve a device can be used to hold the valve closed, the system re-filled with water and heating turned on. Once the water temperature has risen a little the device must be removed.

Some upmarket motorhomes have a wet central heating system with concealed radiators.

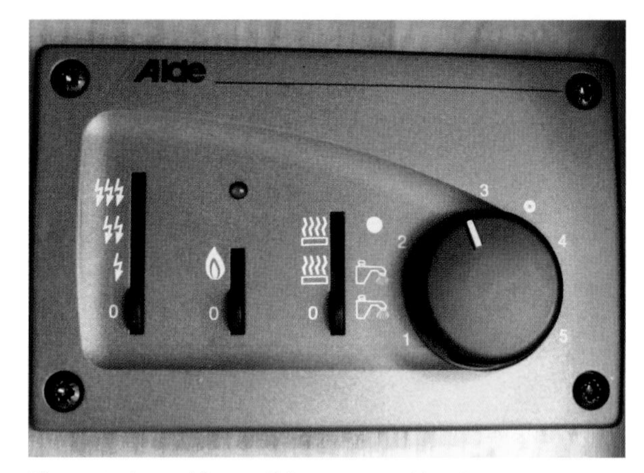

The control panel for an Alde wet central heating system

The most popular boiler for this is made by Alde. Again these are electronically controlled, have all the flame failure devices required and can operate from gas or mains electricity and are almost totally silent. The Alde heater unit has two water jackets, the inner water jacket is connected to the radiators distributed throughout the motorhome and this system is filled with a water/antifreeze mix. The outer water jacket is for hot water supplies and like other water heaters, should be drained down if not in use when the ambient temperature threatens to reach, or go below, freezing. The heating system can be used without the fresh water system being filled.

Webasto also make a diesel-fired blown air heater system.

A balanced flue on the side of a motorhome

BALANCED FLUES

All gas (and diesel) heaters used in motorhomes today have balanced flues - this being where the exhaust gas from the burner and the fresh air intake for the burner enter virtually at the same place on the outside of the motorhome, some flues are fitted in a sidewall, some on the roof and some under the floor. In most cases the external fitting has a co-axial input/output arrangement. The reason for this is to ensure that the wind pressure applied to the burner inlet and exhaust is always equal, so that it always operates with the same effectiveness. Modern heating appliances are very efficient and carbon build-up in the exhaust systems is minimal. However ducts can get damaged by over filled lockers and spiders can do their worst, so it's important that these systems are checked periodically to ensure that both intake and exhaust pathways are clean and in proper working order.

CARBON MONOXIDE

This is a colourless, odourless deadly poisonous gas. It is produced by fossil-fuelled burners that do not have sufficient fresh air to ensure complete combustion. Motorhomes are compact and thus the balanced flue outlet/inlet for a burner is never that far away from a window or door, so in breezy conditions the exhaust gas can sometimes get blown back into the motorhome. Heaters do not last forever, and especially early generation, compact blown air heaters can, after lots of use, burn through the dividing stainless steel or aluminium divisions of the heat exchanger within, resulting in a small amount of the exhaust gas being mixed with the heated fresh air which is routed inside the motorhome. For these and other possible fault scenarios, it is advisable to have a Carbon Monoxide sensor fitted to the motorhome. These look like smoke detectors but cost about five times as much. Follow the instructions supplied with smoke detectors regarding their location and installation.

BARBEQUE POINT.

This is a small brass connector fitted within a housing, which is flush-mounted into the skirt of the motorhome. Only when the mating brass connector on the end of your barbeque hose is fitted to the BBQ outlet will gas pass through it. This makes al fresco cooking very easy, limited only by the length of your gas hose.

Weights and payloads

EVERYTHING YOU NEED TO KNOW BUT WERE AFRAID TO ASK

It's one of the most common topics of conversation on motorhome forums and a constant source of anxiety for some newcomers, but understand the basics and payloads needn't be a pain. **Brian Kirby** explains the basics – with a little help from members of the MMM forum.

THE subject of motorhome weights is one of the most complex and potentially confusing areas of the motorhome ownership experience.

Get it right and you should encounter few problems, get it wrong however and not only will you be driving a vehicle which is unsafe, but you also risk fines – and on the continent – potential impoundment of the vehicle.

It's essential, therefore, that you fully understand what your vehicle weighs unladen and how much payload it's allowed to carry. If you're considering towing a small car or other form of trailer, this may also have an impact.

The key criteria are the Mass In Running Order (MIRO), and the Maximum Technically Permissible Laden Mass (MTPLM, but sometimes called Gross Vehicle Weight or Maximum Laden Weight).

The former (MIRO), is the weight (mass) of the vehicle, as manufactured, "including coolant, oils, fuel, spare wheel, tools, and driver". It usually relates to the basic version of the 'van in question, so any options (engine/chassis upgrades, equipment "packs" etc), will increase the stated MIRO. The weights of these options are usually found in the technical part of the brochure. The mass of the driver is taken to be 75kg. This is augmented, in the case of motorhomes, by the mass of the Essential Habitation Equipment, corresponding to fresh water and gas storage tanks filled to 90 per cent. These loads may vary within plus or minus five per cent. It is therefore prudent to assume the MIRO for your van will be five per cent above that in the catalogue!

Some manufacturers may exclude some – or even all of the essential payload elements in their MIRO figure. If it's not crystal clear in the brochure specification, the only way to be sure is to ask whether the MIRO specifically includes the weight of filled tanks and the driver.

The latter (MTPLM), is the maximum weight to which the vehicle may legally be loaded, and is given (among other important loading information) on a plate attached to the chassis by the maker of the base vehicle and, in a number of cases, on a second plate attached by the motorhome maker/converter. Where there are two plates, both should state the same values. If they do not, one or other of the plates may be wrong, and any error should be corrected. However, it is unlikely either plate will refer to MTPLM as such, so consult the motorhome and base vehicle handbooks for where to find these plates, and what the numbers on them mean. While checking the plates, note also the maximum permissible loads for the front, and rear, axles - you will need these as well. These are absolute limits, and must never be exceeded.

The plate should also have a figure for Gross Train Weight – this reflects the maximum weight of the motorhome plus any trailer being towed. Again this weight should not be exceeded and bear in mind that if the motorhome has been replated at a higher weight – this may reduce the maximum weight of the trailer being towed.

The payload, which is what interests us, is the difference between the two. That is to say, it is the weight allowance for all our camping gear,

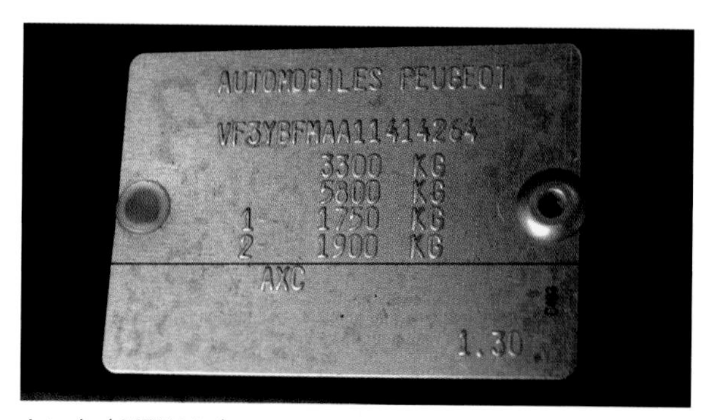

A typical MTPLM plate

clothing, food, bikes toys etc. However, it is also from this allowance that the weight of any options on either base vehicle or conversion, such as awnings, bike racks, satellite dishes etc. must be deducted.

BASIC MATHS

MTPLM	3500kg	
MIRO	2575kg	(925kg)
Essential habitation payload	275kg	(650kg)
Optional extras	120kg	(530kg)
User payload =	**530kg**	

For test and Type Approval purposes, although seldom stated, there is a weight formula for passengers and general baggage, that must at least equal 75kg per belted passenger seat (excluding driver), plus an additional 10 kg for every metre of length and a further 10 kg per passenger - including the driver. For this purpose only belted passenger seats count so, any seats without belts will not have been allocated a load allowance, ditto any berths in excess of the number of belted seats.

All this is intended to ensure is that a vehicle can reasonably function as a motorhome. In other words, it is a minimum requirement. It does not guarantee that it will be adequate for you, or for how you intend using it. You will still need a healthy residual payload for options, additional equipment, bikes, awnings etc. How much?

Well, based upon our own experience, what these figures would give is, very much, a minimum. The actual MIRO of our 2007 Hobby Van T500GFSC measured on a weighbridge is 2,737 kg, which compares quite fairly with the catalogue figure - adjusted for options - of 2,725Kg. Our MTPLM is 3,400kg and the van is 6 metres long. There are two of us: the van is a two-berth fixed rear bed, with four belted seats. Payload (MTPLM minus MIRO) is 663Kg, which looks quite favourable at first sight.

The Type Approval benchmark calculation above would give a load, at the van's MIRO, with driver, three passengers and luggage etc, of 2,737 + 3x75 + 6x10 + 4x10 = 3,062Kg. Our residual payload would thus be 3,400 – 3,062 = 338Kg. Plenty, you might think? Well, read on!

In practice, our actual fully laden weight, with fresh water tank and gas cylinders full, excluding bike rack and bikes, fluctuates between 3,275Kg and 3,320Kg! Our residual payload thus hovers between 125Kg and 80Kg. With bikes, if we can't empty the toilet tank and buy some wine on the way home, this can reduce to 45Kg. Are we profligate? You judge.

Our normal added load of is made up of 45kg of clothing (this includes waterproofs, fleeces, pullovers and walking boots as well as the usual under and outer wear), 40Kg of food and drink (fridge contents, milk, bottled water, some wine, fruit, vegetables, some tins, plus the usual dry packaged foodstuffs), 70kg of general goods (towels, washing kit, cosmetics, soaps etc, general cleaning materials, laptop, books, guides and maps), and 80kg of general camping kit (electric cable, water hose, tools, 'van cleaning materials, levelling ramps, windscreen wash, cab screen cover, camping table and chairs). Thus loaded, were we to carry our permitted two passengers, we should have to shed 25kg to remain legal!

It is almost impossible to compile a rule of thumb loading allowance for a motorhome, there are too many variables. However, I do not think we carry much excess, and even getting the load down to the above level involves some disputes as to what to take and what to leave. We could travel with the water tank empty and only fill on arrival: however, we have found that this is not always practical. We do not always empty the toilet or grey water tanks before leaving. The former simply gallops through the chemical, especially if stops are short; the latter is not always possible.

If the published MTPLM minus the published MIRO (the crude payload) is in the region of 650kg, and there will be two of you, the 'van is probably reasonably viable. If the crude payload is much less than this, or if there will be more than two people using the 'van, do your homework carefully before buying. It would be quite possible for four people to be accommodated within 650kg, I'm sure a number of people will post to say they do this without any difficulty. However, in view of the various posts from people who do find their payload inadequate, it would be well worthwhile checking that you are not trying to get a quart into a pint pot before spending your money.

In a nutshell, there's a lack of consistency over what the manufacturers and converters class as the MIRO and in most motorhomes, an element of hidden weight, seems to creep in; what if you and your passenger weight more than 75kg or both fresh and waste tanks are brimful? But in the eyes of the law, there is no grey area surrounding the vehicle's MTPLM – exceed it and you break the law.

WEIGHBRIDGES

The only way to be sure you are within the law is to take your motorhome to a public weighbridge and get it checked. Your local authority should be able to point you in the right direction and there's usually a fee – but it's a small price to pay for peace of mind.

The procedure is fairly straightforward but you may need to book a slot in advance, so it's worthwhile ringing first rather than just turning up.

Ideally, the motorhome should be fully laden with all the tanks filled, accessories such as bike racks and bikes attached and both driver and passenger (and the kids, if you usually carry them) onboard. This will immediately tell you whether you fall within the vehicles MTPLM.

However, if you fear your payload is marginal, as long as you know the precise capacity of your water tanks (fresh and waste) you may want to leave them empty and add the relevant filled weight to the final readings. Whatever you do, take a precise note of exactly what is stowed on board so you can allow for any extras.

Once on site, you drive the van onto the plate and then drive off, before reversing just the rear wheels onto the plate. This gives you a gross weight and a rear axle weight from which you can then calculate the front axle weight.

The weighbridge operator should give you a certificate containing all the readings – hold on to it for documentary proof of the legality of your vehicle.

Alternatively, simply take along a completely unladen vehicle to the weighbridge to establish its true MIRO (but don't forget to fill the tanks). Subtract this figure from the MTPLM to get an accurate payload. You then have the slightly laborious task of weighing every single item you load on board – including the cat – as you pack the van for a trip.

When calculating weights this way, it's advisable to leave at least 50kg leeway for any items you purchase while you're away – such as the inevitable case of cheeky Bordeaux from the roadside caves.

THE CONSEQUENCES

British Police are getting hotter on the enforcement of weight limits in the motorhome sector and we know of several motorhomers who have been stopped and challenged about their

Lafarge Aggregates Limited
Granite House
PO Box 7392
Syston
Leicester LE7 1XQ
Tel 0870 336 8725
Tel Sales 0870 336 8232
Fax 0870 336 8627
VAT Reg No 238 5560 46

LAFARGE

733/ 314756

CONDITIONS OF SALE

RECEIVED AND APPROVED BY

PLEASE PRINT NAME & COMPANY

WEST DEEPING

M SUTCLIFFE

Non-Aggregate - Source on request

GROSS

TARE

NET

A public weighbridge is the only place to get an accurate picture of your payload

A weighbridge ticket

van's weight. The maximum fine which can be imposed upon drivers of overweight vehicles is £3,000.

Matters could potentially be worse for overweight motorhomes on the continent – where as well as imposing a stiff on-the-spot fine, some forces have the right to impound the vehicle.

It's also worth considering that if you have an accident whilst driving an overweight motorhome, although your insurance company will probably honour Third Party claims, they may refuse to pay out for repairs to or replacement of your wrecked motorhome and its contents.

REAL EXPERIENCES

Posted by kelly58 on www.outandaboutlive.co.uk:

I put our Compass Suntor 115 on a weighbridge today fully loaded as per long trip: full fuel tank, two full gas bottles, full water tank and full toilet flush tank, food and clothing for two people and we grossed at 2910kg - our gross permitted weight is 3000kg which gives us 90kg spare!

We were thinking of fitting a bike rack and by doing so and loading two bikes we would still be just under permitted weight but not a lot to spare if we want to bring some booze back from France - although we could always dump the water once loaded for home I suppose.

Posted by carolh on www.outandaboutlive.co.uk:

We have a Rapido 741 mgw 3500kg - payload is about 350kg, we have a Fiamma awning and a solar panel and bike rack.

I am in the process of having it re-plated to 3850kg, it's only a paper exercise as our vehicle is on the maxi chassis.

We went out for the day today to give the van and run and on the way back called into our local public weighbridge - we had:

- Both of us in the cab - neither of us are porkies - but not slimline either!
- Full fresh water - 90 litres or thereabouts
- Full 6kg Gaslow bottles x 2
- 3/4 tank of fuel.
- Hardly any clothes
- Maybe enough tinned food for 2 days.
- And a mattress topper on the fixed bed.

We were 3480kg! Doesn't bear thinking about does it? OK, so we don't need to travel with full fresh water tank. But it still doesn't give us much to play with. Hence the re-plating.

Posted by alan k on www.outandaboutlive.co.uk:

We weighed our van as we set off for a month in France with 3/4 fresh water (sits over rear axle) and two bikes in the garage at 3500kgs against our plated weight of 3850kgs.

But our rear axle was right up to the limit and the 300kg spare was all on our front axle. I was able to redistribute a bit of stuff out of the garage and had to carry the wine home under the table and in the front seat boxes with a nearly empty water tank.

Our local trading standards office has a free 24-hour free weighbridge at Gildersome just off the M62 near Leeds where the A62 crosses. There's no ticket but it weighs individual axles and then adds them up.

So I'm very careful about how much we carry and where it goes. I've even thought about moving the bike rack from the back wall of the garage to the front, or moving the leisure battery to a side locker to improve matters.

BRIAN KIRBY

Having owned a tent, a trailer tent, and two caravans over the past 20 years, Brian Kirby began his motorhoming career by reading MMM for three years before he retired and imported a Bürstner from France, in April 2005.

His present van, a Hobby, was imported from Germany in July 2007. He and his wife, Carole, generally spend the spring and autumn travelling Europe, with occasional forays around the UK. His initiation into the mysteries of payloads began with the two caravans, both lightweight models with minimal capacity, for which correct loading was critical.

Motorhome electrics

Increasingly complex electrical systems are integral to the functioning of the modern motorhome and while we'd recommend leaving major re-wiring jobs to the experts, it's useful to have an insight into the key elements. Consultant engineer and regular MMM contributor Clive Mott-Gotobed gives you the low-down

Over the years motorhomes have become increasingly reliant on an electrical system to control the various bits of equipment on board. Without electrics, a modern, state-of-the-art motorhome would not have any cooking, heating, lighting, refrigeration or hot water and your motorhome really would become a shed on wheels! Motorhomes built a few years ago would at least allow you to cook and keep warm, as not everything was under the control of a CPU (Central Processing Unit)

The electrical systems employed in a motorhome fall into two categories: 12-volt DC and 230-volt mains equipment with a fair amount of overlap between the two systems, the most important by far being the 12-volt circuits.

All motorhomes will have at least two 12-volt batteries, one in the engine bay associated with starting the engine and running those pieces of equipment associated with the base vehicle and a second battery located elsewhere for running the habitation equipment. Both of these batteries will be charged when the vehicle is in use by the alternator driven by the engine. Most motorhomes have a 'split charge' relay which only closes its contacts when the engine is running and these contacts will connect the second habitation or 'leisure' battery to the alternator connecting it effectively in parallel with the starter battery. The reason for this 'split charge' relay is to ensure that when you are camping and discharging the leisure battery that this battery is separated from the starter battery so you do not discharge it as well, resulting in an engine that cannot be started.

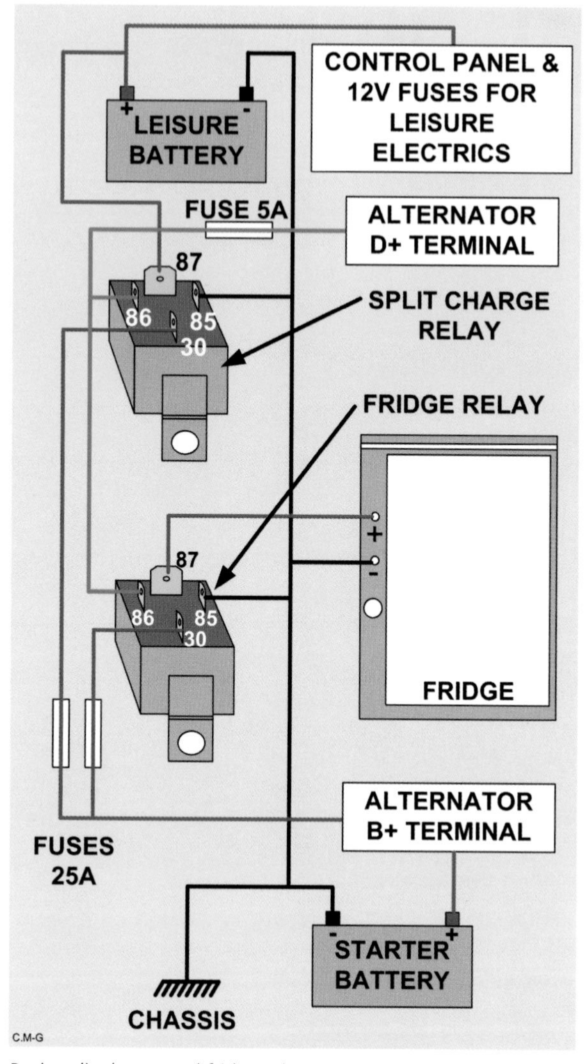

Basic split charge and fridge relay circuits

Your motorhome will most likely have two 'split charge' type relays and the second of these relays will be used to power the 12-volt heater supply of the three-way (Mains, 12-volt and gas) absorption-type refrigerator that most of us have. The reason for this being that you should not drive a vehicle with an operational gas appliance.

In older motorhomes, these relays can be found mounted anywhere from inside the engine bay to under the fridge or in the wardrobe, often with a pair of fuses mounted alongside them. On more

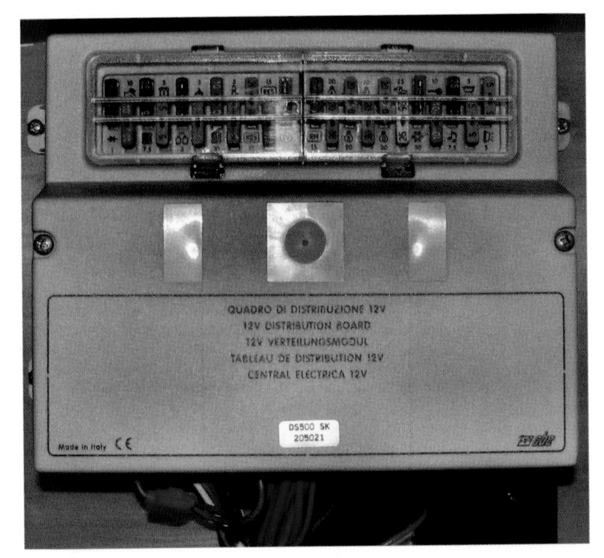

A CBE fuse box

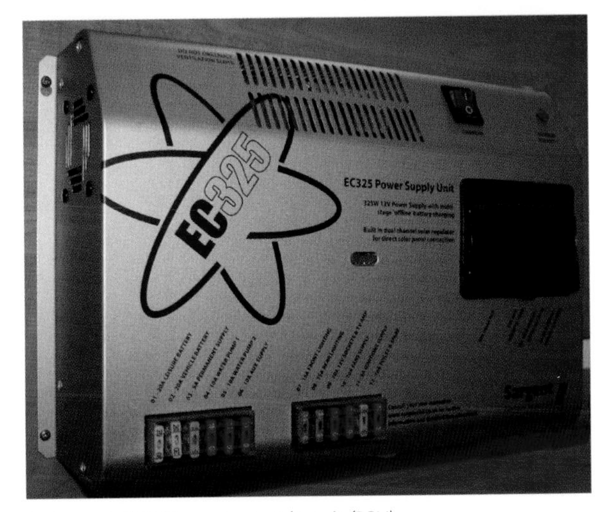

A Sargent EC325 power supply unit (PSU)

modern ones, these relays will be incorporated into an electrical box of tricks with other components and many fuses.

The output from your leisure battery will be routed through a fuse (often in the battery box) and then some sort of master switch before feeding a row of fuses that will supply (via more switches) the various bits of kit in your motorhome.

On older motorhomes the master switch and other switches were simply that: a row of switches in a panel. On more modern motorhomes these switches are replaced by remotely controlled switches called relays.

A CBE control panel

These are often mounted on an electronic printed circuit board and incorporated into the aforementioned 'box of tricks', together with many fuses, and hidden away under a bed or in a wardrobe in many cases. The motorhome user should not normally need to do anything with this box but should be directed by the instruction manual to the 'Control Panel' which is situated inside the habitation area in a clearly visible location - frequently above the entrance door. This Control Panel will have various buttons to turn ON and OFF various functions, it will have some sort of digital display to indicate which devices have been turned ON or OFF but it may be as simple as a few LEDs (light emitting diodes) or an LCD (Liquid Crystal Display) giving accurate readings of various battery parameters, the inside and outside temperature, water levels etc.

Whether your motorhome has a row of switches or state-of-the-art remote LCD control panel, the switches or relays and fuses still control the same basic functions of Main ON/OFF, Water pump ON/OFF, Lights ON/OFF, Heating ON/OFF. It's the additional features that make some systems more comprehensive than others.

MAINS HOOK-UP

All modern motorhomes will have a mains hook-up connection. This is a fixed 16-amp rated blue round semi waterproof plug on or in the side of the motorhome. Using a mains hook-up lead, you plug your motorhome into a suitable mains power outlet point provided on most campsites. It is prudent to connect the van end of the hook-up lead first, so that you are not walking round with a live connector in your hand. Even some

A 16-amp semi waterproof socket which attaches to your motorhome

The plug end of your electric cable and attaches to the distribution post

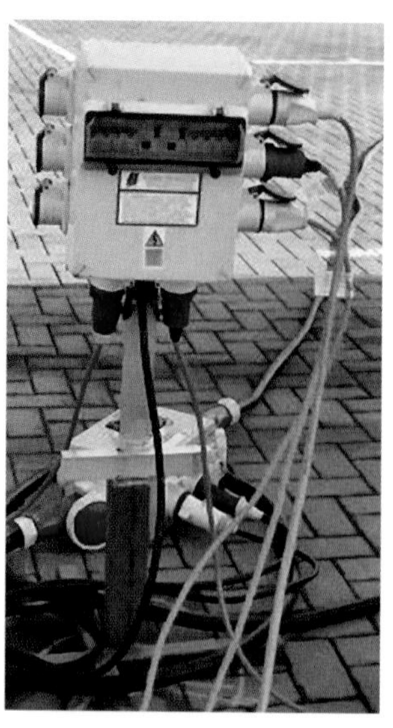
A temporary distribution post at the NEC

The business end of the electric hook-up – a mains distribution post or pylon

temporary campsites provide this facility although most limit your maximum loading by fitting a smaller circuit breaker at the distribution post. In this example 6 amp.

The most important task of a mains hook-up is to run the on-board battery charging system that all motorhomes have. Even the most limited hook-up will be more than adequate to do this. Once safely hooked up, lots more opportunities open up and battery power is no longer a limited resource. You can set your fridge to operate from the mains electrical supply, some fridges (Automatic Energy Selection or AES) switch automatically between 12-volt, gas and mains power. You can turn on the mains part of your water heating system if you have this option, you can charge your mobile phone or laptop battery and use the electrical space heating if you have it.

A typical 16-amp rated main hook-up cable

230 VOLT AC EQUIPMENT

The RCD (Residual Current Device) is the main double pole circuit breaker through which both LIVE and NEUTRAL connections from your mains hook-up connector must pass and an important piece of safety kit. The RCD monitors the current (amps) flowing in the neutral conductor and compares it with the current flowing in the live conductor. If these differ by more than 0.03A (30 milliamperes) the RCD will open and disconnect both live and neutral connections. If you have an earth fault on an appliance then some of the current from the live will flow back via the earth wiring to the substation, this imbalance is then detected by the RCD which switches off. Even if the mains hook-up point has been wired incorrectly by the campsite resulting in the LIVE and NEUTRAL connections being transposed, the RCD still provides a high level of protection.

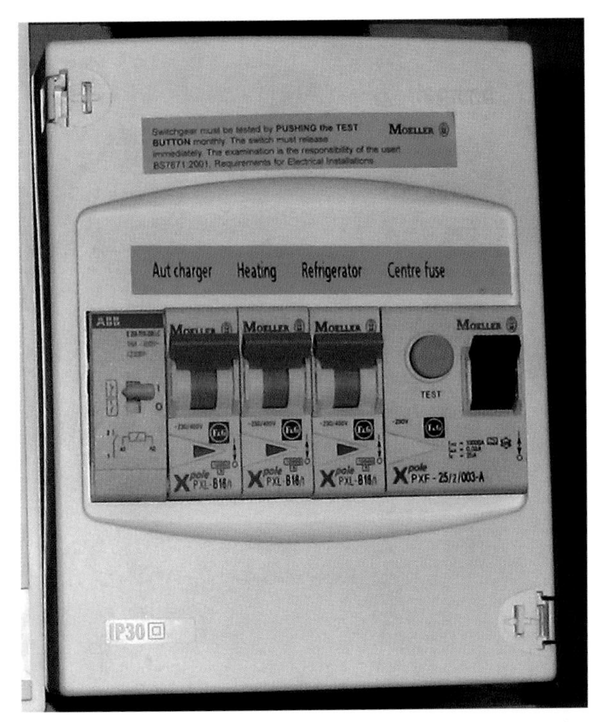

The RCD and MCBs are usually in the mains distribution panel

CIRCUIT BREAKERS

These provide over current protection and are the modern equivalent of fuses. Their main advantage is that in the event of an over current fault they open very quickly. Having removed the offending fault from the circuit they are simply switched back on again.

The first line of defence is an RCD. This device compares the current flowing in the live and neutral wires. If there is the slightest difference a potentially dangerous leakage from live to earth is occurring and it trips and cuts off the mains supply. If this is the one tripping out it needs to be checked as a matter of urgency. It may just be a faulty unit, but could be a serious, but intermittent, fault with a severe risk of electrocution.

Each individual mains circuit has an MCB (Miniature Circuit Breaker). Most 'vans have three in a bank and usually alongside, or close to, the RCD. The purpose of these is to protect the wiring from overheating and the risk of fire if overloaded.

In effect these are re-settable fuses. If one of these is tripping without operating the RCD the MCB is probably faulty, but it needs to be checked, as there could still be a problem with the equipment connected to that circuit.

You need the services of an electrician with a PAT (Portable Appliance Testing) certificate. Most motorcaravan dealers should be able to arrange for one even if they do not have one on their staff.

To turn both RCDs and circuit breakers on, flick the switch to the 'up' position. The mains supply therefore enters the motorhome via the blue hook-up connector, the currents in both LIVE and NEUTRAL are compared to check for any disappearing to earth as it passes through the RCD, is routed to the individual circuit breakers that then connects via the mains wiring within the motorhome to the charger, fridge, electric heaters, mains lighting and socket outlets. The fridge and charger are frequently protected by a 5 amp circuit breaker with other circuits protected by 10 amp breakers.

LEISURE BATTERY

All motorhomes have at least one leisure battery. To increase one's ability to camp away from hook-ups for prolonged periods of time there are several options available. The most cost-effective way to double the time you can survive without hook-up is to double the size of your leisure battery, this frequently being achieved by connecting a similar battery to the existing battery in parallel with it.

Paralleled batteries are best if they are of similar age, ampere-hour capacity and construction, that is, for example one

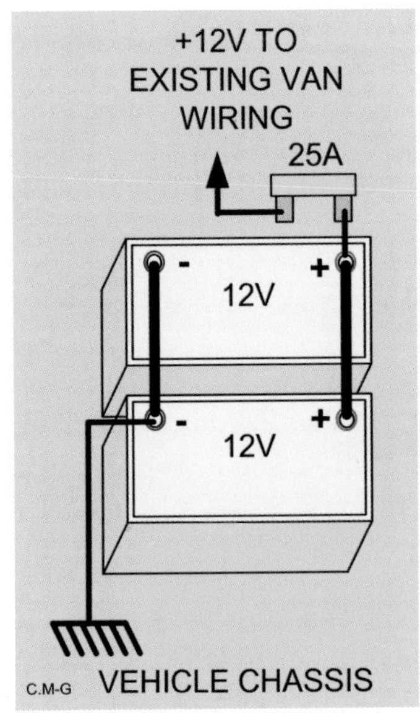

Adjacent 12 volt batteries in parallel

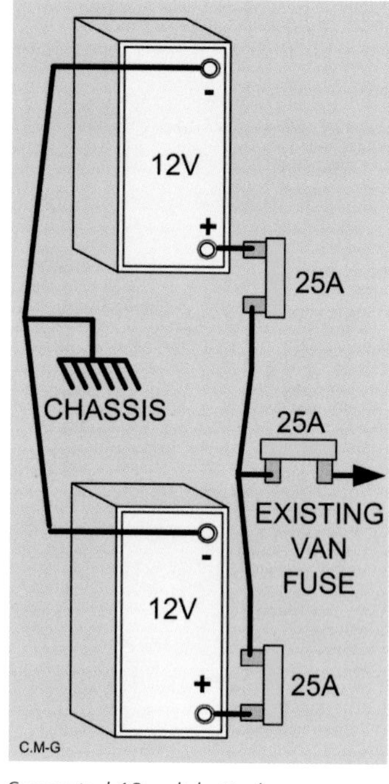

Separated 12-volt batteries connected in parallel

does not connect a maintenance-free (Gel) battery in parallel with a wet electrolyte battery. Indeed if one wants to fit two batteries in parallel it's best if they are purchased together as a pair.

If the two batteries to be connected in parallel are mounted directly alongside each other then it's OK to fit two short stout cables or copper links to join the negatives together and the positives together. The original single fuse should be sufficient. Batteries are heavy however, and there is a limit on how much battery capacity one can carry without seriously compromising payload.

SAFETY

When working on battery systems, be aware that you're working with acid and potentially explosive gasses, as well as very high short circuit fault currents. Take great care and think twice before doing anything. Always disconnect the negative (chassis) cable first as this is already connected to the chassis by the cabling and should you join the negative battery post to chassis with your spanner a fault current should not flow. Once the negative connection has been disconnected, safely insulated and secured, then the battery positive becomes safe. BUT if you have more than one leisure battery then the potential for spanner short circuit faults remains and the circuits remain live until the penultimate battery connection on the final battery is removed.

BATTERY CHARGER

These vary in output size and charging pattern. For many years the built-in charger would replicate the output of the vehicle alternator, providing a current-limited output voltage of 14 volts. More recently, intelligent chargers have been used. These carefully monitor the battery during the charging process and initially charge faster, then for a short time they allow the battery voltage to rise above 14 volts to achieve a 100 per cent charge, reverting to a lower voltage of about 13.8 volts to maintain the battery in a charged state. Slight variations in the charging pattern are used for different battery types.

These battery chargers need to be in a well-ventilated place and never covered up with clothing. Frequently they will include an integral cooling fan to improve cooling air flow as they all generate some heat in use and the harder they work, the more heat they will generate. The better fan-cooled chargers have control of the fan so that it either does not run or operates slowly if the charging current is moderate to minimise fan noise.

Some chargers are incorporated into the main 'box of tricks' like those produced by Sargent Electrical for example, others like CBE have them as separate units.

WATER PUMPS

Foot-operated water pumps have not been fitted to caravans or motorhomes for several years. Today there are two basic types of pump in common use: the small submersible pump that is lowered into a water container on the end of a stiff length of hose, or the larger bulkhead fitted pump that has the ability to draw water from a container below.

All systems with submersible pumps and some systems with bulkhead fitted pumps are used in conjunction with special water taps that operate an electrical switch when the tap is initially turned ON. This is the simplest system and at no time is the water system left pressurised.

The increasingly popular system uses a bulkhead pump which has an integral pressure switch. When the master water system switch is operated

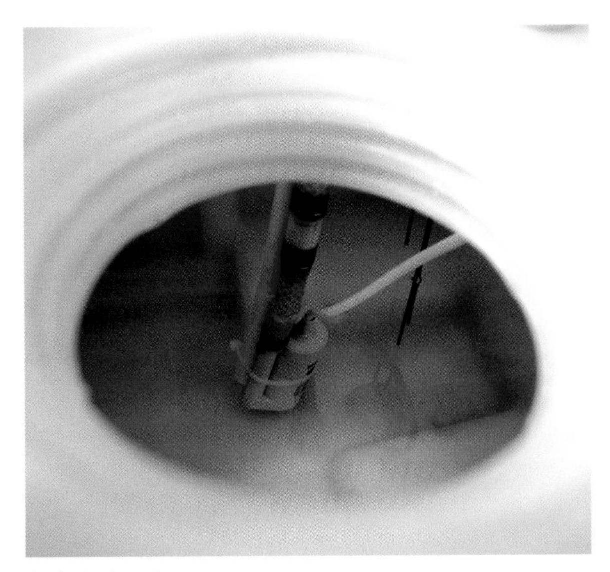

An in-tank water pump

to turn the water system on, the pump will run and pressurise the system then, when sufficient pressure is achieved, a pressure switch will open and turn OFF the electrical supply to the pump enabling simple taps to be used. When any tap on the system is turned ON water will flow and the pressure will fall, causing the switch to close and the pump to run. The water system, hot as well as cold can be just like home.

HOB IGNITION

Nearly all modern gas hobs, ovens and grills have electronic ignition. A small electronic module is powered from the 12-volt supply via a momentary switch or push button. When the switch is closed the module pulses a small spark coil, similar to that in a petrol car, to generate a high voltage that is routed to spark gaps situated alongside each gas burner. The burner gas tap will also include a connection to a thermal sensor so that the gas cannot be left turned ON unless the flame is lit.

HEATING SYSTEMS

These can be split into systems where hot water and space heating are combined in one unit or systems which have independent equipment for hot water and space heating.

The Truma water heater and previously the Carver Cascade water heater are small gas boilers which are fully automatic in operation. A 12-volt electronic module operates the ignition, gas solenoid and fan within the unit, a small control panel inside the van allowing ON/OFF control of the boiler with LEDs indicating its status.

Truma and Carver also made space heaters to warm the air in the motorhome. Early models had piezo ignition but later were electronic. These were frequently supplemented by a large fan that circulated the warm air from the heater through ducting around the motorhome.

The later Truma Combi boiler combines both water and hot air space heating in one unit.

The Alde combination boiler offers gas or 1, 2 or 3kW of electrical heating in a wet central heating system that is almost totally silent. Power consumption from the 12-volt system being modest at no more than 1 amp total including the water circulating pump.

CLIVE MOTT-GOTOBED

Clive Mott-Gotobed worked for 42 years as an electrical/electronic designer and project engineer for the UKs principal manufacturer of battery electric fork lift trucks, Lansing Bagnall/Linde. Clive and Janet's passion for Motorhomes started in 1972 with a Bedford CF-based Dormobile. This was soon quickly re-converted to suit Clive's height and a high top fitted. Then followed a similar conversion on a Bay window VW. Later a total conversion of a 29-seater Duple Vista coach in which they travelled widely over Europe. Clive's experience as a technical writer was honed during his formal working life producing many technical manuals. Clive still provides a consultancy service for his old employer.

Your first night away

FOR some new converts, as we suggested earlier in this section, the first night they spend in their new van could be adjacent to the dealership where they bought it or on a campsite conveniently located just down the road.

It's hard to underestimate the peace of mind this option affords, as the knowledge that if something does go wrong, help is close at hand should make first-timers sleep that little bit easier.

But once you feel confident enough to drive a few miles and set the van up onsite by yourselves, you could just head off into the sunset and see where the road takes you.

It's a romantic notion and very much part of the motorhoming ideal, but planning a few things in advance rather than diving into the wide blue yonder unprepared is likely to make the whole experience that little bit more comfortable, if not quite as spontaneous, unpredictable and exciting.

Not so long ago, meandering around the countryside, footloose and fancy-free, simply turning up at a site 'on spec' would usually be OK as they'd almost certainly have a few vacant pitches. But recent years have witnessed a dramatic increase in demand for camping pitches from growing numbers of retired or semi-retired caravanners and motorcaravanners touring outside peak season, meaning space on popular sites is often tight – even in the depths of winter.

So to avoid disappointment, our advice is always to book ahead. Both Clubs now operate efficient online booking systems and if you want to speak to a real person, you can also do it over the phone. Independent sites are increasingly accepting bookings via their websites or email and are usually happy to accept a telephone reservation without a deposit.

In popular holiday destinations with plenty of capacity, chancing your arm and turning up without a reservation is a strategy that probably will work fine – as long as you are prepared to drive from site to site until you find one which has spaces. But after a long day on the road, do you really want the hassle of those extra anxious miles until you find somewhere. And when you do, what are the chances that the site which does have spaces is as nice as all the ones you called in at en route?

Arriving at a site for your first trip away is an exciting time

When you're off the beaten track in sparsely populated areas with few tourist facilities, turning up at a site without booking can be an altogether more fraught experience, however. If there's no room at the inn, you may be left with a fairly stark choice: drive on for another 30 or 40 miles to the nearest site or park up and wild camp.

When you've identified the destination point for your maiden voyage, the process of finding a campsite is a lot easier than it was a decade or two ago. Club members can search both organisations' websites for the nearest site and book online and more and more of the large groups owning multiple sites have easy-to-use websites.

Independent sites are sometimes hard to locate, although dedicated site search engines such as www.ukcampsites.co.uk and www.outandaboutlive.co.uk/pitchfinder can help in this respect. Even a simple Google search using the locality or nearest large town together with the words 'camping' and 'motorhome' will usually throw up some useful results.

Simply select a site which appeals and give them a ring to secure your space.

PREPARING THE VAN

Assuming your van is fully serviced and has a valid MOT, there shouldn't be too much mechanical messing about involved in getting it ready for your maiden outing.

If you enjoy delving around under the bonnet with a socket set, then by all means give the engine a bit of a once-over yourself, but if it's been a few months since the van has been serviced or MOT tested, we'd advise taking it to an approved van servicing centre or a specialist motorhome centre for a check-up.

If you're happy that the mechanicals are in good working order, then it's simply a case of checking the basics like oil levels and tyre pressures. The former should be self-explanatory, but the subject of motorhome tyres is a little more involved.

Most motorhomes are fitted with specialist 'camper' tyres which are designed to be inflated to significantly higher pressures than standard car tyres and also to operate at a wider range of pressures according to seasonal temperature factors and the payload being carried.

Check carefully in the owners' manual which pressures the tyres are designed to operate at and make sure they are correctly inflated. It's worth purchasing a simple tyre pressure gauge and keeping it somewhere handy within the van and checking inflation pressures every trip. It's an essential safety measure and will also extend the life of the tyres and ensure the van returns the most efficient fuel economy figures.

PACKING

When it comes to packing, motorhomers broadly tend to fall into one of two categories: those who painstakingly pack everything into its allotted space in the van and tick every individual item off on their checklist prior to heading off – a process which can take several hours - and those who leave the van fully provisioned and ready to leave at the drop of a hat.

Which approach you take is largely dependent on how frequently you aim to get away in the van, but if you're hoping to escape at least once a month – we'd suggest adopting the second strategy will save a lot of time and hassle.

At the end of every trip, all that's needed is to make a brief inventory of what you've used and add it to your next weekly shopping list so you can replace it ready for the next excursion. Obviously, extended trips will require additional provisions, but if you're going to be away for a long time, remember that, unlike Transatlantic yacht crews, you are more than likely to encounter the odd supermarket on your travels!

The 'pre-loading' approach also allows you greater control over your payload limits as you can either take the fully provisioned van to a weighbridge to make sure its within its limits or – if you have a clear indication of how much user payload you have remaining after the essential habitation payload plus any extra items are accounted for – you can simply weigh every additional container on a set of bathroom scales.

Yes, we know it's complicated, so if you are in any doubt, please read the chapter on payloads before adding the kitchen sink to your provisions list. In the checklist below, we've split a typical motorhome inventory into three sections: permanent fixtures, consumables and perishables, but only the first two categories remain on board at all times. For European touring, especially over extended periods, the list gets significantly longer. Consult the chapter on European touring for further details.

BEDDING

Duvet or sleeping bags? Go for the latter and once you've rearranged the cushions, bedtime is a breeze. It's far from romantic however and most couples opt for the full compliment of bed linen – including underlays, mattress-toppers, fitted sheets and variable-TOG duvets.

The duvet option is fine, especially if you have a fixed bed

Much depends on whether your sleeping quarters are of the fixed bed variety or need to be made up each night from seat cushions. With the former, it's straightforward enough, just treat it like the bed at home, although you may want to invest in some fitted sheets and mattress underlay.

The underlay – particularly when the base of the bed is a solid sheet of ply rather than slatted, will improve the flow of air underneath the mattress and reduce any condensation. Mattress toppers are also becoming increasingly popular – especially the memory foam versions - as they smooth out the contours that are inevitable in any mattress constructed from multiple seat cushions.

Fitted sheets with elasticated edges are a must and if your bed is an unusual size or shape, there are specialist suppliers who will make them to order.

CLOTHING

While you will come across the occasional sticklers for standards who insist upon keeping up appearances, encounters with 'golf club' types decked out in twin sets and pearls or blazers, slacks and brogues are increasingly rare – although if you do meet these folk, they usually mix a mean G&T around 5:37pm.

Most motorhomes do have some form of wardrobe space, so it's entirely feasible to transport a smart outfit to wear during an indulgent meal at a swanky seafront restaurant and if so, don't forget the coat-hangers.

Light, comfortable, easy to wash, fast-drying and non-iron are the watchwords – together with warm and waterproof when touring outside the summer season. The ideal is to exist in shorts, T-shirts and flip-flops, but this isn't always possible in the UK, so some additional items are usually required.

The one golden rule relates to footwear. If it's wet underfoot, remove outside shoes at the door and replace with slippers, flip-flops or those garish plastic moulded monstrosities which seemed to have taken over the planet. This will save a lot of cleaning and keep the interior of the van looking presentable for far longer.

SAFETY

All motorhomes should be fitted with the following items as a matter of course: dry powder fire extinguisher, fire blanket, smoke alarm and a carbon monoxide alarm. In addition, those who drive A-class type motorhomes with only a single cab door may want to consider having a glass-breaking safety hammer attached to the cab wall on the non-opening door side to facilitate escape from the vehicle if, in the event of an accident, it rolls onto the side with the opening door.

Anyone taking essential prescription medicine or requiring an inhaler should ensure they take adequate supplies with them.

HANDY CHECKLIST

You're almost certain to forget some essential item or other, but here's a handy checklist of important items which first-timers often overlook. We've deliberately omitted discretionary luxuries or more expensive items such as televisions, DVD players, satellite TV systems, MP3 players and lap-tops, but more and more people regard these as essential equipment these days…

Handy Checklist

Permanent fixtures

- [ ] Duvet or sleeping bags
- [ ] Bed sheets
- [ ] Pillows
- [ ] Corkscrew and bottle opener
- [ ] Tin opener
- [ ] Chopping board and sharp kni
- [ ] Breadknife
- [ ] Kettle
- [ ] Non-stick deep-side frying pa
- [ ] Small saucepan
- [ ] Oven-proof casserole
- [ ] Large salad bowl
- [ ] Cutlery
- [ ] Crockery
- [ ] Hand and bath towels
- [ ] First aid kit
- [ ] Coat hangers
- [ ] Spirit level (for getting level on pitch)
- [ ] Basic toolbox
- [ ] Gaffer tape
- [ ] Torch
- [ ] Dustpan and brush (or mini vacuum cleaner)
- [ ] Barbecue and utensils

ARRIVAL

You're unlikely to receive the warmest of welcomes if you arrive at the site reception shortly after breakfast having set off in the wee small hours 'to avoid the traffic'. Most sites operate an arrivals and departures procedure which smoothes out the change-over to make best use of the available pitches.

On sites which are popular with motorhomers, the resident population tends to be highly transient, with up to 30 per cent of pitches changing hands every day. This proportion will increase still further in peak season and at weekends, so you won't be thanked for throwing a spanner in the works.

Consumables

- ☐ Loo roll
- ☐ Matches or lighter
- ☐ Washing up liquid
- ☐ Pan scourer and dishcloth
- ☐ Soap (bar or pump action liquid)
- ☐ Shower gel
- ☐ Disinfectant wipes
- ☐ Coffee
- ☐ Tea
- ☐ UHT milk
- ☐ Tinned and packet food
- ☐ Prescription medication
- ☐ Spare batteries
- ☐ Bin liners (recycled supermarket carrier bags work well)
- ☐ Toilet chemical
- ☐ Flush chemical

Perishables

- ☐ Fresh food and drink
- ☐ Butter or margarine
- ☐ Bread
- ☐ Fruit juice
- ☐ Fresh milk

Don't arrive too early or you could get a frosty reception

Most site wardens expect new guests to arrive after midday and certainly later than 10am to give them a chance to get their morning chores out of the way and the site looking ship shape before welcoming the next intake.

Arrive before10am and you're almost certain to be politely asked to go away and return after a few hours, or at the least park up in the late arrivals area (about which more later).

Aim to arrive mid to late afternoon and you should be assured of a warm welcome and have the pick of the vacant pitches. Leave it much later and you may have to sit in a queue of campers waiting to check and face something of a scrum for the last remaining pitches with a sea view.

If you have no alternative but to arrive late in the evening, most sites have a 'late arrivals' area. If there are no signs of life in reception, it's best to park up here for the night and check in at reception the following morning – although you may still have to wait for existing campers to vacate a pitch before you can move onto the site.

After checking in (or even while one of you checks in) it's a good idea to split up with one walking around the site to locate a suitable pitch while the other manoeuvres the van. You may want to head straight for the motorhome service point (MSP) if the site has one, to top up the water tank and dump any grey water you may have acquired – but if you are only stopping for a couple of days and then returning home, think carefully about how much water you're likely to need. Rather than filling the fresh tank to the top, work out how much water you're going to use on the basis of between 10 litres and 20 litres per person, per day – possibly less if you are using site facilities to wash the pots and shower.

Most sites have 5mph speed limits which are rigorously enforced by the wardens and fellow campers – and it's also a good idea to have the windows wound down to give advance warning of other hazards.

Once the pitch has been selected, follow the protocols and checklists in the 'First Steps' chapter to get set up, but bear the following guidelines about positioning in mind.

The Caravan Club advises leaving at least 20 feet between the side walls of adjoining units and at least 10 feet of clearance behind your van and any other vehicle in any direction – i.e. to the front or rear. These guidelines may seem a bit prescriptive and on some sites, the size and spacing of the pitches may prevent observance of them, but they do help preserve not only your neighbours', but also your own privacy.

SITE ETIQUETTE

Expectations of campers' conduct on site vary enormously, but the process of choosing a site will hopefully mean that you've pitched up somewhere that you are comfortable with your fellow residents.

Regarding other basic safety guidelines, some sites adopt a completely laissez-faire attitude to rules and regulations and allow campers largely to police themselves. On some sites, you may find large groups of youngsters gathering around campfires and listening to ghetto blasters until the early hours is perfectly acceptable and if the owners are comfortable with this, it's difficult for individual campers to challenge. At the other extreme, Club sites expect all outdoor activity and noise to cease at 10.30pm, which when the evening is warm and the drink is flowing as easily as the conversation, can seem a little draconian. But by the same token, how would you feel about a gaggle of noisy kids kicking off a football match at 8am while you nurse you head?

In practice, it's about striking a balance between tolerance and respecting fellow campers' space and privacy. Most well-run sites have a list of guidelines and make it fairly clear as to their expectations of campers' conduct. Stick within these and you shouldn't go far wrong.

Make an effort to establish amicable relations with your neigbours, don't wander across other people's pitches to get to the shower block, keep the radio down to a reasonable level and be equally considerate about the volume of outdoor conversation in the evenings – especially after a couple of glasses have been consumed!

DEPARTURE

Most sites like to have their pitches vacated by between 10am and 12pm on the designated day of departure and reserve the right to charge an extra night's pitch fees if the pitch isn't empty by the set time.

In practice, as long as the site isn't full to capacity, most wardens will give campers a little leeway here, but it's always best to check before lingering on the pitch.

Whilst packing up, it pays to have – you've guessed it – another checklist to tick things off before upping sticks. With practice, you'll soon get into the swing of things and learn which jobs you can leave and which absolutely, positively need to be done before vacating your pitch.

Make sure any loose items are safely stowed and catches on all the lockers properly engaged. Switch off the gas and electricity together with all appliances although if the fridge still contains perishables, select an alternative power source – ideally the 12-volt system.

Shut all windows and rooflights and turn off the master power switch on the consumer unit before unhooking the mains cable – following the exact reverse of the safety guidelines i.e. remove the cable from the pillar first, then unplug from the van, coil up the cable and stow carefully.

Have a final wander around the outside of the vehicle to check for things you may have missed then drive slowly off the pitch, recover any chocks used and off you go.

As previously discussed in the 'First Steps' chapter, if your onward journey is a lengthy one and you know there are motorhome service facilities at the other end, we'd recommend a visit to the service point to drain down the

Check with the wardens when you are expected to vacate your pitch

fresh and waste water tanks and empty the toilet cassette if it needs it. Similarly, if you're returning home, it's usually easier to deal with these jobs at a purpose-built MSP than on your driveway at home.

Finally, if you are only vacating the pitch for the day while you explore the delights of the surrounding area, leave some form of indication clearly visible to new arrivals looking for a place to park. Some people leave a plastic step or a windbreak in place, but the politest way of letting fellow campers know that you'll be back later is to buy a purpose-made 'pitch occupied' sign with your vehicle registration number included. Simply stick this into the grass at the back of the pitch and you've effectively marked out your territory.

Toiletiquette: rules of engagement

TRADITIONAL English reserve means in-depth discussion of the practicalities of using the typical motorhome toilet is something of a no-go zone, meaning many guides gloss over this delicate subject in a flurry of vague euphemisms.

We're going to tackle it head-on, so if you're of a nervous disposition, you may want to skip this chapter, but you do so at your peril, because there's nothing more embarrassing than having to deal with the fallout from a toilet malfunction in front of your fellow campers on a busy site.

At home, you simply flush and forget it, but it isn't that simple when you're the one who is ultimately responsible for disposing of waste products in a safe and hygienic fashion.

GROUND RULES

Many motorhomers evolve an unwritten understanding about what constitutes reasonable use of the motorhome's toilet. When staying on well-equipped sites, there's arguably no need to use the toilet at all – save for the odd nocturnal emergency visit – particularly after a convivial evening spent around the table.

Adopting a 'fluids-only' policy makes the whole process of waste management a great deal easier and with some sensible maintenance, should ensure the toilet and its cassette remain in tip-top condition for many seasons. It also means you can use just a fraction of the recommended dose of chemicals in the cassette.

FILLING AND EMPTYING

Priming the loo for active service is easy enough. If there's a separate flush tank, fill it with water, add the requisite volume of flush chemical and top up with water – usually around seven litres. Flushing systems which draw directly from the freshwater tank pretty much look after themselves.

The cassette needs to be primed with around a litre of water and chemical for full spectrum use, but for liquids-only, just a cup of water and a quarter of the recommended dose of chemicals ought to be sufficient.

The liquids-only approach really pays dividends when it comes to emptying, as the cassette just needs a quick rinse and you're back in business.

If this is an entirely new experience to you, it may be worth perfecting your emptying technique in the privacy of your own home with a cassette filled with water. It's also worth emptying the cassette for the first time before it gets completely full as it will be easier to handle.

Angle the emptying spout at 90 degrees to the cassette, press the air release button and pour the contents into the disposal bowl. **DON'T**, whatever you do, pop the screwcap on the side of the bowl, as retrieving it when you inevitably knock it into the bowl it is not a pleasant undertaking.

USING

There will be times when the motorhome loo is the only option for all your toilet requirements (although if you are that far off the beaten track, you could simply go behind a tree and bury it.

Prior to sitting down, close the blade and flush a little water into the bowl and cover it with a few pieces of toilet roll arranged flat to cover the entire surface, rather like lily pads.

Once you've finished, open the blade and the whole package disappears down the hole enclosed neatly in a tissue wrapper. Why bother with this rigmarole? Well it stops the bowl and the seals getting soiled and stained, minimising the need for additional scrubbing and cleaning later.

SOG SYSTEMS

A smart alternative to using chemicals in the cassette is the SOG toilet, which is becoming increasingly popular with motorcaravanners. This simple innovation involves wiring a small fan into the cassette compartment which vents odours outside the van and by drawing in air through the toilet bowl, prevents them getting back in while the cassette blade is in the open position.

SOG toilets render toilet chemicals redundant, which is better for the environment and, in the long run, should work out cheaper for long term touring on the continent.

Greener motorhoming tips

Splashing out on solar panels and low energy lighting systems are great ways to help the environment if you can afford it, but we can all do our bit for the environment without breaking the bank. Adopt some of these 20 tips and as well as reducing your carbon footprint, you'll save money too

ON THE ROAD

Work out your fuel consumption

It sounds simple, but it's surprising how many people don't keep track of their fuel consumption – and if you don't measure it – how do you know whether you're reducing it?

Many modern 'vans have a fuel consumption setting on the trip computer, but it's still worth doing your own calculations to establish its accuracy. Get into the habit of working out your fuel consumption on a regular basis then try some of the tips below and see how much of a difference they make.

If you're not mathematically minded, the Which? website will do the maths for you and work out the CO2 used on every trip: www.which.co.uk/advice/fuel-calculator

Stay below 60

As your speed increases up to 60mph, your level of pollution decreases. Travelling over 60mph increases your level of pollution again. It can cost you up to 25 per cent more in fuel to drive at 70mph compared to 50mph. If your 'van has cruise control – make use of it!

Switch off

Guidance from fuel-saving experts varies, but the consensus is that you should switch off the engine if you are likely to be stationary for more than two minutes.

Travel light 1

For shorter trips - do you really need to take all that clutter with you? If the roof rack is packed with holiday gear you're unlikely to use on a weekend break in Spring, lighten the load and you'll also ease the strain on your wallet!

Travel light 2

Empty your tanks – travel with a half-full fresh water tank and an empty waste water tank and you'll save as much as 150kg – which will have a significant impact on fuel consumption.

While this may not be feasible for itchy-footed nomads overnighting on basic sites, for those pitching up for extended periods on well-appointed sites with good motorhome service points, it makes a lot of sense to offload this excess baggage before embarking on a long journey.

Plan your journey

Don't rely on the Sat Nav – they aren't 100 per cent reliable and they could land you in a tight spot, meaning a lengthy detour, wasted fuel and a lot of stress. Use the route-planners on the AA or RAC websites or do it the old-fashioned way – with an up-to-date road map – they are still available! Check traffic reports before you set off by logging onto www.trafficengland.com

Air conditioning

Switch off the air conditioning unless you really need it and although this may seem like a contradiction, don't travel for long distances with the windows open – this significantly increases drag and with it, fuel consumption.

If you're confused about when to use the air con and when to simply open the window: at motorway speeds, flick on the air con to cool down the cab, but in town, when the air con makes a greater demand on the 'van's power system, you're better off opening the window.

Check your tyre pressure

Driving on under-inflated tyres can increase your fuel bills by two per cent, so invest in a pressure gauge and check them regularly. Motorhome tyres are usually inflated to significantly higher pressures than standard car tyres – so check the pressures carefully in your owner's manual. There are also likely to be different figures for summer and winter motoring and unladen and fully laden weights.

Look into the possibility of fitting low-rolling resistance radials next time you're due to replace the tyres. Fleet operators running vans fitted with energy tyres report fuel savings of up to five per cent.

Travel off-peak

As well as being frustrating, sitting in rush traffic increases both fuel consumption and emissions. Unless you absolutely have to set off first thing in the morning, plan your trip so that you set off after 9am and arrive at your destination by 4pm.

ON THE PITCH

Don't abuse the hook-up

Most sites charge a flat-rate for a hook-up so your energy usage isn't accurately reflected in the price of the pitch, but this shouldn't be treated as a licence to leave the lights and heating on in the 'van when you pop out to the pub.

In response to steeply rising energy costs, some sites have started metering electricity on a pitch-by-pitch basis and seen spectacular savings on their energy bills. Campers may be tempted to 'get their money's worth' when they've paid a couple of quid for a hook-up, but as long as energy prices remain high, deliberately leaving appliances on in a deserted motorhome is likely to hasten the introduction of metered hook-ups throughout the sites network.

Install LED lights

Yes, they're expensive and the cheap ones cast an unappealing, thin light, but LEDs will make a huge difference to your energy consumption – conserving the battery's charge and drawing less power from a hook-up. The cheaper, multiple source bulbs will improve energy efficiency, but the illumination tends to be a bit anaemic. Look for the bright single source bulbs, which use around a fifth of the energy of a halogen bulb and should last for up to 100,000 hours.

Walk or cycle

A motorhome will use twice as much fuel over the first couple of miles of any journey and the engine doesn't have the time to get up to efficient operating temperature on short hops, so if you're only popping into town, consider the alternatives.

Many campsites are well-connected to the surrounding towns and villages by a network of footpaths, bridleways or cycle-tracks. Ask for details of these at reception and you'll often get a little map with directions to local points of interest. It may take a little longer, but you'll see more by exploring on foot or by bike and you can still feel virtuous after having that extra slice of cake in the café if you've cycled there!

Check out www.sustrans.org.uk for further information about the National Cycle Network.

Use public transport

Despite their rural locations, many sites have good public transport links and we know of at least one site which persuaded its local bus company to create a bus stop at the site gates. Town and city centre parking is often unsuitable for larger units and it's getting more and more expensive. Many sites are located on a bus route or near to railway stations. Ask for a timetable at reception or call the National Traveline for travel information: 0871 200 22 33.

Renewable recharging

Buy a solar or wind-up charger to keep your mobile phone topped up. Some of the more expensive versions will also recharge your laptop and iPod. Log onto www.ecofreak.co.uk for motorhome-friendly products.

Recycle

More and more people are recycling at home and it's easy enough to do it on site too. Sites are increasingly making provision for recycling, so it's easier to do your bit. Invest in a set of plastic recycling boxes and you can keep glass, metals and plastics separate.

Take an old bag shopping

Don't discard supermarket carrier bags – re-use them. Most supermarkets offer a 'bag for life' scheme where they make a nominal charge for a sturdy carrier bag and then replace it when it wears out. Keep a few of these in the 'van and take them with you when you do the groceries run.

Look after your batteries

Investing in a quality leisure battery and buying a smart charger to keep it topped up when the 'van is in storage plus a battery-to-battery charger to keep it in tip-top condition on the road will pay huge dividends. The key point about batteries is that you need to replace the power you've taken out of them as quickly as possible without over-charging them. Invest in a couple of devices which ensure this happens and you'll significantly improve your battery's efficiency and prolong its life. The Environmental Transport Association recommends Varta as the greenest batteries around.

Clean and green

Try to use low-impact cleaning products,110 both for washing up and washing the 'van. It's also a good idea to convert to lower impact toilet chemicals like Thetford Aquakem Green or Dometic's new Special CARE range.

Avoid bottled water

Plastic water bottles can take up to 500 years to break down, yet every year, millions of them go into landfill. Tap water is completely safe in most western European countries, so avoid buying litres of expensive branded water and invest in a cool Sigg water flask which you can top up from the tap to keep yourself hydrated. With tap water costing less than a hundredth of the price of bottled mineral water, it'll pay for itself in less than two weeks, so as well as saving the planet, you'll be saving yourself money into the bargain.

Shop local, eat local

Part of the fun of exploring a new area is seeking out local delicacies which you can't buy in your local supermarket and having a kitchen on wheels provides the perfect opportunity to try locally sourced produce for yourself.

Organic meat, freshly baked bread, organic vegetables and, of course, local ales are all on the local menu and many sites take pride in promoting products from local suppliers by stocking them in site shops.

Shopping locally brings much needed income into the hard-pressed rural economy and keeps local traditions alive, but it also drastically reduces 'food miles' - for more information, log onto: www.fwi.co.uk/gr/foodmiles

▶ *Got any more tips for saving the planet? Share them with other motorhome enthusiasts at www.outandaboutlive.co.uk/forums.*

▶ Compiled with the assistance of the Energy Saving Trust. Visit their website for more ways to reduce your carbon footprint - www.energysavingtrust.org.uk

Solar systems

The vexed question of whether to invest in a solar panel for your 'van often generates more heat than light.

It sounds like a great way of doing your bit in these environmentally enlightened times, but in the harsh light of day, the fact is that a solar panel only make sense for a minority of motorhomers

For serious nomads who spend protracted periods on spartan sites in the next valley over from the back of beyond – particularly in southern European climes – a sizable solar array could potentially keep them self sufficient for weeks at a time. But if you only manage to escape for the odd weekend break in Bognor, it's unlikely you'll get a sensible return on your investment.

Visit a reputable solar installation specialist and they should ask you a number of questions about how much time you spend in the 'van, how much electricity you use when pitched up and how far you take your motorhome.

If they don't ask these questions and simply try to sell you the biggest panel you can afford – our advice is to look elsewhere.

The object of this exercise is to establish how much demand for electricity you are creating and how much generating capacity are you likely to need. So if you spend three months of the year in Southern Spain, only occasionally watch TV, and eat out every other evening – you could probably get away with a relatively small panel to meet your needs.

If however, you enjoy exploring quieter parts of the UK during the winter months and spend every evening snuggled up in the lounge, drinking cups of tea in front of the telly, you're going to need a much bigger array.

While cheaper products abound, meaningful membership of the solar club starts at around £450 for a small panel and the equipment necessary to connect it up and regulate the flow of power to the battery.

It's also worth upgrading your leisure battery from the typical 80Ah capacity unit to a 125Ah version which will store a lot more of that lovely free power from the sun.

Upgrade to the most popular size of panel (80-watt) and it'll cost around £550, while the biggest panels (120-watt) are £700. Some people link a 120-watt panel with an 80-watt panel to give them 200 watts – an investment of around £1,000.

But you can spend a lot more. Some people swear by sun-tracking systems from Alden or Oyster which use GPS technology to follow the sun across the sky and maintain the solar panel at it's most efficient angle to the sun. These clever systems start at around £2,000, but as well as the expense, they do have a downside.

As well as costing significantly more, sun-tracking systems can be vulnerable if the wind gets up. The manufacturers say they shouldn't be used above a certain wind-strength, but what happens if the wind gets up suddenly when you're two hours away from the van? It could be very expensive repair job if a gust catches your expensive roof-mounted array and rips it off the roof.

Auto shutdown systems are available, but these cost around £250 – adding even more expense to what is already an expensive system.

If you have the space on the roof, you may be better off installing a bigger array of standard flat panels. They may not work as efficiently when the sun is low in the sky, but they'll generate the same amount of power and they'll still be cheaper than a tracking system.

So the choice of equipment is far from clearcut and it's crucial that individual needs are taken into account. Our advice is to visit a specialist and make sure they take your individual needs into account before making any recommendations.

SOLAR PANELS

WHAT DO YOU GET FOR YOUR MONEY?

Price	Type	Output
£450	Single flat panel	65-watt
£550	Single flat panel	80-watt
£700	Single flat panel	120-watt
£1100	Combined flat panels	200-watt
£2000-plus	Sun tracking system	100-watt

▶ *Compiled with the help of Solar Solutions, Bournemouth www.solarsolutionsltd.co.uk. Tel: 01202 632488*

Trouble-shooting

Motorhome habitation equipment varies enormously so it's all but impossible to dispense general advice which will be relevant to the majority of owners. Suffice it to say that it's important to read ALL the manuals which accompany each individual appliance (usually at least half a dozen) and familiarise yourself with the workings before heading off into the sunset.

Every month, MMM Magazine receives dozens of technical enquiries from motorhome enthusiasts looking for solutions to their motorhoming dilemmas.

The following pages offer some solutions to common problems from MMM Magazine's Interchange experts.

For more practical advice on all aspects of owning a motorhome, consult MMM's monthly Interchange pages or log onto: www.outandaboutlive.co.uk/open/?page=MMMinterchange

WATER

Q In cold weather, we sometimes wake up in the morning to find there's no hot water and the water heater tank has mysteriously emptied itself. What's going on?

A Most water heaters are fitted with a safety valve which automatically opens and empties the tank if temperatures approach freezing. If temperatures drop much lower than eight degrees centigrade, this activates the safety valve, which is designed to prevent damage from water freezing in the system.

If the water pump is switched on, once the water tank starts to empty, this will usually activate the pump, but I assume you switch the water pump off overnight.

To re-set the safety valve, a device can be used to hold the valve closed, the system re-filled with water and heating turned on, but once the water temperature has risen, the device must be removed.

WATER WORRIES

Q My motorhome is experiencing intermittent but regular problems with the water system. Basically it appears that the pump is sucking air into the system along with the water. This results in an air bubble in the pipes against which the pump often has no success - and keeps running! The only way to shift this bubble is to draw yet more water! We then hear a very loud gurgling noise as the air makes its way into the hot water tank. To avoid wasting a large portion of our supply, we now resort to switching the pump off until water is required.

Any ideas about diagnosing and fixing this intermittent problem?

A First check the pump filter for debris. The screen is quite coarse and debris from holes being cut into the tank can sometimes get under the pump inlet valve and cause problems.

Air can only leak in on the suction side of the pump - which includes its filter and the hoses all the way back to the tank. Filters are usually transparent and you may be able to see a stream of bubbles passing through as the pump is working. Over-tightening its tapered thread can crack the filter, as can frost damage. Leakage can occur at hose clips or connections into the tank and are very difficult to find.

A while ago I had problems when valves in the pump hardened and during repair I slightly under-tightened screws holding the pump's internal diaphragm in place and air bled past them.

STINK STOPPER!

Q The water from our fresh water tank is tainted with a chemically sort of smell when it emerges from the taps.

Being new to motorcaravanning, we were using a garden hose purchased specifically for the job, to fill the tank, and we attributed the problem to this. However, changing to food grade hose made no difference.

I now use Certisil Microbox products regularly to clean out the tank and pipes, and this does help, but if we don't use the 'van for a week or two, the smell reappears.

I did initially, also in ignorance, use Puriclean a couple of times and I do know that Milton had been used in the past, so I wonder if this has damaged the pipes in some way.

As a result, we never use tank water to drink or cook with, although we do use it for washing up and even toothbrush rinsing, without suffering any ill effects. We carry two five-litre spring water bottles, which we refill directly from a mains water tap, but this is a nuisance and I wish we didn't need to.

A Drain off as much water as possible with the motorhome static but then leave the drain tap open. Any small amount of water remaining will then slosh around and come out as you travel.

If possible, angle the drain outlet to point slightly to the back of the 'van. If you have left the drain open, the forward motion of the motorhome will create a negative pressure at the outlet and hence draw fresh air through the tank for the whole of the journey.

Use standard washing up liquid rather than bio-degradable. I have no idea why this makes any difference but it certainly does.

Avoid washing up any excessively greasy items in the sink.

Occasionally, before setting off on a journey, close the waste outlet and put some Thetford Tank Freshener down the sink with about two gallons of clean water. This will slosh around during the journey and clean the tank. We do this two or three times during the season and it seems to work very well.

LPG OUTLETS

Q I have recently purchased a refillable gas cylinder and find I am fortunate enough to have a bulk supplier with an Autogas pump local to me. Because they distribute LPG for domestic use we were able to take advantage of the lower rate of VAT - £8.55 for 11Kg. I have been trying to locate other such suppliers in the UK on the Internet without success, can you point me in the right direction please?

A The Liquid Petroleum Gas Association web site (www.lpga.co.uk) details both refuelling stations and bulk suppliers. You can download a list of these and keep it in your motorhome (type in the post codes to your satnav system for the easiest way to find these). The Autogas web site (www.autogas.ltd.uk/whereToBuyMap.htm) also has a search facility that allows you to easily find retailers. Another useful web site is www.golpg.co.uk which has information added by reviewers (it would be wise to telephone the retailer before making a special trip). Given the recent hikes in the cost of diesel and petrol, LPG is looking increasingly appealing.

HEATING

HOT TIP

I bought my first ever motorhome 17 months ago and have referred to the instruction manual many times for the water and heating controls. So for us oldies with poor memories, I have come up with this solution. It may not be very 'high tech' but I hope it will help other fellow travellers. Owning a motorhome has been a steep learning curve.

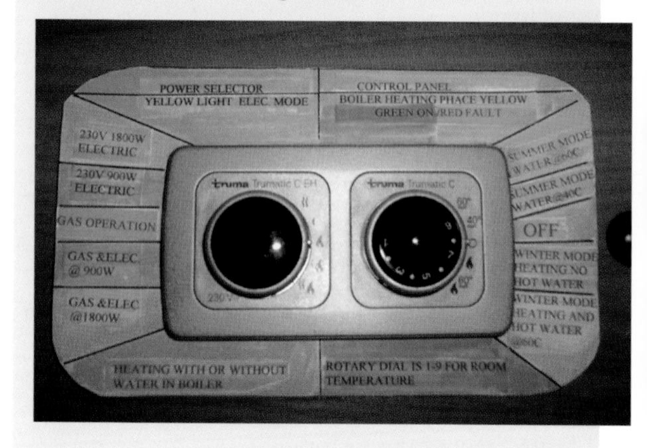

ELECTRIC HEATING

Q When we bought our van we were told the heating was both gas and electric, but when we have the heating on we think it is running on gas only. The heating system is a Trumatic C6002. We also have a EC200 electronic control system PSU 2007. Neither of us are very technical and the instruction book is not very clear. I would be grateful for any information regarding this.

A There are two versions of the Trumatic C6002. The C6002 (EL) provides electric and gas-powered water heating, but only gas-powered blown-air heating. To have electric-powered heating you need to have the C6002 EH which offers either 900W or 1800W of electric heating. While it would be preferable to save a little gas and have the electrically-powered heating version, it still won't give anywhere near the heat output when you're running on gas, which can output up to 6kW of heat on maximum.

Running any appliance of 1800W on a campsite (especially one with 10amp hook-ups rather than 16amp versions), will also mean that you'll only have a limited amount of spare power to play with. For example a 10 amp hook-up can only cope with a total load of 2400W – and the 600W left to power the lighting and charging circuits, the radio, TV etc may give issues with the hook-up tripping out. On 16amp hook-ups you'd be fine.

To conserve gas and provide a little localised heat, I'd suggest investing in a small fan heater and running it on a setting of around 1000W. These can be bought for under £20 from a wide range of outlets. For safety, don't run fan heaters while you're sleeping, or when the van is unoccupied.

The power supply unit (hence PSU) is made by Sargent Electrical Systems and controls the supply of 240V AC current to all the systems in your vehicles, together with the supply of 12V DC current from your leisure battery. It merely supplies the current to the combined Truma water boiler heating unit and does not control the Truma unit. There will be a wall-mounted thermostat control to actuate the heating system.

DEALING WITH DAMP

Q What is the most effective method of keeping the inside of the 'van free from damp during the winter months when most motorhomes are laid up?

I have toyed with the idea of using a dehumidifier. How would this compare with my present set-up, I wonder? Would it be necessary to leave it on all the time and how powerful should the dehumidifier be; also how safe are such contraptions if left unattended for a period of time?

A Humidity is a complex relationship between air, water vapour and temperature. The higher the temperature the more water vapour air can hold before condensation occurs on relatively cold surfaces. If a vehicle remains damp for prolonged periods it provides ideal conditions for moulds and other organisms to become established.

TOWING

Q Can I legally tow a small car behind my motorhome and if so, do I need a trailer or can I simply attach an A-frame with a towing hitch to the front of the car

A The law in the UK is complicated in this area and it's difficult to offer a definitive answer without some important qualifications. The Gross Train Weight and payload of your motorhome are critical factors, and, depending on the size of your motorhome your driving licence may impose further restrictions. Consult the chapters dedicated to driving licence restrictions and payloads for more information.

In general, as long as the combined weight of the car and the A-frame don't exceed 750kg, and the combined weight of the car and motorhome don't exceed the motorhome's Gross Train Weight and your licence permits it, you can legally tow a small car attached to an A-frame behind your motorhome.

However, in most European countries, this arrangement is illegal and a car needs to be towed on a dedicated trailer with all four wheels off the road.

The same situation prevails in the UK for small cars which exceed 750kg as the upper limit for any unbraked trailer on British roads is 750kg. Any vehicle weighing more than 750kg needs to be braked.

▶ *For more practical advice on all aspects of owning a motorhome, consult MMM's monthly Interchange pages or log onto: www.outandaboutlive.co.uk/open/?page=MMMinterchange*

Touring in the UK

The British Isles are blessed with more than five thousand campsites meaning that wherever you may roam, you're never very far away from somewhere to park up and bed down for the night. And what better way to reach those far-flung destinations over the hill from the back of beyond than in your very own home on wheels, allowing you to explore the backroads and byways at your own pace?

THE Great British countryside has undergone something of a renaissance in recent years as the public's interest in its own back yard has been rekindled by peak time television programmes like 'Coast' and 'Britain's Favourite View'.

After years of jetting off to increasingly exotic short, medium and long-haul destinations worldwide, suddenly it's cool to stay home and explore the wonderful sights you never knew existed in the British Isles.

And what better way to reach those far-flung destinations over the hill from the back of beyond than your own home on wheels, which allows your to roam the backroads and byways at your own pace without any obligation to fit in with the timetable imposed by tour guides, holiday reps or intimidating landladies.

The British Isles are blessed with between five and ten thousand designated campsites; nobody knows the exact figure, but it's an awful lot, meaning you're never very far away from somewhere to park up and bed down for the night.

The recent resurgence of interest in domestic holidays and camping in particular mean that in peak holiday periods, it's increasingly essential to book pitches well in advance rather than risk rolling up and expecting to find a space.

The general ambience, quality and feel of British campsites varies immensely to meet the differing preferences of Britain's growing army of campers and caravanners. Many folk are happy with a flat grass field with a standpipe, while others demand all mod cons such as fully serviced pitches with electricity, running water, dedicated drains and satellite television. Some expect cafes, bars, shops and discos while the only entertainment others require is a decent view and a bit of wildlife to watch.

Numerous sites directories exist to offer guidance to motorcaravanners on where to stay in parts of the UK which are unfamiliar to them, but the quality, accuracy and usefulness of advice dispensed therein is variable. 'Unspoiled, out of the way location' usually equates to a barren field miles from civilisation. 'Lively nightlife' may mean the onsite disco goes on until shortly before dawn' and 'family-friendly' may indicate that a dozen kids start playing football beside your pitch as soon as breakfast's over.

The key to finding campsites which suit your individual needs is to know what you are looking for and understand how to translate the 'lingua franca' employed by the guides into plain English.

Unlike continental Europe, the UK has fewer municipal sites and 'Aires de Service' which allow motorhomers to park overnight for free. It is however blessed with two absolutely wonderful institutions dedicated for meeting the needs of their members as opposed to faceless corporate shareholders – the Caravan Club and the Camping and Caravanning Club.

CERTIFICATED SITES AND LOCATIONS (CS AND CLS)

Between them, these two member-owned organisations operate more than 300 sites nationwide – most of which are open to non-

CLs and CSs can be tranquil havens

ENGLAND
SWIFT
Kon-tiki

The Camping and Caravanning Club's site at Devizes

members. Many motorhome enthusiasts join both however – entitling them to discounted rates, a full range of support services and access to both clubs' vast network of smaller certificated sites and locations – tiny five-pitch sites with limited facilities in away-from-it-all locations.

These intimate little outfits – often attached to farms, country houses or even pubs – have something of a cult following among seasoned campers and the locations of the most picturesque examples often remain a closely guarded secret among the cognoscenti who want to ensure they stay that way.

The best way to find your own favourites is by getting out there and exploring. It's sometimes a bit of a hit and miss affair and you may end up sharing a farmer's paddock with a psychotic cockerel and a bolshy old billy goat, but when you stumble across a little gem of a rural retreat which nobody else seems to know about, it's well worth the time and trouble.

Some CS and CLs evolve into affiliated sites, which are tied into one of the clubs and agree to provide facilities of a standard prescribed by the club, but are free to set their own agenda in other areas. These sites can strike a happy balance between the regimented feel of a full-blown club site and the more laid-back ambience of a CS/CL.

CLUB SITES

Fully fledged club sites are a very different proposition to the certificated sites. They are bigger operations of between 50 and 150 pitches usually run by full-time wardens who are employees of the club.

Both clubs insist that very high standards of cleanliness are maintained throughout their sites and this applies in equal measure to the shower blocks, reception area and pitches themselves.

Most club sites restrict commercial activities on site to a simple shop selling only the basics and very little else, so you are highly unlikely

The Caravan Club's site at Tintagel

to find bars, cafes and discos within the site's perimeters.

They are almost universally well-run and superbly manicured, but maintaining these high standards means club sites are run along quite strict guidelines, and a long list of dos and don'ts are often enforced by a proliferation of polite little signs. This necessarily regimented approach doesn't suit everyone – particularly the more subversive breed of motorhomer who wants to stay up late and put the worlds to right around the barbecue over a few bottles of Rioja. Such anarchic behaviour is likely to be greeted with the odd disapproving glance from club stalwarts the morning after.

FOREST HOLIDAYS

Forest Holidays is a joint venture between the Forestry Commission and The Camping & Caravanning Club which operates a network of 'back to nature' sites in the heart of some of Britain's most unspoiled environments. You're unlikely to find fancy facilities or organised on-site entertainment at these sites, but they have one commodity in abundance: easy access to acre upon acre of woodland to explore and enjoy at their patrons' leisure.

Originally wholly owned by the Commission, these sites were remained a well-kept secret until the Club brought its expertise to the operation and began marketing them more aggressively. As a consequence, the facilities have improved in the last couple of years and some sites offer a programme of wildlife or environmental discovery programmes, but these simple sites in beautiful surroundings are a long way from becoming commercialised.

COMMERCIAL SITES

Commercial sites vary enormously in terms of ambiance and appeal, ranging from gigantic seaside holiday complexes to quiet family-owned sites to which regular guests return year after year.

The former have their following and for people with children who need to be entertained when the Great British Weather does its best to wreck

The Loch Ness Caravan Park has fabulous views

the annual vacation, they do make a degree of sense. Many have quite spectacular facilities – including bars, restaurants, cafes, swimming pools, amusement arcades and health clubs – so there's never a shortage of things to do and the best examples succeed in separating the commercial aspects of their operation from the camping pitches. They are often located on the edge of popular holiday resorts with direct access to the beach and outside the main holiday periods, when the crowds subside, they are pleasant enough places to spend a few days by the sea.

However, you're likely to be sharing the facilities with the owners of static caravans and park homes – or the people who rent them - and if you do visit in peak holiday periods, chances are the place will be heaving with young families.

Smaller, commercial sites are likely to be just as busy in peak season and the quality of your experience is inevitably going to be dependent to a large extent on the sort of clientele a particular park attracts. There are some outstanding examples of privately operated sites designed specifically for touring caravans and motorhomes and managed to a very high standard.

Some of the more prestigious sites are affiliated into marketing organisations like Best of British and the whole commercial sector is represented by the trade association known as the British Holiday Homes and Parks Association.

Identify the type of site with which you are comfortable and learn how to spot them in the guides by using criteria which exclude aspects you don't want or need as a benchmark. For example, if you're looking for a quiet country escape, you're unlikely to find it on a 300-pitch holiday park with an entertainments complex, supermarket and three themed bars.

RALLIES

Outgoing social types may find the camaraderie of the rallying scene right up their street. This involves a group of motorcaravanners arranging to meet up at a given location for a bit of a weekend knees-up. The venue might be a huge national rally, an official campsite's dedicated rally field or somewhere as simple as a friendly farmer's spare paddock, but it's an ideal way to meet fellow motorcaravanners and extend your social and touring horizons.

Many of these rallies are organised under the auspices of the two club's regional committees, special interest sections or the different motorhome manufacturers' owners' clubs.

But whatever the unifying factor which brings participants together, rallies are a great way to meet new motorhoming friends and see different parts of the country without spending a small fortune on pitch fees.

If you join either of the main clubs, you should get information about local rallies and special interest groups in the post and when you buy a new motorhome, you may be invited to join a dedicated manufacturer's owners' club.

Rallies are a great way to pick up useful advice and information if you're new to the game and you may well make friends with whom you can link up on an informal basis to explore further afield in the UK and Europe.

WILD CAMPING

This is a complex and potentially controversial subject, but one which inspires almost religious fervour among hardcore motorhomers, and as such, is worthy of exploration in some depth.

Wild camping or 'free parking', as it's sometimes referred to, is staying in your van somewhere overnight without paying pitch fees. It might be a deserted spot by a lake in the wilds of Scotland or a lay-by in the heart of a city where it's not expressly forbidden.

The spectrum of responses to the concept of wild camping ranges from: 'it's illegal, so don't do it' to: 'if you think you can get away with it, give it a go.'

The truth, as always, lies somewhere between these two extremes, and for the independently-minded motorhomer who is geared up for self-sufficiency, it's an appealing alternative to a formal campsite – largely because it's so cost-effective.

Britain is a densely populated nation with relatively few tracts of genuine wilderness and the opportunities for wild camping tend to be fairly limited. Look carefully and the vast majority of specifically designated parking spaces off the public highway have signs which expressly forbid overnight camping. Attempting to spend the night here will almost certainly attract the attentions of the local constabulary. Similarly, private land-owners who permit parking during daylight hours are usually less comfortable with motorhomers who overstay their welcome – although if you seek permission politely – it's sometimes granted.

There are, of course, safety considerations to be taken into account and the motorhome enthusiasts' internet forums are littered with lurid accounts of modern day highway robbery in which campers recount tales of being rudely awoken in the middle of the night by local hoodlums intent on trashing their vans and stealing their valuables.

One particularly alarming style of attack has attracted a huge amount of attention in recent years and some heated debate over the accuracy – well-intended or otherwise – of these accounts. Many unfortunate subjects of these crimes reported a strange smell when they awoke to find themselves under attack, leading to speculation that a form of gas was being employed to render the hapless victims unconscious.

In the ensuing debate over the likelihood of this being effective, a number of respected experts – a consultant anaesthetist amongst them – concluded that the volume and concentration of gas needed to knock out a couple of healthy adults while their van was ransacked would stretch the resources of the typical A&E department and it was highly unlikely that such a modus operandi would prove effective.

Irrespective of the facts of the matter though, if there is any doubt over the safety of a potentially free pitch, find somewhere more secure. Discretion is always the better part of valour.

Wild camping isn't always an option in the UK

Unless you are confident that you are parked legally and safe from the unwanted attentions of the criminal fraternity, wild camping in the UK is a practice which should be undertaken with a healthy amount of discretion.

Attitudes to wild camping in Europe tend to be more liberal – although there are exceptions – and there are places where motorhomes gather in surprising numbers to enjoy the spectacular natural surroundings of a dense forest or alpine pass without paying a penny. It's even possible to park overnight in the middle of some European cities without the risk of being moved on.

Forget about putting up the awning, lighting the Barbie and setting out the table and chairs, however. Except on well established free camping grounds, such ostentatious displays are unlikely to go down well with either the locals or fellow campers. The whole idea of free-parking is to maintain as low a profile as possible and be ready to up sticks and off at very short notice. In this way, motorhomers maintain the impression that they are little different from other motorists taking a quiet roadside nap before continuing their journeys – minimising the likelihood of being disturbed and thus sustaining the privilege of free camping for years to come.

Wild camping locations – rather like favourite fishing spots among anglers – can become jealously guarded secrets, but the rise of the internet has facilitated a lively exchange of information between a network of diehard free camping aficionados, so the information is out there for those who want to give it a go.

Touring in Europe

Owning a motorhome opens up a whole continent of touring opportunities to the adventurous. With a bit of planning and preparation, your first European tour is just a short ferry trip away

BRITAIN has much to offer the motorhomer and it would be easy to spend many months exploring the further flung reaches of these sceptred isles. For many motorhomers however, the lure of the continent proves too strong and sooner or later they bite the bullet, book a ferry and embark on the 21st Century equivalent of the Grand Tour.

The motorhome is the ideal vessel for such an undertaking, in fact, it could almost have been designed specifically for the purpose, and our continental cousins have been swifter to embrace the concept than us Brits.

Levels of motorhome ownership are significantly higher in most western European countries than in the UK and the infrastructure which has evolved to service this nomadic constituency is consequently much better developed.

When you learn that many European countries have a network of dedicated stopover locations for motorhomes and many small towns have subsidised municipal campsites to encourage motorhomes to visit them, you begin to understand that spending time touring Europe can actually be cheaper and easier than staying in the UK.

Recent shifts in the value of the Pound have obviously made Europe significantly more expensive in the last year or so – particularly for those who enjoy the laid-back café lifestyle, sitting outside a French bistro drinking an espresso which has just cost around £2.50 is less relaxing than it used to be!

Avoid eating out, stick to wine and look for local seasonal produce in the markets and supermarkets however, and a motorhome tour of Europe is still probably the cheapest way of seeing the continent - with the possible exception of a tandem and touring tent!

CAMPER STOPS

Although the continentals don't quite have equivalents to the Caravan Club or the Camping & Caravanning Club, they do have a fantastic network of sites to choose from.

Many towns and cities have municipal sites which offer decent pitches and good facilities at very reasonable rates, but the jewel in the continental touring crown has to be the European network of Camper stops.

Known variously as 'Aires de Service' in France or Stellplatz in Germany, these wonderful inventions are basically glorified lay-bys, but the facilities on offer for motorhomers can rival those of a well-appointed campsite in the UK. Electric hook-ups, toilets and showers, dedicated motorhome parking, picnic areas and even Motorhome Service Points. Many are completely free while the better equipped ones may charge a few Euros, but with thousands of them across the continent, with extensive prior planning, it's feasible to tour most of Western Europe and spend only €20-€30 a week on accommodation.

Aires de Service sign to look out for

Numerous guides to the thousands of camper stops throughout Europe exist, and one of the most comprehensive resources for motorhomers is available online at www.eurocampingcar.com/uk.

Aires like this superb one in Kirkel, Germany, can be found in many countries on the continent

RESTAURANT

Sites like this one near Calais can have a transient feel about them which often means disturbance in the wee small hours when someone is leaving to catch a ferry

The English is a little stilted, but you should be able to glean plenty of useful information. A number of English language guides are also available and for the technically savvy, it's possible to upload camper stop locations into a satellite navigation system.

Once on the road, talking to other motorhomers will often yield really useful information about camper stops and other forms of free-parking locations – so it pays to be sociable.

While France alone has an estimated 5,000 Aires de Service, they are virtually unheard of in the UK and although the Europeans take them for granted, we Brits tend to get very attached to our favourite camper stops. The whole free- or very cheap parking thing has been elevated to something of an artform and many a conversation with fellow continental nomads will inevitably be studded with references to fantastic hidden-away camper stops with breath-taking views and superb facilities.

CONTINENTAL CAMP SITES

With no equivalents of the two big British clubs upholding standards, European sites can vary widely in quality terms. The UK clubs do play a role on the continent however. The Caravan Club www.caravanclub.co.uk produces two excellent guides to European sites which are regularly updated by its members. These useful guides are invaluable companions on any extended European tour and the Club's website has more useful tools to help you prepare for a continental trip www.caravanclub.co.uk.

Both the Caravan Club and the Camping and Caravanning Club www.campingandcaravanningclub.co.uk have affiliative arrangements with more than 200 sites in Europe, allowing British motorhomers to book continental sites through their UK reservations systems.

For first-time European tourists, having the support of a major organisation such as one of the big clubs can be reassuring. They will not only offer guidance on finding sites with which you should feel comfortable, but they can also offer the full range of support and ancillary services such as insurance, break-down recovery, legal advice and ferry bookings

Perhaps the closest Europe gets to the concept of Club sites are those affiliated to the two big 'loyalty card' schemes – Camping Card International www.campingcardinternational.com and ACSI www.eurocampings.co.uk

The former is a neat way of booking into European sites without producing your passport

Relaxing on site at Trois Rois, Les Anderlys, Normandy

and may secure discounts on some sites, while the latter is the biggest discount pitches scheme in Europe. Valid at some 1300 sites throughout Europe, this card won't always secure the holder a discount – particularly in high season – but it's a valuable resource for spring or autumn touring. The 2010 ACSI cards go on sale in December – get yours early because they do sell out.

Attitudes to camping and the standard of facilities vary considerably across the continent – particularly in the former Eastern Bloc countries, but on the whole, the Europeans are probably better disposed to it than us Brits. If you decide to 'wing it' and go where the mood takes you, it's unlikely that you'll encounter too many complications outside the main summer season. Most campsites are entirely comfortable with motorhomers turning up on spec, having a look around the site and if it doesn't appeal, heading off to another one down the road. Do bear in mind though that between the end of October and the beginning of March, your accommodation options will be more limited as many sites shut down for the winter.

If you're planning a long trip, it's worth getting in touch with the relevant countries tourist authorities and obtaining details of recommended sites in advance. Most tourist offices publish campsite booklets in English, but it's probably easier to get hold of one in advance via post than expect to find one readily available on arrival. There's a list of tourism contacts for most European countries towards the back of the book.

FREE PARKING

Free parking, or wild camping, as it's sometimes referred to, is staying in your van somewhere overnight without paying pitch fees. It might be a deserted spot by a lake in the wilds of the Alps or a lay-by in the heart of a European capital where it's not expressly forbidden to stop overnight.

The spectrum of responses to the concept of wild camping ranges from: 'it's illegal, so don't do it' to: 'if you think you can get away with it, give it a go.'

The truth, as always, lies somewhere between these two extremes, and for the independently-minded motorhomer who is geared up for self-sufficiency, it's an appealing alternative to a formal campsite – largely because it's so cost-effective.

As evidenced by the network of camper stops, with the notable exception of Spain, free parking is more tolerated in continental Europe than it is in Britain, but it's still important to be considerate of others and keep as low a profile as possible.

There are, of course, safety considerations to be taken into account. Try to park in an area illuminated by streetlights and be ready to leave at a moment's notice. Other motorhomes parked up is a good sign and it's sensible to have a chat with their occupants – even if they aren't English and your French/German/Croatian isn't wonderful. Get to know the locale by wandering around it and if the place feels wrong, find somewhere else.

When parking in quiet village squares overnight, do make an effort to establish when and where the weekly market takes place, or you may find yourself surrounded by blokes in berets unloading Citroen vans come the morning. This is ideal for shopping but less than ideal for making onwards progress!

If the authorities do choose to 'notice' your van, you're more likely to find a polite note on the windscreen requesting that you move on in the morning than get 'knocked up' by the local constabulary in the middle of the night.

In the unlikely event that you are asked to move on by the authorities, bewilderment and polite compliance are usually the best policies.

If there is any doubt over the safety of a potentially free pitch, find somewhere more secure. Discretion is always the better part of valour.

Motorhomes lined up in La Place St Martin in Josselin, Brittany

There are places in Europe where motorhomes gather in surprising numbers to enjoy the spectacular natural surroundings of a dense forest or alpine pass without paying a penny. It's even possible to park overnight in the middle of some European cities without the risk of being moved on.

Forget about putting up the awning, lighting the barbie and setting out the table and chairs, however. Except on well-established free camping grounds, such ostentatious displays are unlikely to go down well with either the locals or fellow campers. The whole idea of free-parking is to maintain as low a profile as possible and be ready to up sticks and off at very short notice. In this way, motorhomers maintain the impression that they are little different from other motorists taking a quiet roadside nap before continuing their journeys – minimising the likelihood of being disturbed and thus sustaining the privilege of free camping for years to come.

Wild camping locations, rather like favourite fishing spots among anglers, can become jealously guarded secrets, but the rise of the internet has facilitated a lively exchange of information between a network of diehard free camping aficionados, so the information is out there for those who want to give it a go.

SAFETY

Every year you can read horror stories of motorhome holidays from hell in which innocent Brits abroad are subject to the modern equivalent of highway robbery by despicable hoodlums hell-bent on stealing their last cent.

Some of the more lurid accounts detail how motorhomers were 'gassed' while they slept and their vans ransacked while they were unconscious. It's all good tabloid fodder, but the reality is that only a very tiny minority of motorhomers experience these unfortunate incidents. For a little reassurance in this area, have a look at the MMM forums here: http://www.outandaboutlive.co.uk/forums/forums/thread-view.asp?tid=5565&start=1

Safety is a serious issue however – particularly for folk on extended tours – but if you follow a few golden rules, the chances of getting into difficulties are minimal.

Don't carry large quantities of cash

Credit cards are accepted across most of Western Europe and increasingly in Eastern Europe while the network of ATMs just keeps expanding, so there really is no need to treat your motorhome like a bullion van. Open a bank account which allows you access to your money overseas without charges and use your credit card for petrol, meals out and pitch fees.

You'll need some cash of course, but be discrete and consider using a money belt if you are travelling in the more remote areas of Eastern Europe.

Keep valuables out of sight

Don't advertise the fact that there's an expensive mobile, posh laptop and fancy digital camera on board. Keep them hidden away. Think about installing a safe somewhere inaccessible and use the old false tin of beans ploy to store petty cash. Treat your passport in the same way as valuables – never surrender it unless you're sure there is no other option

Secure your vehicle

Make sure all the external doors, windows and skylights shut securely before you set off and secure them at night. Temperatures may stay high at night in southern Europe, but resist the temptation to leave windows open at night – especially when free parking. If you need extra ventilation, use the extractor fan on induction setting.

Drive defensively

Standards of driving vary from country to country and it's almost impossible to familiarise yourself with all the local rules and conventions, so always take the safest option in traffic. Some countries frown on the use of the horn in built-up areas, whereas in others, it's an alternative to the indicator. Similarly, using the headlights during daylight hours will get you flashed in some countries but it's mandatory in others. The most up-to-date resource can be found online at www.theaa.com and it's also available in book form, which is highly recommended for serious nomads.

Keep a camera handy

In the event of an accident, have a disposable camera or cheap digital camera handy and take multiple shots of the vehicles involved, the scene and any damage

Know the emergency service numbers

There is a general pan-European number to call the emergency services – 112 – but this doesn't work everywhere. Emergency numbers vary from country to country – either write them down or programme them into your mobile phone. It's also worth noting the local British Embassy's contact details for emergencies. For more info and up to date information for travellers, visit www.fco.gov.uk/en/travelling-and-living-overseas

Don't drive when you're tired

It's actually an offence in some countries, so take regular breaks on long journeys and don't be tempted to 'press on' to make it to an overly ambitious destination

Always wear a seat belt and make sure other passengers do

Again, the seatbelt rules vary across Europe, but belting up in the front and back is safer and eliminates the risk of a hefty fine

Don't drink and drive

In many countries, the alcohol limit is often lower than in the UK and in some countries there is zero tolerance of drink driving. Some police forces may issue an on the spot fine, impose an immediate ban or even impound your vehicle for drink driving

Don't stop if people try to flag you down

In some parts of southern Europe, opportunist thieves target foreign tourists by flagging them down under the pretence that their vehicle, or your van, has a problem. It's possible their intentions may be entirely honourable, but it's safer to keep on driving until you get to a service station or built-up area where you can pull over and check your vehicle.

Learn the language

Try to learn just a few key phrases in French, German, Spanish and Italian and they will stand you in good stead. If you have any health issues, learn the phrases that accurately describe them.

There's safety in numbers

If you're looking for a rest or overnight stop and you see other motorhomes parked up – join them

HEALTH

Long-standing health issues or the fear of falling ill abroad deters many motorhomers from venturing outside the UK, but the fact is that continental healthcare standards are comparable to and even exceed those we've become accustomed to in Britain.

The key to access to healthcare in Europe is the EHIC card – a credit-card sized passport to most countries' health services. The card doesn't guarantee free healthcare across the continent, but when combined with a comprehensive travel insurance policy which includes healthcare provision, you are unlikely to be asked to produce a credit card before receiving any treatment.

Pick up a form at the post office or apply online at www.dh.gov.uk/travellers .

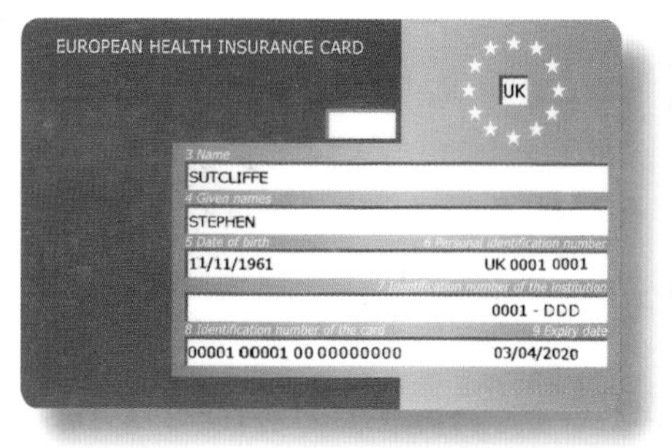

An EHIC card is your passport to healthcare in EU countries

If you have a pre-existing medical condition, Foreign and Commonwealth office advises the following:

- Tell your travel insurer about your condition
- Carry a doctor's letter and a copy of any prescriptions
- Ensure your medication is legal in the country you are visiting – the British Embassy can advise you
- Learn key words and phrases in the local language for your condition, medication and emergency help

INSURANCE

All European countries require drivers to have at least third party insurance and the best way to prove this is by applying for a Green Card from your insurer. Don't assume that any breakdown recovery policies included as part of your deal will extend to the continent – or that the terms and conditions are identical to those which apply in the UK. Check the small print very carefully and top up if necessary.

On top of this, we'd also recommend taking out travel and personal insurance policies to cover you against accidents, theft or other mishaps and also cover you for healthcare. Don't forget to factor in the estimated value of your accessories and personal effects whilst travelling and make sure the sum insured covers these too.

BREAKDOWNS

This is the biggie – tantamount to your hotel falling down and the flight back home being cancelled on a package holiday – so it's important that you are properly covered as your travel or personal insurance policies aren't likely to pay out.

Many general insurers simply aren't geared up to fix or recover broken down motorhomes because they often require specialist technicians and larger recovery vehicles. In the event of a major mechanical failure, the only option may be repatriation, which can be very costly if the breakdown happens on one of the more remote Greek islands. Add to this the nightmarish logistics of providing an adequate replacement vehicle should you want to continue your odyssey and you begin to get the picture.

For these reasons, it's best to deal with a specialist insurer which intimately understands the motorhomer's insurance needs. When shopping around, ask the agent exactly what's included and check carefully over the details covering replacement vehicles, provision of alternative accommodation and repatriation of unrepairable motorhomes.

Another important factor to check is the definition of a 'competent driver' in the event of the principal driver being incapacitated by illness or injury. If your partner is legally able to drive the motorhome in Europe, but is unwilling to drive it back to the UK, the insurance company may refuse to pay for repatriation.

MAPS VERSUS SATELLITE NAVIGATION

The advent of satellite navigation has made the prospect of a European tour infinitely more appealing to couples whose previous experience of driving abroad is somewhat clouded by the odd disagreement over navigation.

In our experience, far from eliminating rows, sat nav initially deflects and then just defers these arguments. Drivers tend to disagree with the unit then start shouting at it when they get hopelessly lost before redirecting the blame onto the co-pilot when they struggle to identify the correct motorway exit from the 1:500000 scale map in the back of their diary. Some of the fancier units which include speed camera detectors could also land you in hot water with the law in some countries.

Our advice is to invest in some decent maps of the countries you are visiting and familiarise yourself with the legend (symbols and icons) in advance. Plan your routes using the AA's routefinder www.theaa.com/route-planner/index.jsp or ViaMichelin www.viamichelin.co.uk.

Sat nav is good on motorways and should be seen a handy back-up, but it's no substitute for knowing exactly where you are and precisely where you are heading.

WHEN SHOULD WE VISIT?

European sites get very busy from the beginning of July until the end of August, so if it's at all possible, visit outside the peak summer season. Many motorhomers escape for a few weeks in Spring, then stay in the UK for summer before heading off on another European jaunt in Autumn. Look for special deals during these 'shoulder season' periods – particularly on the ferries – but also on sites.

In southern Europe, temperatures soar from June onwards and they can be especially oppressive inland, where a combination of global warming and the continental climate conspire to keep temperatures high for days on end. If you struggle in the heat or have any respiratory issues, it may be best to steer clear of the continent in summer.

There's more space on sites outside the July-August peak but often you may have fewer facilities such as on site restaurants and entertainment

But when the temperatures are struggling to get above freezing in Britain during the depths of February, Spring is already starting take hold in southern Europe and a quick jaunt down to the south of France, Italy or Spain does wonders for the spirits.

Many motorhomers take advantage of cheap ferry deals and head off in search of the sun at this time of year and one of the most popular journeys is to follow spring as it slowly works its way north.

If this idea appeals, find a cheap deal on one of the long crossings to northern Spain operated by Brittany Ferries or P&O from either Portsmouth or Plymouth and head down to Andalucia. Even in the middle of February, the weather down here can resemble a really warm spring day in the UK. It's then simply a case of taking your time to meander north through Spain and France and by the time you return to the UK, you'll have brought spring back with you.

MANDATORY DRIVING ACCESSORIES

Before leaving the UK, it's a good idea to give the van a comprehensive mechanical service and get any niggling problems sorted out. Pay particular attention to tyres, exhaust systems and other components which might be suffering from wear and tear as you are likely to be covering several thousand miles if you plan to move from site to site.

Buy some headlamp converters even if you don't intend to drive at night as you may need to use headlights during the day time in some countries and many tunnels require vehicles to use dipped headlights.

Precise requirements vary from country to country, but the following inventory should ensure you comply with local rules across Europe:

- Fire extinguisher
- First Aid kit
- Fuses
- GB stickers
- Headlight deflectors
- Jack and wheelbrace
- High vis jackets for driver and passengers
- Snow chains
- Spare bulbs (base vehicle and habitation)
- Spare set of keys
- Spare wheel
- Steering wheel lock
- Tool kit
- Tow rope
- Warning triangle x 2

HABITATION CHECKLISTS

A full habitation service is a must before setting off to make sure all the van's key services are in tip-top condition. For summer trips to southern Europe, make sure your fridge is working at peak efficiency, while for winter trips, check the heating and hot water systems are running properly.

In summer, two full gas bottles should last you several weeks, but for extended tours, it's worth buying an additional regulator to allow the use of Campingaz www.campingaz.co.uk cylinders, which are widely available throughout Europe – unlike Calor cylinders. Bear in mind though that you probably won't be able to exchange Campingaz empty cylinders bought in one country for a full cylinder in another.

Europe does have a good gas refuelling infrastructure however - see the chapter dedicated to gas for details on installing refillable cylinders for extended trips, but steer clear of outfits which offer to refill exchangeable cylinders.

You may also want to take a mains polarity tester and a reversed polarity adaptor to deal with sites whose hook-ups are wired differently to those found on UK sites. A continental two-pin adaptor may also come in handy.

- Bucket
- Calculator (for currency conversion)
- Campingaz regulator
- Dustpan and brush or mini vacuum cleaner
- Gas bottles
- Hook-up cables x 2
- Continental 2-pin plug adaptors
- Insect repellant
- Levelling chocks x 4
- Overlength food grade water hose
- Polarity tester
- Prescription medicines
- Reverse polarity adaptor
- Safe
- Smoke/carbon monoxide alarms
- Spare pair of glasses
- Spirit level
- Toilet liquids
- Torch

Essential Documents

- Bank details
- Breakdown cover agreement

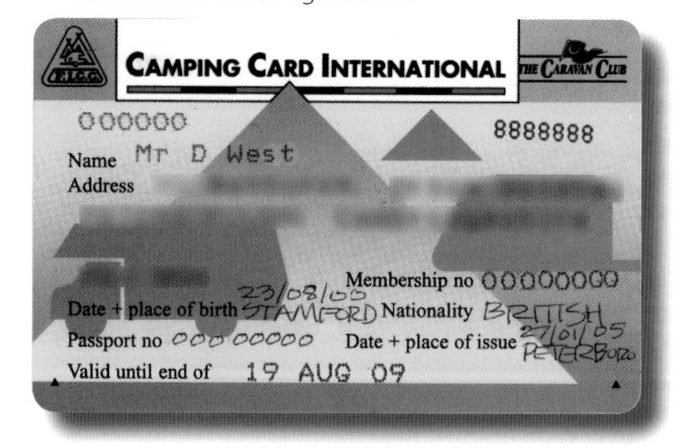

- Camping Card International

- Club membership cards
- Details of any prescription medicine
- Details of next of kin
- EHIC card
- Full driving licence and counterpart
- Insurance details and/or Green Card
- International Driving Permit (where required)
- MOT Certificate
- Original vehicle registration document
- NHS medical card
- Passport
- Pets passports

AND FINALLY...

We've outlined the essentials, but we also asked members of the MMM Forum at outandaboutlive.co.uk which items they wouldn't be without when touring on the continent. Here's a compilation of the best suggestions

LordThornber

A contract mobile phone containing every possible number you may need in case of breakdown/accident/illness etc. Plus a hard, CD or paper, (or both) copy of the numbers too. I can't imagine anything worse than any of the above scenarios and your phone has no credit, you're boiling hot and Pedro has just run into you on his scooter.

spospe

Phrase books for the languages you are going to encounter.

catinou

We have laminated copies (for ease of handling/writing notes etc.) of the road regulations, which gives details of most common road signs, speed limits etc. together with emergency nos. (e.g. Police) for each country we visit/drive through in Europe.

2nd most useful item (after husband, who does the driving!) is our Remoska cooker - a godsend for baking and grilling, especially fish, which can be cooked outside and the pan in the cooker is non-stick so it's easier to use and wash up than a BBQ.

malc d

Most indispensible: good maps.

Most useful: corkscrew

We also carry one of those little fold-up gadgets for making toast on the gas hob. Wouldn't like to leave that at home.

Tracker

A very long hose for getting water in unusual places - without water life becomes difficult - with water all problems are solvable!

alan k

Both indispensible and useful is my dear wife, formerly chief navigator (now usurped by Tom, so she can have a nap on those long hot afternoons), but still site/aire picker, chief tea maker/G&T mixer, for when we arrive at site and companion. I could go on ....

Usinmyknaus

A 'Nature Pure' portable water filter kit which removes all taint, chemicals, spores, cysts and bacteria from the water we use for drinks or washing salad items. The first time you see (and you will) someone stick the spout of their sewage cassette firmly over the drinking water outlet on the only Aire for miles around, at the very moment your on-board tank is extremely short of water, you'll be very glad you bought one!

Rapido-lass

For driving: cruise control
For sleeping: a memory foam mattress topper
For cooking: a double skillet
For relaxing: a corkscrew
For memories: a digital camera
For bathroom freshness whilst wild camping: a SOG fitted to the toilet

Mandy&Andy

Hi, I have a few to be honest,
Cadac BBQ
External BBQ point

Nature Pure water system
Strap down and wind break from Lillypad Leisure (sounds like adult shopping!)
Oval mop bucket for easy reach under van for grey waste drainage
Lap Top and Tom Tom for keeping on straight but not narrow
Non-slip mat on table for children's play things whilst on move

Archiesgrandad

An old bicycle inner tube: chop out the bit where the valve is, and use it to get to grey water drains when you can't quite get close enough. The cut end will stretch over the drain tap, and provided you open the valve carefully, it's just the job.

Barbarian

In some countries drivers who wear spectacles MUST have a second pair and be able to produce them on request, this is not something we would think to carry.

Barbarian

Hi, me again. Something very important that I forgot to mention I only found out recently regarding the European Health Insurance Card (Formerly the E111). It is only valid for 3-5 years dependent on when issued. Check the expiry date in the bottom right hand corner. Renew it free on www.nhs.uk/Healthcareabroad and follow the links to renew. You will need your National Insurance Numbers handy.

WARNING: Do not Google E111 because you gain access to firms that charge £9.95 for the (Free) service.

Hope you do not need to use it, but in 2006 I dislocated a finger in Italy, all the Hospital were interested in was the EHIC card, not even my Passport. Because my problem was an emergency, there were no charges. I made a donation to the Bonnasola Ambulance Service.

Brambles

Just remembered another accessory which is needed on many continental camp sites: A long extension lead for electric hook-up (and 2 pin adapter).

It can be a long way on some camp sites from electricity points. I have a 15-metre and 25-metre cable and it's still not quite enough joined together on some sites when they are busy.

Ranger

Don't forget a roll of the 'old faithful': DUCT TAPE.

Ferry guide

BRITAIN has an awful lot to offer motorhomers, but many people feel an irresistable urge to cross over to mainland Europe and join the legions of continental motorhomers exploring this diverse continent.

For most people, leaving Britain automatically means crossing over to France. But there are dozens of routes and ferry operators out there, keen to take you and your motorhome to pastures other than La Belle France.

If you're feeling a tad more adventurous, you could jump on a ferry to Iceland or Spain (www.spain.info); take enough time out and you can book a one-way trip to Bilbao then enjoy a lengthy drive home through Europe.

However, we're not trying to dissuade you from paying a visit to our Gallic neighbours. With largely empty roads and a much more relaxed pace of life, it's always a pleasure spending time in France. It's a large country and there are some fabulous areas worth visiting; whether you spend time in Northern France or drive further south, there are some great places to pitch your van and you'll be spoiled for choice when it comes to sightseeing.

CHOOSE YOUR CROSSING

While the principal channel ports see huge volumes of traffic, there are regional options which will save you a long drive if you live north – or for that matter – a long way west of the Watford Gap. Scottish motorhomers now have a service from Rosyth to Zeebrugge and there's also a service operating between Newcastle and Amsterdam and two services to Holland operating out of Hull. It will cost significantly more than a short hop across the Channel, but you'll save diesel – not to mention the stress of negotiating the south-east of England's notorious motorway network.

It's a similar story at the other end of the crossing. One of the most popular areas to tour is

north-west France, and unless you live just minutes from Dover, you're almost always better off sailing from Plymouth, Poole or Southampton to Dieppe, St Malo or Roscoff. You'll save huge amounts of driving, which also means you'll cut down the fuel cost as well as the time taken to get to your destination. You'll pay more for the sailing, but on balance you'll almost certainly be better off choosing the longer crossing and shorter drive. That's assuming of course that you're not going to enjoy a leisurely amble between Calais and your final French destination.

It's worth bearing in mind that just because you take one route on your way out, you don't have to retrace your steps on the way back. In most cases you'll have to opt for one-way tickets if you choose to do this, but Brittany Ferries allows you to mix and match between outgoing and return crossings.

CHOOSE YOUR OPERATOR

Before you book your tickets, think long and hard about your trip. Working out your destination is the obvious first move and you may also have a choice of carriers – but it's unlikely on all but the most popular cross-channel routes and prices tend to be broadly similar anyway. That's assuming you go by the standard, advertised fares. Different companies have different offers at various times of the year; shopping around should save you some money.

Most ferry operators are happy to cater for motorhomes, but sometimes there are restrictions. DFDS has a 10-metre limit on total length, so a long tag-axle motorhome with towed car may pose a problem.

ROUTE PLANNING

Planning your route before you set off is a good idea, as it's likely to reduce the likelihood of problems occurring later. Your plans don't need to be cast in stone as you can always change course during the holiday – but things will be made a lot easier if you're carrying a decent atlas or your sat-nav is up to date. On that note, sat-nav is becoming increasingly popular with Brits travelling in Europe, but we advise against sole reliance on sat-nav and recommend you take a good map as back-up.

Sat-nav systems have had a rather negative press in recent months, with tales of caravanners being sent down narrow cul-de-sacs or over to France via Ireland. Sometimes it's down to how the preferences are set, but they're generally superb as long as they're DVD-based. CD-based ones aren't so great because they're slow to work out a route, slow to recalculate if you get it wrong and you have to carry lots of discs to cover Europe. DVD-based systems are far quicker to do their job, and the whole of Europe can fit onto one disc.

Then there are the hand-held units of course. You can now buy one for under £100, although something nice is closer to £250. That gets you a compact unit that's well built and does a great job of getting you to your destination; stick to recognised brands such as TomTom or Garmin and you can't go far wrong. However, if you do buy a hand-held unit, remember to remove it from the car when you get out – or someone might do it for you. Sat-nav units have become increasingly popular with opportunist thieves.

One thing we'd strongly recommend is an up to date listing of camp sites and Aires de Service in the areas that you'll be travelling through. At peak times there's a good chance that you won't be able to get a pitch at no notice, but if your plans go horribly awry and you find that you haven't covered ground at the rate you expected to, you might just need to find somewhere to stay in an area where you didn't think you'd be stopping.

Before you set off, if you haven't driven in Europe before, it's worth buying a copy of *Driving Abroad* (www.haynes.co.uk), which contains a massive amount of useful information. Some of it is general while much of it is specific to countries all over the world; its ISBN is 1-84425-048-2.

However, if you've got a decent European atlas there will probably be some information in the front which should cover any key rules for the main countries. If you find the idea of driving on the right rather daunting, there's no need to be frightened by the prospect – especially as European roads are invariably rather less congested than the UK's, so you needn't feel pressured.

Before you leave you should also ensure you have a recovery scheme in place should your van

Torshavn
Seydisfjordur
Lerwick
Bergen
Haugesund
Stavanger
Hanstholm
Rosyth
Esbjerg
Stranraer
Belfast
Newcastle
Dublin
Holyhead
Dun Laoghaire
Hull
Rosslare
Cork
Fishguard
Pembroke Dock
Amsterdam
Harwich
Hook of Holland
Rotterdam
Dover
Zeebrugge
Folkestone
Dunkerque
Poole
Portsmouth
Calais
Weymouth
Newhaven
Boulogne
Plymouth
Dieppe
Le Havre
Cherbourg
Caen
Roscoff
St Malo
Santander
Bilbao

break down or you're involved in an accident. If you did your homework when you bought your insurance, you should be adequately covered when travelling in Europe. But don't just assume that you are; check the policy documents and make sure there are no restrictions before you set off. The last thing you want is to break down and find yourself stranded.

GETTING THE RIGHT ROUTE

There are masses of ferry routes to and from mainland Britain. To save space, we've listed the main ones below in one direction only; all are available as return trips. There are lots more minor routes offered as well; to find out more about any of them, take a look at www.cross-channel-ferry-tickets.co.uk. It's also worth looking at the ferry route map on www.cheap4ferries.com while there's all the port information you could need at www.ferrybooker.com

OPERATORS AND ROUTES

Brittany Ferries

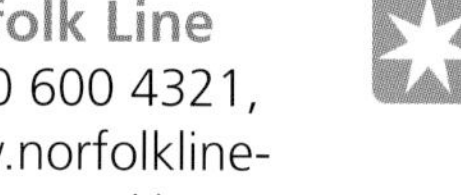

(08703 665 333, www.brittanyferries.co.uk)
Portsmouth – Caen
Portsmouth – St Malo
Portsmouth – Cherbourg
Poole – Cherbourg
Plymouth – Roscoff
Cork – Roscoff
Portsmouth – Santander
Plymouth – Santander
Cork – Roscoff

Caledonian Macbrayne

(08705 650 000, www.calmac.co.uk)
Ferry links between mainland and Scottish Islands (except Shetland and Orkney)

Condor Ferries

Condorferries

(0870 243 5140, www.condorferries.co.uk)
Weymouth to Channel Islands and St Malo
Poole – Channel Islands
Portsmouth – Channel Islands
Portsmouth – Cherbourg

DFDS Seaways

(08702 520 524, www.dfds.co.uk)
Newcastle – Amsterdam
Harwich – Esbjerg

Eurotunnel

(08705 35 35 35, www.eurotunnel.com)
Folkstone to Calais

IOM Steam Packet

(08705 523 523, www.steam-packet.com)
Heysham – Isle of Man
Liverpool – Isle of Man
Isle of Man – Dublin
Isle of Man – Belfast

Irish Ferries

(08705 17 17 17, www.irishferries.com)
Holyhead – Dublin
Pembroke – Rosslare

Norfolk Line

(0870 600 4321, www.norfolkline-ferries.co.uk)
Dover – Dunkirk
Liverpool – Belfast
Liverpool – Dublin
Rosyth – Zeebrugge

Northlink Ferries

(0845 6000 449, www.northlinkferries.co.uk)
Aberdeen and Scrabster to the Orkneys and Shetlands

P&O

P&O Ferries

(08705 980 333, www.poferries.com)
Dover – Calais
Hull – Rotterdam
Hull – Zeebrugge
Portsmouth – Bilbao

P&O Irish Sea

(0870 24 24 777, www.poirishsea.com)
Liverpool – Dublin
Cairnryan – Larne
Troon – Larne

Red Funnel
(0870 444 8898, www.redfunnel.co.uk)
Ferries from Southampton to the Isle of Wight

Seafrance
(0870 443 1653, www.seafrance.com)
Dover – Calais

Stena Line
(08705 70 70 70, www.stenaline.co.uk)
Harwich – Hook or Holland
Fishguard – Rosslare
Holyhead – Dun Laoghaire
Holyhead – Dublin
Stranraer – Belfast
Fleetwood – Larne

Transeuropa
(01843 595 522, www.transeuropaferries.com)
Ramsgate – Ostend

Transmanche Ferries
(0800 917 1201, www.transmancheferries.com)
Dover – Boulogne
Newhaven – Dieppe
Portsmouth – Le Havre

Wightlink
(0870 582 7744, www.wightlink.co.uk)
Ferries from Portsmouth and Lymington to the Isle of Wight

USEFUL WEBSITES

- www.1st4ferries.co.uk
- www.aferry.co.uk
- www.allferries.co.uk
- www.bluedogferrytickets.co.uk
- www.cheap4ferries.com (0870 111 0634)
- www.cross-channel-ferry-tickets.co.uk
- www.eurodrive.co.uk
- www.ferries-trains-planes.co.uk (020 8989 3437)
- www.ferrybooker.com
- www.ferrycrossings-uk.co.uk (0871 222 8642)
- www.ferryoffers.co.uk (0871 566 1596)
- www.ferryprice.co.uk
- www.ferrysavers.com (0844 576 8835)
- www.ferrysmart.co.uk
- www.ferryto.com (0870 1129 374)
- www.ferry-to-france.co.uk
- www.intoferries.co.uk

GET BOOKING

All these companies offer the ability to book a ferry between one port and another. They're effectively brokers; they deal with all the ferry operators on your behalf, so you're dealing with an intermediary rather than the ferry company itself. While their websites are easy to use, they offer varying amounts of information.

Finally, make sure you book your ferry as early as you can. Not only does the price usually go up as the crossing date draws closer, but there are only a certain number of spaces available for bulky vehicles. Leave your booking until the last minute, and the chances are that you won't find a space – and certainly not if you're crossing during peak periods such as the school holidays.

European country guides

ANDORRA

ANDORRA sits high up in the Pyrenees which separate France from Spain, making this tiny little Principality Europe's highest country.

Blessed with 65 peaks topping 2000m within an area of less than 200 square miles, Andorra is popular with tourists due in part to its tax-free status. Despite adopting the Euro as its currency, the Principality is not part of the EU and has established something of a reputation as an international duty-free shopping mall. Fuel is cheap and summer and shoulder season tourism is now well established in the ski resorts, but free-parking is frowned upon and sites can be expensive.

The traffic in and around the capital – Andorra La Vella – is horrendous

Motorhomes tend to park up near the border and explore this tiny country from its periphery to avoid the congestion, so if you see groups of vans parked up en masse, join them!

GETTING THERE: There are only two major routes into this mountainous country from France (N22) or Spain (N-145). You'll need to show your passport at the border.

CURRENCY: Euro

LANGUAGE: Catalan, but French, Spanish and English widely spoken.

ROADS NETWORK: Only one decent road (CG-2) and lots of mountain passes. Congestion in the capital is notorious and native standards of driving can be scary.

SPEED LIMITS: 40km/h in built-up areas; 90km/h elsewhere

TOLLS: No

DRIVING LICENCE REQUIREMENTS: Minimum age is 18

USE OF LIGHTS: Use dipped headlights in poor daytime visibility

SEATBELTS: Compulsory for front seat occupants

FINES: On the spot

DRINK DRIVING LIMIT: 0.05 per cent (UK: 0.08 per cent)

SITES NETWORK: Limited and expensive – most motorhomers visit on a day trip.

NEED TO KNOW: Andorrans enjoy highest life expectancy in the world at 83.5 years!

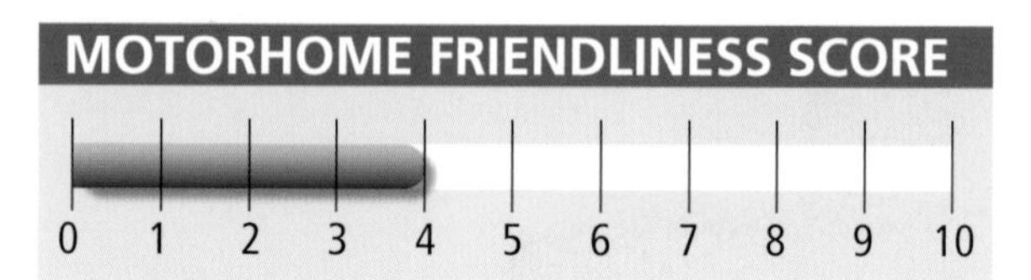

AUSTRIA

Rich culture and glorious alpine scenery are the highlights of this spectacular corner of Europe – which is a conduit between Western and Eastern Europe. While the decline of Austria's powerful Habsburg Empire ushered in turbulent times to the east, the influences of Austria's rich heritage and history are still visible today in the fascinating cities of Vienna, Salzburg, Graz and Linz.

In the 18th and 19th Centuries, Austria was the undisputed hub of Europe's cultural life where classical music was virtually invented by such luminaries as Haydn, Schubert and one Wolfgang Amadeus Mozart.

More recently, Austria has capitalised on its pristine natural environment to attract skiers, walkers and nature lovers to its fantastic national parks – including Tirol – the largest national park in Europe.

Motorhomers often bypass Austria because of its reputation for high prices and the potentially expensive Vignette system in operation on its motorways. But it's difficult to find anywhere else in Europe blessed with such a potent concentration of culture, heritage and natural history.

GETTING THERE: Excellent motorway links from Germany, Switzerland or Italy.

Alpbach in Austrian Tirol © Österreich Werbung - Mallaun

CURRENCY: Euro

ROADS NETWORK: Excellent – but you pay for using the motorways via a pre-purchased Vignette which costs €7.70 for 10 days which can be bought at the border, in post offices and some filling stations. However, vehicles of over 3.5 tonnes are classed as HGVs and pay by the kilometre using a form of tracking system.

SPEED LIMITS: Built-up areas 50km/h; standard roads 100 km/h; motorways 130km/h

TOLLS: Payable to use some Alpine tunnels

DRIVING LICENCE REQUIREMENTS: Minimum age 18. UK licences without a photo need to be accompanied with a passport

USE OF LIGHTS: Mandatory in daylight

SEATBELTS: Compulsory for front and rear seat occupants

FINES: On the spot

DRINK DRIVING: 0.049 per cent (UK: 0.08 per cent)

SITES NETWORK: Very good but can be pricey. Free parking is allowed outside Vienna – although local restrictions do apply – especially in the national parks

NEED TO KNOW: Vienna has the highest quality of life of any of Europe's major capital cities

BELGIUM

Grand Place, Brussels, Belgium

Belgium gets a bit of a bad press, but it's a civilised little country often overlooked in favour of it's bigger neighbours. Belgium's compact towns and cities like Brussels, Bruges, Ghent and Antwerp are all well worth a visit.

Beer and chocolate are two of Belgium's specialities and there's a generally laid-back feel to the cafés and bars. The culture and architecture will exceed most expectations and a visit to the WW1 battlefields – most notably Ypres – is a poignant reminder of this country's turbulent past.

GETTING THERE: Ferries direct to Zeebrugge or Ostend from Hull, Ramsgate and Rosyth. Fast motorway routes from France (E17/E19), Germany (E40), Holland (E19)

CURRENCY: Euro

ROADS NETWORK: Good – but can get busy at peak times.

SPEED LIMITS: Built-up areas 50 km/h; standard roads 90 km/h; motorway/dual carriageway 120 km/h. Also minimum speed on motorway of 70 km/h

TOLLS: No – although a flat fee is being considered

DRIVING LICENCE REQUIREMENTS: Minimum age 18

USE OF LIGHTS: Use dipped headlights in poor daylight visibility

SEATBELTS: Compulsory for front and rear seat passengers

FINES: On the spot

DRINK DRIVING: 0.049 per cent (UK: 0.08 per cent). On the spot fine and immediate three or six-hour ban

SITES NETWORK: Well-developed network of several hundred sites – although prices vary widely. Roadside overnight parking permitted for short periods.

NEED TO KNOW: Look out for road signs banning the use of cruise control on busy roads and in roadworks

CROATIA

Blessed with arguably the least developed coastline on the European side of the Mediterranean, Croatia is rapidly establishing itself as a Bohemian alternative to the increasingly crowded coastlines further west.

But as well as some stunning coastline – studded with pretty coves and rocky outcrops with more than 1,000 islands close inshore – there's a rich seam of history dating back to the dawn of civilisation.

Ancient coastal fortresses such as Split and Dubrovnik are must-see destinations – before the relentless onslaught of commercial tourism makes them almost completely indistinguishable from other European tourist magnets.

Motorhomers are welcome in Croatia and the campsite network is well established, but it's advisable to visit outside of the peak summer holiday season as prices of everything tend to rocket between July and September.

GETTING THERE: Hop over the border into Croatia from Northern Italy via Slovenia or take a ferry from Venice, Bari, Ancona or Pescara – but check first as services are subject to seasonal variations and cancellations at short notice.

CURRENCY: Kuna

ROADS NETWORK: Good on the whole, but rural roads may be unsuitable for larger motorhomes.

Dubrovnik, Croatia

SPEED LIMITS: Built-up areas 50 km/h; standard roads 90km/h; expressways 110 km/h; motorways 130 km/h

TOLLS: Yes – on motorways, bridges and tunnels

DRIVING LICENCE REQUIREMENTS: Minimum age 18. Further speed restrictions and zero alcohol policy for drivers under 24. Driving whilst taking prescription medicines which may affect your ability to drive is also prohibited.

USE OF LIGHTS: Mandatory daytime lights between end of October and end of March.

SEATBELTS: Compulsory for front and rear seat occupants

FINES: On the spot payable within eight days. Police may hold passport until fines paid.

DRINK DRIVING: 0.05 per cent. (UK: 0.08 per cent). Police can suspend driving licence for eight days and may confiscate vehicle in some cases.

SITES NETWORK: Extensive and developing and the tourist authorities are keen to promote it. Free-parking is expressly forbidden.

NEED TO KNOW: Border guards may want to record any damage to your vehicle when you enter the country on a certificate which must be produced when leaving the country.

CZECH REPUBLIC

Among Europe's many new states formed after the break-up of the Soviet Union, the Czech Republic is very young – formed in 1993.

But its origins as the old countries of Bohemia and Moravia give it huge depth and a proud heritage reflected in the modern capital Prague, which is deeply sophisticated fare. The hilly countryside with Prague at its heart boasts a richness of castles and country homes so touring could be a stop-start affair as you take in the views.

Find a site on the outskirts and bike or bus to the bars, for here are some of the world's finest beers – Pilsner style beer was invented here and the 'real thing' that was aped by America's insipid Budweiser.

Avoiding the tourist crowds isn't difficult, with so many heading straight for Karlovy Vary and its other cities. Prague in particular has suffered at the hands of Stag Weekenders intent on taking advantage of low beer prices. But hectic though they can be, the cities are chocca with cultural delights. Prague's Archbishop's Palace, the Basilica of St George, monastereries, museums... the list spans days of interest.

In winter, Czech people head for the ski slopes but out of season, there are precious few tourists about and almost complete peace and quiet.

GETTING THERE: Excellent motorway links from Germany, Poland and Austria.

CURRENCY: Czech Crown

ROADS NETWORK: Roads vary according to classification but are generally sound. You'll need a motorway vignette obtainable at the border for a week, month or year, and it has to be displayed. Border guards will also check and note vehicle damage on your way in and, if you have any further damage on the way out, you have to produce evidence that the police attended the accident.

SPEED LIMITS: Built-up areas 50km/h; standard roads 90 km/h; motorways 130km/h

TOLLS: Other than motorway vignettes, none

DRIVING LICENCE REQUIREMENTS: Minimum age 18. UK licences without a photo need to be accompanied with a passport

USE OF LIGHTS: Mandatory, dipped, in daylight

SEATBELTS: Compulsory for front and rear seat occupants

FINES: On the spot

DRINK DRIVING: NIL per cent (UK: 0.08 per cent)

SITES NETWORK: Very good and great value but many don't take credit cards. Roadside parking is limited.

NEED TO KNOW: Good King Wenceslas was a Czech, or Bohemian. He's the country's patron saint.

DENMARK

If you're looking for high standards in Europe, they don't come much higher than those in Denmark.

Now done with invasion and debauchery, the Danes peacefully go about the business of ensuring their country looks its best – not easy with a country that is largely flat and watery. Copenhagen is proof that they succeed. It reflects the fact that Danes have the highest per capita GDP of any country in the EU.

Denmark helped invent Scandinavian cool in design, whether furniture, architecture, art or even buses. Not surprising with a standard of education which includes a 100 per cent literacy rate.

On the touring front. Denmark is great, if a little pricey. The cities all have well-organised sightseeing of every kind, with royal palaces and country piles, cathedrals and wildlife parks. Night life is much improved on years gone by, with welcoming bars and cafes.

Dotted all over the countryside are 500 top-quality sites that cater for the Scandinavian obsession with outdoor life, whether in motorhomes, caravans tents or log cabins. For anglers, Denmark's a paradise with lakes round every bend.

And if you want to get around without your motorhome, relax in the knowledge that the Danes have one of the best public transport systems around... and a zeal for bicycles.

GETTING THERE: By ferry with DFDS from Harwich to Esbjerg, or by motorway from Germany. You can cross an incredible 10-mile bridge across the sea into Sweden

CURRENCY: Danish Krone (DKK/kr)

ROADS NETWORK: Excellent.

SPEED LIMITS: Built-up areas 50km/h; standard roads 90 km/h; motorways 110/130km/h

TOLLS: Tolls payable for the Oresund and Storebaelt Bridges

DRIVING LICENCE REQUIREMENTS: Minimum age 17. UK licences without a photo need to be accompanied with a passport

USE OF LIGHTS: Mandatory, dipped, in daylight

SEATBELTS: Compulsory for front and rear seat occupants

FINES: On the spot

DRINK DRIVING: 0.05 per cent (UK: 0.08 per cent)

SITES NETWORK: Very good in number and quality.

NEED TO KNOW: Wind turbines produce 20 per cent of all Denmark's power.

MOTORHOME FRIENDLINESS SCORE

0 1 2 3 4 5 6 7 8 9 10

Aarhus, Denmark

FINLAND

Think of Finland and crazy rally drivers, reindeer, Nokia and possibly a commercial Santa Claus holiday come to mind.

It's a veneer. Endless forests and lakes, some of Europe's most spectacular wildlife and an absence of people are the hallmarks of this Scandinavian outpost which has so much to offer. You can enjoy the delights of its capital, Helsinki, knowing you've encountered an entire fifth of its population. Take in a few more of its southern coastal towns and you've seen where half of its population lives. The remaining 2.5 million are scattered in a country which, north to south, would take 18 hours to drive.

Finland has a passion for rock music. And on its day off, Finland takes to the great many caravan sites it has on offer, at little expense. Nothing's cheap – in any sense – in Finland but you may be staying in a forest park through which a moose could wander at any time. You may even see a beaver. Just hope you don't encounter a brown bear or wolf.

The Finns are keen hunters so it is normal to see game on the menu, especially in winter when – in the north – the sun doesn't show for two months. In summer, though, the sun doesn't set, except for an hour or so in the south.

Finland is one of Europe's unsung destinations. It deserves far more attention.

GETTING THERE: There are no direct ferries to Finland but you can reach it from Sweden and Germany. The alternative is a drive to Talinn, in Estonia, to the ferry or more of a marathon, without a ferry, via Russia.

CURRENCY: Euro (€)

ROADS NETWORK: In the south, great but as you travel north, they are fewer and of lower standard.

SPEED LIMITS: Built-up areas 50km/h; standard roads 80 km/h; dual carriageways 100km/hr; motorways 120km/h

TOLLS: None.

DRIVING LICENCE REQUIREMENTS: Minimum age 18. UK licences without a photo need to be accompanied with a passport

USE OF LIGHTS: Mandatory in daylight, dipped

SEATBELTS: Compulsory for front and rear seat occupants

FINES: On the spot fines up to €115 are issued but you pay at the bank

DRINK DRIVING: 0.05 per cent (UK: 0.08 per cent)

SITES NETWORK: There's a network of excellent sites but be aware that many close for the winter and not all have mains hook-ups.

NEED TO KNOW: Finland only gained independence in 1917, and celebrates this release from Russian rule on December 6

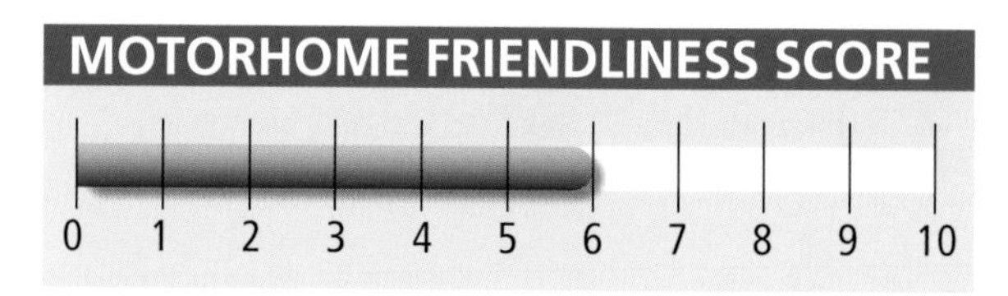

FRANCE

Our nearest neighbour, France is the jumping off point for most trips into mainland Europe so there's no avoiding it.

Not that you'd want to. There's a definite feeling of entente cordiale these days – a softening of old rivalries which goes beyond the language. If you haven't crossed the Channel yet, do it, because in most of France there's a warm welcome awaiting you.

Explaining Paris would be overkill; it's the darling of 'romantic' destinations with every possible service on tap, at varying levels of good taste. What does taste good is the food but, even outside of Paris, you can be assured of the real thing.

The British seem obsessed with Brittany and Normandy but other regional gems include Lorraine on the German border – scene of horror in WW1 – northern Languedoc-Roussillon and Aquitaine stretching down to the Pyrenees. The fact is, there's a lot of France to explore and the 65 million inhabitants are spread fairly thinly.

Blois, Loire, France © E Mangeat-CRTCentre

To comfort you along the way there are not only a great many well-appointed holiday sites but the famous 'aires' – motorway lay-bys specifically for overnight stops, some with mains hook-ups and sewerage. It's a kind of motorhome heaven.

Mitigating against all this is are the toll roads. Take them all to reach the Med and you could be looking at a £150 bill. But if you're not in a hurry to get somewhere, driving through France is the joy of near-empty roads, heavenly roadside cafes and probably the most varied countryside in Europe.

GETTING THERE: Ferries and the Eurotunnel from Dover, or from Portsmouth, Poole and Plymouth into Brittany.

CURRENCY: Euro (€)

ROADS NETWORK: Superb though most motorways are péages (toll roads).

SPEED LIMITS: Built-up areas 50km/h; standard roads 90 km/h; dual carriageways 110km/hr; motorways 130km/h

TOLLS: Everywhere. If you want to avoid them, sat-nav really comes into its own.

DRIVING LICENCE REQUIREMENTS: Minimum age 18. UK licences without a photo need to be accompanied with a passport

USE OF LIGHTS: Only in poor weather in daylight, dipped

SEATBELTS: Compulsory for front and rear seat occupants

FINES: On the spot and can be very severe. Break the limit by 40kph and you lose your licence. Don't even think about using a radar detector; they'll seize your motorhome

DRINK DRIVING: 0.02 per cent (UK: 0.08 per cent)

SITES NETWORK: An extensive network of very good sites and the addition of more than 1,000 aires along the major roads.

NEED TO KNOW: France is divided into 22 regions and 96 départements. On average, each département has 10 unique cheeses…

GERMANY

Germany is simply the most unavoidable country in Europe, slap-bang in the middle of the continent.

It shares borders with France, Belgium, Poland, the Czech Republic, Netherlands, Denmark, Poland, Luxembourg, Austria and Switzerland – you don't get more central than that. And it's also got a little of everything, from big cities like Berlin to ancient forests, from the lowlands near the North Sea to the 9,000-foot Zugspitze in the south.

German cities offer some of Europe's best shopping and night life, whether you visit Hanover or Hamburg, Munich, Nuremburg or Cologne. If you're after some culture you'll find plenty, but don't miss the small historic towns such as Regensburg, former home of Oscar Schindler, and Meissen, the cradle of European porcelain manufacturing.

It is no surprise to regular motorhomers that the Germans are fanatical about them, to the extent of making some of the best you can buy. This is reflected in the sheer number of sites in every part of the country and the roadside 'Stellplatz'

St Mark's Tower, Rothenburg, Bavaria, Germany

– overnight laybys dotted through Rhineland and the south.

The most obvious aspect of any journey through Germany is that here are a people who care about their environment. Absorbing East Germany cost it a fortune but how many other countries would find the money to block-pave their village roads?

GETTING THERE: Excellent motorway links from all border countries and super-fast autobahns to get through Germany.

CURRENCY: Euro (€)

ROADS NETWORK: Germany's road network is famed and won't disappoint – although they do get congested in urban areas at peak hours

SPEED LIMITS: Built-up areas 50km/h; standard roads 100 km/h; motorways a recommended, but not compulsory 130km/h

TOLLS: Payable to use some tunnels

DRIVING LICENCE REQUIREMENTS: Minimum age 18.

USE OF LIGHTS: Compulsory in fog, snow or rain in daylight

SEATBELTS: Compulsory for front and rear seat occupants

FINES: On the spot and covering a variety of offences

DRINK DRIVING: 0.05 per cent (UK: 0.08 per cent)

SITES NETWORK: Plenty of sites in all grades to choose from, some at the top end of the market quite pricey. For touring, Stellplatz are cheap and good, many having waste disposal facilities

NEED TO KNOW: In common with most European countries, Germany has excellent healthcare under the EHIC (formerly E111) scheme. The only cover not provided by EHIC is emergency repatriation, which should be the focus of any travel insurance you buy.

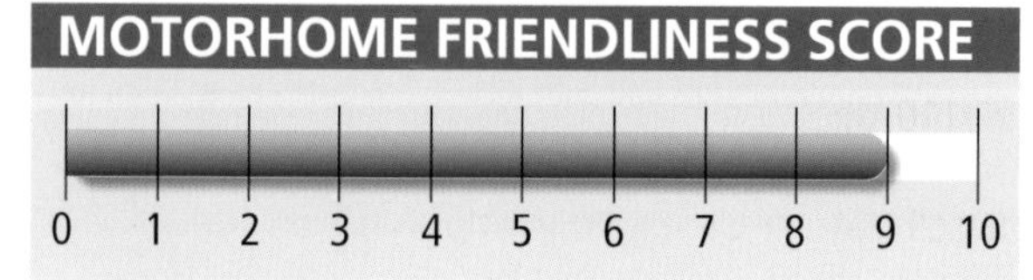

GREECE

Greece once sent the tendrils of its empire into every corner of the Mediterranean but if you really want to see its legacy you have to visit the country itself.

Greek temples pop up all along the southern Med and many are very impressive. But until you have climbed up to the Parthenon in Athens you probably have no idea of the scale of Greece's intellectual dominance of the western world.

So Greece is worth a visit for its antiquities alone but it has a much lighter side. The sun is relentless so it's perfect for a beach holiday, whether you stay on the mainland or take one of the frequent ferries which interlace the country's huge number of holiday islands.

Greece is also about its food. It's based around lamb, chicken and fish, olives, superb breads, salads, pulses, nuts, yoghurt and the ubiquitous aubergine. It couldn't be healthier. But don't pass by the sweets such as the honey-soaked pastries full of nuts – baklava. And don't eat too early – 9pm is the starting block for most Greeks.

The standard of Greek roads has improved massively in the last 20 years but it's still not for the faint-hearted. Locals drive fast and seem to ignore limits, towns are crammed with mopeds overtaking on both sides, and some of the mountain passes need nerves of steel. And fill up as often as possible – fuel stations usually close at 7pm and rarely open on Sundays.

GETTING THERE: You can enter Greece from the north through Macedonia and Bulgaria but there are a huge number of ferry services from Italy into Athens and Patra, starting as far north as Venice (www.ferries.gr lists them all)

CURRENCY: Euro (€)

ROADS NETWORK: The E-marked motorways are fine but, off that beaten track, road quality is very variable. .

SPEED LIMITS: Built-up areas 50km/h; standard roads 90/110 km/h; motorways 130km/h

TOLLS: Payable on sections of the E75, E65, E55 and E94, but very cheap

Zakinthos Navagio, Ionian Island

DRIVING LICENCE REQUIREMENTS: Minimum age 18.

USE OF LIGHTS: Compulsory in fog, snow or rain in daylight

SEATBELTS: Compulsory only for front seats but rear seat occupants should belt up, too

FINES: Handed out on the spot but paid later

DRINK DRIVING: 0.05 per cent (UK: 0.08 per cent)

SITES NETWORK: There are plenty of sites open in summer but many close in winter. Despite hefty penalties for truly wild camping, the Greeks are fairly relaxed about roadside overnighting; buy dinner at a restaurant and negotiate to park outside for the night.

NEED TO KNOW: All Greek camping and caravan sites are regulated and should display an 'EOT' roundel.

Skaftafell, Iceland © Ragnar Sigurdsson

ICELAND

Given the difficulty of getting there, you'd think that Iceland didn't have much to offer the motorhomer.

But whether you take the long drive north to the only UK crossing – via northern Scotland and the Faroes – or opt for a flight and motorhome hire, the rewards make the trip worthwhile. It's the land of fire and ice, with spectacular scenery of a kind found nowhere else in Europe.

Iceland heats most of its houses by drilling a few metres down and pumping water through the ground, because it sits on a bed of volcanic magma which is just itching to show itself. Not that the energy demand is great with fewer than 300,000 inhabitants.

Iceland's reputation of being expensive is deserved, though prices have come down in recent years. The price of alcohol, though, doesn't stop Icelanders living it up at bars through the long summer nights.

There's not much driving to be done in Iceland. Or rather, the ring road which follows the shoreline is more or less your lot, and even that was only finished 30 years ago. From what road there is, though, the glaciers and astonishing landscape make the journey worthwhile.

Icelanders are Great Outdoors types; to get the best from the available entertainments, it's worth joining in.

GETTING THERE: Smyril Line sail from Scrabster, northern Scotland, in mid summer, via the Faroes, though on the return trip, you're in the Faroes for three days before returning to the mainland. Or fly and hire.

CURRENCY: Krona (kr)

ROADS NETWORK: Aside from a few spurs, in essence a ring road round the island, and not all of it surfaced.

SPEED LIMITS: Built-up areas 50km/h; standard roads 80 km/h; major road 90km/h

TOLLS: None

DRIVING LICENCE REQUIREMENTS: Minimum age 18.

USE OF LIGHTS: Dipped headlights mandatory all day

SEATBELTS: Compulsory for front and rear seat occupants

FINES: On the spot fines but usually payable later

DRINK DRIVING: 0.05 per cent (UK: 0.08 per cent)

SITES NETWORK: Few and far between. There are 68 official sites in all, many without services but most with waste water disposal. There's a directory at www.visiticeland.com

NEED TO KNOW: Short summers mean Icelanders have learned to make meat and fish their staple food, and dried or pickled fish and meat a speciality. Most is delicious but Greenland shark, buried for six months then eaten raw, and pickled ram's testicles, are both acquired tastes

MOTORHOME FRIENDLINESS SCORE

0 1 2 3 4 5 6 7 8 9 10

IRELAND

Ireland is the best European destination people have never visited. More UK citizens have visited Spain than Ireland.

Yet in every respect it's perfect motorhoming territory. For a start, Ireland drives on the UK side of the road. There's a fair selection of sites of varying quality but in some of the most spectacular places you could imagine. That's as well because Ireland goes out of its way to deter overnight car-park parking for historic reasons.

The compensations are some of the most gently beautiful landscapes in Europe, greened by the Gulf Stream rain and warmth. It's a land of soft hills and slate-grey lakes, rivers and dramatic coastlines, castles, loughs and legends.

The famed Irish welcome isn't a myth. While Dublin's become an international city with international standards, Ireland's other 'cities' – and none are very big – have retained a great deal of charm. Sing-songs still randomly start up in pubs and, in the country districts, the pace of life is still heart-rate-lowering.

Loughs, crustaceans and the Craic – three great reasons for visiting Ireland

Ireland grows food like nowhere else; the quality of its meat, fish and vegetables make meals out a divine pleasure and shopping much less disappointing than in UK supermarkets.

No visit would be complete without a delve into Irish history, kissing the Blarney stone, seeing some Irish dancing or a game of 'hurley.' Just don't forget to sit down and smell the flowers.

GETTING THERE: Three operators cross the Irish Sea, one from Liverpool overnight, the rest day sailings from Fishguard, Pembroke and Holyhead.

CURRENCY: Euro (€)

ROADS NETWORK: Much improved with more motorway but the real joy is to be had exploring the local roads.

SPEED LIMITS: Built-up areas 50km/h; standard roads 60-100 km/h; motorways 120km/h

TOLLS: Tolls are payable on: M4 Kinnegad-Kilcock; M50, which serves Dublin Airport; M1 Gormanston-Monasterboice; N8 Rathcormac/ Fermoy Bypass; the East Link Toll Bridge (Dublin); and the Dublin Port Tunnel.

DRIVING LICENCE REQUIREMENTS: Minimum age 18.

USE OF LIGHTS: Dipped headlights daytime in poor weather

SEATBELTS: Compulsory for front and rear seat occupants

FINES: On the spot fines payable to officers

DRINK DRIVING: 0.08 per cent (UK: 0.08 per cent)

SITES NETWORK: Ireland has a good peppering of caravan sites in some impressive locations, including six approved by the Caravan Club.

NEED TO KNOW: Ireland's roads were largely built pre-potato famine by the Board of Public Works – which gave employment to the depressed population – and, post-independence, by a new but similar organisation. The massive programme trained large numbers of road builders, many of whom migrated to find work.

MOTORHOME FRIENDLINESS SCORE

ITALY

A journey through Italy is a trip through history, charting the rise of the Mediterranean culture from the Roman Empire onwards.

It's a country with far more than its fair share of ancient monuments, whether Roman or religious, and a variety of countryside which ranges from the dramatic mountains in the north to the sun-bleached landscape of the south, taking in lush Tuscany on the way.

Anversa degli Abruzzi, Italy © Vito Arcomano-Fototeca ENIT.

No less iconic is Italy's cuisine. The simple, fresh tastes of Italian cooking have swept through the world. Pasta and pizza are just the fast foods of Italy; slow-cooked rich casseroles like osso bucco also feature on a menu that's recognised for its health-giving nutritional balance. Do not, ever, visit Italy without eating out and, if the menu is confusing, just ask for 'due piatti, per favore' and see what the kitchen conjures up.

Italy is a country which has such fervour for the family that it welcomes children everywhere. Join Italian families in the evening, when the heat has gone from the day, as they promenade in their gladrags in search of gelateria and cafes. Sit with the oldies round the fountain in the town piazza. Drink in Italy's atmosphere.

It does have a reputation for madcap driving and Italy's a country that revolves around roads. Motorways abound but don't miss out on a few rail journeys into areas of the country you otherwise wouldn't see.

GETTING THERE: Italy is well-served by motorways from France, Switzerland and Austria, crossing through the Alps. Any number of ferries reach Sardinia, and Sicily is served by ferries into Messina from the toe of Italy's boot and from Naples and Salerno (see www.traghettionline.com)

CURRENCY: Euro (€)

ROADS NETWORK: Major trunk roads are excellent and regional roads variable but mostly good. In hilly districts, single-lane roads are common.

SPEED LIMITS: Built-up areas 50km/h; standard roads 90-110 km/h; motorways 130km/h

TOLLS: Tolls are payable on a large number of Italian motorways and bridges, and must be budgeted. You could pay as much as £150 to make a round trip through the country. Milan has a congestion charge on weekdays.

DRIVING LICENCE REQUIREMENTS: Minimum age 18. Use of lights: Dipped headlights mandatory in daytime and in poor weather

SEATBELTS: Compulsory for front and rear seat occupants

FINES: On the spot fines (very high for speeding) payable to officers

DRINK DRIVING: 0.051 per cent (UK: 0.08 per cent)

SITES NETWORK: Italy has a huge number of 'camper' sites. The 'aree di sosta' motorhome overnight stops can be located at www.turismoitinerante.com Also, Fattore Amico (www.fattoreamico.it) offers free motorhome parking on farms and vineyards

NEED TO KNOW: Italy is a nation of coffee drinkers. It's been said that every Italian drinks an average two cups a day. Espresso (not expresso!) is taken on the move, latte (with milk) to relax and macchiato (with very little coffee) if you need liquid more than caffeine. Cappuccino is named after capuchin monks, with their black robes and white caps.

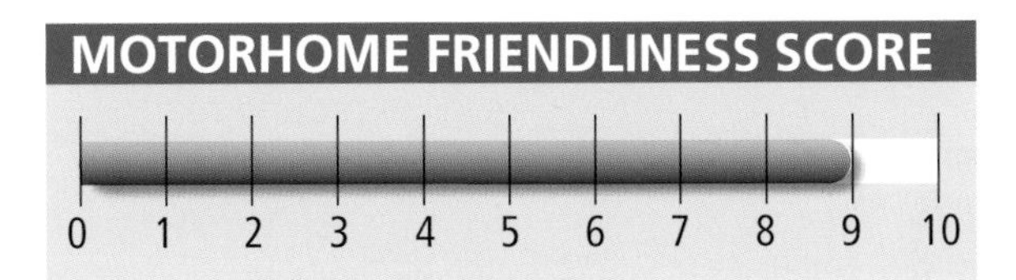

LUXEMBOURG

Luxembourg is not so much a touring region as a destination, too small to offer more than a couple of days' driving pleasure.

But that's not to say the Luxembourgers don't pack a lot into their little banking enclave. One of Europe's richest countries, with the world's highest per capita GDP, it has preserved itself wonderfully, with Luxembourg City, Echternach and Vianden particularly pretty.

Luxembourg City © Luxembourg City Tourist Office

It's done so against a backdrop of strife and invasion, periods of apparent neutrality and occupation. It was at the centre of the WWII Battle of the Bulge. But it has emerged triumphant.

Luxembourg City has some of Europe's finest museums of art and culture, and is itself on the UNESCO World Heritage List. The National Museum of Military History in Diekirch is also worth a visit.

Moselle wine-making is another activity of which Luxembourg is proud, and a visit during the harvest in September is fascinating. The urban myth that Luxembourgers drink 2.8 gallons of pure alcohol a year – while statistically correct – reflects the fact that low taxes on alcohol attract huge numbers of 'booze cruisers' from adjacent countries.

GETTING THERE: All the major routes from the neighbouring countries of France, Belgium and Germany are good, fast roads which converge on Luxembourg city.

CURRENCY: Euro (€)

ROADS NETWORK: Major trunk roads are excellent and regional roads variable but mostly good. In hilly districts, single-lane roads are common.

SPEED LIMITS: Built-up areas 50km/h; standard roads 90 km/h; motorways 130km/h

TOLLS: None.

DRIVING LICENCE REQUIREMENTS: Minimum age 18.

USE OF LIGHTS: Dipped headlights mandatory in daytime in poor weather. Headlights must be flashed before overtaking

SEATBELTS: Compulsory for front and rear seat occupants

FINES: On the spot fines (very high for speeding) payable to officers

DRINK DRIVING: 0.051 per cent (UK: 0.08 per cent)

SITES NETWORK: Around 30 sites are listed for Luxembourg – plenty for such a small country

NEED TO KNOW: A detour through Luxembourg from France, Germany or Belgium is almost a ritual, entering through borders which have ranks of fuel pumps – road fuel is cheap in Luxembourg. Once you're there, you really should take an overnight stop and see what you've been missing…

MOTORHOME FRIENDLINESS SCORE

THE NETHERLANDS

The Netherlands – Holland is just the western bit – doesn't appear to have many credentials for great touring country.

It's a myth that it's devoid of hills but you won't find anything approaching a mountain. Most of the country is in agriculture. But what makes The Netherlands so special is an utter devotion to motorhoming and caravanning.

Touring holidays among the Dutch have many other compensations, too. Relaxed and liberal, the Dutch love speaking English and are culturally very similar to Brits. You'll recognise the food and the shops and you'll be welcomed in the informal way peculiar to the Dutch. The big draw is Amsterdam and it shouldn't be missed; put aside all you've heard about red light districts and dodgy coffee bars, and dive into the deep cultural pool of sightseeing.

Away from the cities, there's the spectacular sandy North Sea coastline peppered with lovely towns, while further north is the delightful Groningen, and everywhere are the splendid and clean waterways which beg to be fished and sailed. Most importantly, take your bicycles; no country in Europe is better equipped for safe cycling.

The Netherlands is a home from home but one which will give you a few surprises along the road.

GETTING THERE: Get to Calais and turn left! Reaching Holland from the short-sea crossings is an easy journey through Belgium but if you want to cut driving time, there are sailings direct from Newcastle, Hull and Harwich.

CURRENCY: Euro (€)

ROADS NETWORK: On a par with UK roads and well-signed.

SPEED LIMITS: Built-up areas 50km/h; standard roads 80 km/h; major road 100km/h; motorways 120km/h

TOLLS: The only toll is for the Westerschelde Tunnel between Terneuzen and Middelburg

DRIVING LICENCE REQUIREMENTS: Minimum age 18.

USE OF LIGHTS: Dipped headlights recommended in daylight

SEATBELTS: Compulsory for front and rear seat occupants

FINES: Handed out and collected on the spot

DRINK DRIVING: 0.05 per cent (UK: 0.08 per cent)

SITES NETWORK: A superb network of well-appointed sites and absolutely no need to use laybys or service areas

NEED TO KNOW: Holland's windmills – there were once 10,000 – were mainly used for pumping water,

The windmill at one side of the Keukenhof Gardens, Holland

not milling corn. The technology of land drainage was exported by the Dutch to England in the 17th Century.

NORWAY

With its fjord-riven western coastline and mountain range separating it from its nearest neighbour, Norway offers plenty of scenic drama.

In Europe but not in the EU, Norway has been fiercely independent, especially since German occupation in WWII. During the war, the Norwegian government lived in Rotherhithe, Kent, while the Norwegian resistance collaborated with us on many acts of sabotage, so the UK has strong ties with Norway.

Norway has prospered with the advantage of oil reserves, and has the third-highest per capita GDP in the world. Prices in the shops, restaurants and bars reflect this; nothing is cheap in Norway.

Norway is not renowned for its culinary past, with the exception of having exported preserved fish – both cod and salmon. The salmon is cured and packed with dill as gravadlax. And the

Springtime in the Fjords © C H-Innovation Norway

Norwegians also eat meat – reindeer, moose, duck, sausages, lamb and pork are on menus.

Tour Norway by motorhome and you must be prepared for very long drives – particularly if you want to visit Europe's most northerly point at Nordkapp and earn the right to display the iconic moose sticker on the back of your van. Head up into the Arctic Circle and you stand every chance of seeing the Northern Lights as the long winter nights close in around September and again in March. It is a truly unique experience. There are plenty of sites open in summer but there's also the 'Allemansrett' – the principle that anyone can 'wild camp' overnight freely.

If you don't fancy the drive, meandering from Bergen north is still great fun, with the kind of winding roads that reveal another breathtaking view every few miles.

GETTING THERE: With the end of the Newcastle-Bergen ferry route, you must now sail DFDS to Sweden and either enter by road or take an onward ferry.

CURRENCY: Krone (Nkr)

ROADS NETWORK: Major trunk roads are excellent and regional roads well maintained.

SPEED LIMITS: Built-up areas 50km/h; standard roads 80 km/h; motorways 90-100km/h

TOLLS: Many major routes, bridges and tunnels have tolls, but they are fairly cheap at an average 20Nkr (£1.90). City tolls are payable (at any Esso station) for Bergen, Oslo, Stavanger and Trondheim

DRIVING LICENCE REQUIREMENTS: Minimum age 18.

USE OF LIGHTS: Dipped headlights mandatory in daytime

SEATBELTS: Compulsory for front and rear seat occupants

FINES: On the spot fines payable to officers

DRINK DRIVING: 0.02 per cent (UK: 0.08 per cent)

SITES NETWORK: There are around 1,000 registered campsites – in various grades – in Norway. Some are seasonal. Buy a Camping Card to get big discounts.

NEED TO KNOW: Salt cod is an ancient delicacy in Norway.... and in the Mediterranean. Norway traded its cod for the Italian and Spanish salt used to cure it which is why salt cod is popular in places like Portugal and Italy even though it cannot be caught there.

PORTUGAL

For a European country which once trailed way behind its neighbour, Portugal has come a very long way.

While the Algarve has long been a favourite holiday destination, the rest of Portugal was once largely unexplored. New prosperity has opened up much more of the country as a destination, from its capital Lisbon to the main ferry port, Porto, but there's still a lot to see.

The coast is still a major attraction. It's the Atlantic, not the Med, so has the lively feel of the tide, ensuring there's surf enough for boarders, wave-battered rocky coves and long sandy beaches, more akin to Cornwall than the Costas. But inland, there are real treasures to be found.

Coimbra, Portugal's university city, has a lovely blend of ancient and modern, from its Roman ruins and medieval streets to lively cafes and bars, stretching down to the River Montego and its leafy parks.

Portugal specialises in ancient towns and villages – Sintra, Evora, Mertola, Alcoutim. But if it's the beach life you're after, Lagos is a fine a resort.

Portugal's cuisine is actually a feast of imports – Europe's most intrepid 15th Century explorers brought home the vegetables and fruits they found in the Americas and assimilated spices from the Far East. Try bacalao, salt cod, imported since the 16th Century but regarded as a national dish.

Lunch is the big meal of the Portuguese day, lasting a couple of hours while the sun's at its peak, and dinner starts after 8pm

GETTING THERE: Brittany Ferries' service into nearby Santander, in Spain, is the best option. Or you can drive down through France and northern Spain.

CURRENCY: Euro (€)

ROADS NETWORK: Major trunk roads are excellent and regional roads variable.

SPEED LIMITS: Built-up areas 50km/h; standard roads 90-100km/h; motorways 120km/h

TOLLS: Many major routes and two bridges in Lisbon have tolls, with widely varying prices. Because many minor roads are of poor quality, they are probably worth paying.

DRIVING LICENCE REQUIREMENTS: Minimum age 18.

USE OF LIGHTS: Dipped headlights mandatory in daytime if conditions are poor

SEATBELTS: Compulsory for front and rear seat occupants

FINES: On the spot fines payable to officers

DRINK DRIVING: 0.05 per cent (UK: 0.08 per cent)

SITES NETWORK: Not as extensive as its neighbours and the best-equipped sites tend to be large commercial complexes

NEED TO KNOW: Cork is one of Portugal's major exports but the industry has been hit by screw-top bottles and plastic corks. This has devastated rural communities and the felling of cork oaks is now destroying wildlife habitat.

SLOVENIA

Along with Croatia, Slovenia is one of the jewels in the east-European crown and a must-visit destination for motorhomers. With a population of just two million, Slovenia is a country with plenty of open spaces and little industrial blight.

It's a superb holiday destination, with an alpine climate in the north, Mediterranean climate in the south, low prices in the bars and restaurants and plenty to see and do. Many people would be hard-pushed to identify it on a map, yet it's just over the border from northern Italy.

Its main attraction is the countryside – outdoor types will revel in its hill-walking and lakeside rambles, ski and snowboarding scene in winter and its canoeing and fishing along the rivers.

If you're after a more placid holiday, the capital Ljubljana is a dazzling hilltop city with architecture to marvel at and a night life boosted by its 56,000 student population – lively but very classy.

Lake Bled, Slovenia © J. Skok www.slovenia.info

Museums abound and there's enough to keep you there for a couple of days.

It's a small country, and many of its other major towns are compact rather than imposing, studded with medieval streets. They just beg to be explored, and the Slovenes are keen to help to share their heritage.

But Slovenia is really all about its hills and mountains. Tour them by motorhome but don't pass up the opportunity to park up and walk.

GETTING THERE: Slovenia is served by major routes from Italy and Austria

CURRENCY: Euro (€)

ROADS NETWORK: Major trunk roads are excellent and regional roads variable.

SPEED LIMITS: Built-up areas 50km/h; standard roads 90-100km/h; motorways 130km/h (minimum 60km/h)

TOLLS: No tolls but you must buy a six-month vignette for €35.

DRIVING LICENCE REQUIREMENTS: Minimum age 18.

USE OF LIGHTS: Dipped headlights mandatory in daytime

SEATBELTS: Compulsory for front and rear seat occupants

FINES: On the spot fines payable to officers

DRINK DRIVING: 0.05 per cent (UK: 0.08 per cent)

SITES NETWORK: Slovenia isn't overburdened with serviced sites but the 50 or so available are of a good standard and great value

NEED TO KNOW: If you're not taking your bikes (but you should) Slovenia is awash with great bus and coach services, allowing you to confidently leave your motorhome parked.

SPAIN

It's hard to say anything new about Spain – it's far and away Britain's most popular overseas destination.

But if you've only been to the Costas, Spain's interior holds a great many surprises. Its cities are world-renowned but not just for their cosmopolitan nature and wonderful architecture. In the costas everything is brought down to a level, while in Barcelona, Madrid, Jerez, Seville and Granada, the Spanish show pure class.

Spain is also a country of real contrast, from the alpine north to the sun-drenched south. If you've not toured the Pyrenean region from Pamplona – home of the famous street bull run – to spectacular Andorra, you're missing something.

The centre of Spain around Madrid is home to many of its national parks but the backdrop to most of the southern resorts are high mountain ranges that beg to be explored, though not by motorhome. Take a jeep safari or pony-trek into the cool high sierra.

We all know, too, about Spain's food. Or at least, we think we do. Most of our knowledge is of a few regional dishes like paella and Spain's passion for tapas but every town and region will have its own specialities. Budget to eat out frequently and enjoy local produce served fresh.

A February expedition to Andalucia not only gives visitors a taste of spring several weeks early, but visit Tarifa – Europe's most southerly point – and you also earn the right to display the famous Andalucian bull on the back of your van.

GETTING THERE: If you don't fancy the drive down through France, Brittany Ferries sails from Portsmouth or Plymouth into Santander.

CURRENCY: Euro (€)

ROADS NETWORK: Major trunk roads are excellent and regional roads usually very good.

SPEED LIMITS: Built-up areas 50km/h; standard roads 90-100km/h; motorways 120km/h (minimum 60km/h)

TOLLS: Many Spanish motorways are tolled but at fairly reasonable rates. The Tunel del Cadi near Andorra is, though, a whacking €11.

DRIVING LICENCE REQUIREMENTS: Minimum age 18.

USE OF LIGHTS: Dipped headlights must be used in tunnels. Daytime use is not required

SEATBELTS: Compulsory for front and rear seat occupants

FINES: On the spot fines payable to officers

DRINK DRIVING: 0.05 per cent (UK: 0.08 per cent) but be aware that your driving licence may be seized

SITES NETWORK: All of Spain's coastal resorts have ample sites as do areas around its national parks. It is also developing a system of aires for 'autocaravanas'.

NEED TO KNOW: If you're looking for a guide to Spanish aires try http://www.furgovw.org/mapa_furgoperfecto.php. It's all in Spanish (dictionary at the ready!) but the red 'lollipops' mark the serviced sites.

SWEDEN

The closest many motorhomers have been to Sweden is IKEA but there is no shortage of incentives to make a trip.

The big problem is that DFDS no longer operates direct to Sweden, though the crossing into Denmark leaves you with a relatively short – and very enjoyable – drive into Sweden's gentle charms.

Sweden may be famous for blond people and furniture but it's a country of huge contrast. In the south, it's all undulating and lush farmland peppered with hills. Further north, you cross into the arctic circle, the hills rise higher and the terrain takes on an alpine feel.

Move further north still and head west and you reach the mountain range which it shares with Norway and encounter the lean landscape of a region that has 24-hour sun in summer, 24-hour darkness in winter. And everywhere you look in Sweden there is water.

There is so much water running west into the Baltic that this sea is brackish; sea fish like cod live alongside freshwater pike and perch. And the little ports which border the Baltic are achingly lovely.

Stories about sky-high prices in Sweden are more myth than reality; food and household items are on a par with much of Europe, though alcohol can be expensive. Supermarket beer is very weak but 'international' hotels have a license to sell the real thing – and there are a surprising number of small breweries in Sweden.

Above all else, the best reason for visiting is the Swedes – always courteous, civilised beyond compare and happy to talk in English, especially in the south.

GETTING THERE: There are no longer any direct ferry services from the UK but you can get to Sweden through Denmark with DFDS. Many other ferries serve Sweden from mainland Europe.

CURRENCY: Kroner (Skr)

ROADS NETWORK: Major trunk roads are excellent and regional roads usually very good.

SPEED LIMITS: Built-up areas 30km/h; standard roads 70km/h; motorways 110km/h but Sweden has a policy of varying speed limits according to road safety.

TOLLS: None apart from Oresund Bridge which connects it with Denmark.

DRIVING LICENCE REQUIREMENTS: Minimum age 18.

USE OF LIGHTS: Dipped headlights must be used at all times

SEATBELTS: Compulsory for front and rear seat occupants

FINES: On the spot fines, payable later

DRINK DRIVING: 0.02 per cent (UK: 0.08 per cent) with very severe penalties

SITES NETWORK: Sweden is crazy about camping and there are a huge number of sites. Northern sites are seasonal. Buy a Camping Card before departure – the discounts are excellent.

NEED TO KNOW: The infamous 'elk test' which European car makers give to every new car has its origins here.

Sweden hosts many of the world car makers' winter test tracks. The risk of needed to swerve to avoid a moose or reindeer is very real in Sweden.

SWITZERLAND

There's really only one reason to go to Switzerland – mountains. And for most people, that means skiing.

Parked as centrally as possible in Europe, Switzerland shares borders with France, Germany, Italy and Austria. Around its capital, Zurich, the landscape is lush and hilly but as you head south, the Alps loom huge and impressive. The experience of driving through them is legendary.

Then, of course, there are Swiss towns and cities. Basel has some of the best modern architecture in Europe, Geneva's a cosmopolitan place while Zurich pushes the boundaries a little. Yes, Switzerland is expensive. Very expensive. But the gap between it and the rest of Europe has narrowed in recent years.

The compensations for your excess spending are some of the best-preserved medieval towns in Europe, pretty-as-you-like alpine villages, outstanding views and – if you're out of season – some lovely mountain walking. If you go for the skiing, be aware of the need to carry snow chains but look forward to saving a bundle on the price of accommodation.

GETTING THERE: Access Switzerland from any of its borders, though the quickest way is through France.

CURRENCY: Francs (Sfr)

ROADS NETWORK: Major trunk roads are excellent and regional roads usually very good.

SPEED LIMITS: Built-up areas 50km/h; standard roads 80km/h; dual carriageways 100km/h; motorways 120km/h (lower limit 80km/h).

TOLLS: A vignette must be purchased at the border for any motorway use. Two alpine tunnels have tolls - Munt La Schera Tunnel and Saint Bernhard Tunnel.

Lake Lucerne with Mount Pilatus, Switzerland © swiss-image.ch STS0409

DRIVING LICENCE REQUIREMENTS: Minimum age 18.

USE OF LIGHTS: Dipped headlights are recommended at all times

SEATBELTS: Compulsory for front and rear seat occupants

FINES: On the spot fines, payable immediately

DRINK DRIVING: 0.05 per cent (UK: 0.08 per cent) with very severe penalties

SITES NETWORK: Switzerland is very well served by campsites, the Swiss being very comfortable with the outdoor life. There are more than 500 – many of extremely high quality and numerous camper stops

NEED TO KNOW: Switzerland is famous for its chocolate, with Suchard, Lindt and Tobler particularly well-known. Indeed, milk chocolate was invented in Switzerland. Each year, Switzerland exports 80,000 tonnes of the stuff.

Tourist offices and websites

ANDORRA
Andorra Turisme SAU
C/ Doctor Vilanova, 13
Edifici Davi, esc. B, 3er
AD500 Andorra la Vella
Principat d'Andorra
www.andorra.ad

AUSTRIA
Austrian National Tourist Office
9-11 Richmond Street
London W1D 3HF
0845 101 1818
www.austria.info

BELGIUM
Belgian Tourist Office
217 Marsh Wall
London E14 9FJ
0800 954 5245
www.visitbelgium.com

CZECH REPUBLIC
Czech Tourist Authority
13 Harley Street
London
W1G 9QG
0207 631 0427
www.czechtourism.com

CROATIA
Croatian National Tourist Office
2 Lanchesters
162-164 Fulham Palace Road
London
W6 9ER
0208 563 7979
www.croatia.hr

DENMARK
VisitDenmark
55 Sloane Street
London
SW1X 9SY
www.visitdenmark.com

FINLAND
Finnish Tourist Board
PO Box 33213
London W68JX
www.visitfinland.com

FRANCE
French Government Tourist Board
Lincoln House
300 High Holborn
London WC1V 7JH
09068 244123
www.franceguide.com

GERMANY
German national Tourist Board
Nightingale House
PO Box 2695
London
W1A 3TN
0207 317 0908
www.germany-tourism.co.uk

GREECE
Greek National Tourist Organisation
4 Conduit Street
London
W1S 2DJ
0207 495 9300
www.gnto.co.uk

IRELAND
Irish Tourist Board/Bord Failte
103 Wigmore Street
London
W1U 1QS
08000 0397000
www.tourismireland.com

ITALY
Italian State Tourist Office
1 Princes Street
London W1B 2AY
0207 408 1254
www.enit.it

LUXEMBOURG
Luxembourg Tourist Office
Suit 4.1
Sicilian House
London
WC1 2QH
0207 434 2800
www.luxembourg.co.uk

THE NETHERLANDS
Netherlands Board of Tourism
PO Box 30783
London
WC2B 6DH
0906 8717 777
www.holland.com

NORWAY
Norwegian Tourist Board
Charles House (5th Floor)
5 Lower Regent Street
London SW1Y 4LR
0207 839 2650
www.visitnorway.com

PORTUGAL
Portuguese Tourist Office
11 Belgrave Square
London
SW1X 8PP
0845 355 1212
www.visitportugal.com

SLOVENIA
Slovenian Tourist Office
South Marlands
Itchingfield
Horsham
West Sussex
RH13 0NN
0207 222 5277
www.slovenia-tourism.si

SPAIN
Spanish Tourist Office
79 Cavendish Street
London
W1W 6NB
0845 940 0180
www.spaininfo.info/www.tourspain.co.uk

SWEDEN
Visit Sweden
Stortorget 2-4 Se-83130
Ostersund
Sweden
0207 108 6168
www.visit-sweden.com

SWITZERLAND
Switzerland Tourism
30 Bedford Street
London
WC2E 9ED
00800 1002 0030
www.myswitzerland.com

Further reading

Camperstop Europe
Facile Media
£24.99 ISBN 978-9-0760-8014-7

Caravan & Camping Europe
The AA/Camping and Caravanning Club,
£10.99 ISBN 978-0-7495-6063-8

Caravan Europe 1 & 2
The Caravan Club
£15.99 each (members' price £9.00 and £8.50)
Tel: 01342 327410 to order

The European Driver's Handbook
The AA
£9.99 ISBN 978-0-7495-5643-3

The Motorcaravanning Handbook
John Wickersham/Haynes Publishing,
£12.99 ISBN 978-1-84425-428-6

USEFUL WEBSITES

lpgas.bpgas.co.uk
Advice and information on BP Gas Light cylinder availability

www.calor.co.uk
Advice and information on Calor Gas availability

www.campingandcaravanningclub.co.uk
Sites and touring information plus practical and technical advice

www.campingaz.com
Information on Campingaz distribution and availability across Europe and general advice

www.campingcardinternational.org
More information on the huge number of European sites affiliated to this popular discount and accreditation scheme

www.campingcheque.co.uk
Details of this popular scheme offering discounted pitch fees at sites across Europe

www.caravanclub.co.uk
Packed with UK sites information and practical advice for touring at home and abroad

www.davenewell.co.uk
Specialises in all manner of add-ons, accessories and motorhome modification

www.dh.gov.uk/travellers
Apply for an EHIC card here and check latest Government advice for travellers

www.dvla.gov.uk
Always a good idea to consult over any driving licence restrictions and queries

www.fco.gov.uk
Find a list of consulates and embassies in countries you intend to visit on the grand tour

www.lonelyplanet.com
Some useful overviews and practical information on touring in Europe

www.outandaboutlive.co.uk
Warners Group Publications' magazines portal and home of MMM Magazine online. Articles, roadtests, reviews advice and very lively motorhome forums

www.roadpro.co.uk
Friendly advice on all things electrical

www.theaa.com
Excellent resource for route-planning and regularly updated information on driving in Europe

www.vosa.gov.uk
Technical information on issues such as vehicle modifications and payload issues

www.wildcamping.co.uk
Lively forum for motorhome enthusiasts